Java For Testers

Learn Java fundamentals fast

Alan Richardson

Java For Testers

Learn Java fundamentals fast

Alan Richardson

This book is for sale at http://JavaForTesters.com

This version was published on 2015-08-26

ISBN 978-0-9567332-5-2

First published in Great Britain in 2015 by Compendium Developments Ltd (http://www.compendiumdev.co.uk)

contact details: alan@compendiumdev.co.uk

e-book ISBN : 978-0-9567332-4-5

paper book ISBN : 978-0-9567332-5-2

As ever. This book is dedicated to Billie and Keeran.

Contents

Introduction 1
- Testers use Java differently 1
- Exclusions 2
- Windows and Mac supported 2
- Supporting Source Code 3
- About the Author 4
- Acknowledgments 4

Chapter One - Basics of Java Revealed 7
- Java Example Code 7

Chapter Two - Install the Necessary Software 11
- Introduction 11
- Do you already have JDK or Maven installed? 12
- Install The Java JDK 14
- Install Maven 14
- Install The IDE 16
- Create a Project using the IDE 16
- About your new project 17
- Add JUnit to the `pom.xml` file 19
- Summary 20

Chapter Three - Writing Your First Java Code 23
- My First JUnit Test 23
- Prerequisites 24
- Create A JUnit Test Class 24
- Create a Method 31
- Make the method a *JUnit test* 32
- Calculate the sum 33

Assert the value 34
Run the `@Test` method 36
Summary 37
References and Recommended Reading 40

Chapter Four - Work with Other Classes **43**
Use `@Test` methods to understand Java 43
Warnings about `Integer` 50
Summary 52
References and Recommended Reading 52

Chapter Five - Working with Our Own Classes **55**
Context 55
First create an `@Test` method 58
Write code that doesn't exist 59
New Requirements 63
Now Refactor 64
Summary 70

Chapter Six - Java Classes Revisited: Constructors, Fields, Getter & Setter Methods **71**
Context 71
Constructor 72
Getters and Setters 79
Summary 81
References and Recommended Reading 82

Chapter Seven - Basics of Java Revisited **85**
Comments 85
Statement 87
Packages 87
Java Classes 88
Importing Classes 93
Static Imports 93
Data Types 94
Operators 98
Strings 105
Summary 107
References and Recommended Reading 107

Chapter Eight - Selections and Decisions **109**
Ternary Operators 109
`if` statement 111
`else` statement 112
Nested `if else` 114
`switch` statement 116
Summary 119
References and Recommended Reading 119

Chapter Nine - Arrays and For Loop Iteration **121**
Arrays 121
Exercises 138
Summary 139
References and Recommended Reading 140

Chapter Ten - Introducing Collections **141**
A Simple Introduction 141
Iterating with `while` and `do...while` 143
Interfaces 146
Summary 172
References and Recommended Reading 173

Chapter Eleven - Introducing Exceptions **175**
What is an exception? 176
Catching Exceptions 179
An Exception is an object 181
Catch more than one exception 182
JUnit and Exceptions 183
Throwing an Exception 184
`finally` 185
Summary 188
References and Recommended Reading 188

Chapter Twelve - Introducing Inheritance **189**
Inheritance 189
Inherit from Interfaces and Abstract Classes 194
Summary 195
References and Recommended Reading 195

Chapter Thirteen - More About Exceptions **197**
Unchecked and Checked Exceptions 197
Difference between `Exception`, `Error` and `Throwable` 200
Create your own Exception class 201
Summary 202
References and Recommended Reading 202

Chapter Fourteen - JUnit Explored **205**
`@Test` 206
Before & After 208
`@Ignore` 208
JUnit Assertions 209
Asserting with Hamcrest Matchers and `assertThat` 210
`fail` 213
`static` importing 213
Summary 214
References and Recommended Reading 215

Chapter Fifteen - Strings Revisited **217**
`String` Summary 218
`System.out.println` 218
Special character encoding 219
`String` Concatenation 220
Converting to/from a `String` 220
Constructors 221
Comparing Strings 222
Manipulating Strings 231
Basic String parsing with `split` 235
Manipulating strings With `StringBuilder` 236
Concatenation, `.format`, or `StringBuilder` 241
Summary 242
References and Recommended Reading 242

Chapter Sixteen - Random Data **245**
`Math.random` 246
`java.util.random` 246
Seeding random numbers 251
Using Random Numbers to generate Random Strings 252
Discussion random data in automation 252

Summary . . . 254
References and Recommended Reading . . . 254

Chapter Seventeen - Dates and Times . . . 255
`currentTimeMillis` and `nanoTime` . . . 255
`Date` . . . 258
`SimpleDateFormat` . . . 260
`Calendar` . . . 262
Summary . . . 268
References and Recommended Reading . . . 269

Chapter Eighteen - Properties and Property Files . . . 271
`Properties` Basics . . . 272
Java's `System` Properties . . . 275
Working with Property files . . . 278
Summary . . . 281
References and Recommended Reading . . . 281

Chapter Nineteen - Files . . . 283
Example of reading and writing a file . . . 284
File . . . 286
Writing And Reading Files . . . 297
Additional File Methods . . . 299
Files . . . 301
Summary . . . 303
References and Recommended Reading . . . 303

Chapter Twenty - Math and BigDecimal . . . 305
BigDecimal . . . 306
Math . . . 311
Summary . . . 311
References and Recommended Reading . . . 312

Chapter Twenty One - Collections Revisited . . . 313
Set . . . 314
Map . . . 325
Implementations . . . 330
Summary . . . 331
References and Recommended Reading . . . 331

Chapter Twenty Two - Advancing Concepts **333**
Interfaces 334
Abstract Classes 335
Generics 335
Logging 336
Enum 337
Regular Expressions 337
Reflection 337
Annotations 338
Design Patterns 339
Concurrency 339
Additional File considerations 340
Summary 341

Chapter Twenty Three - Next Steps **343**
Recommended Reading 343
Recommended Videos 347
Recommended Web Sites 348
Next Steps 348
References 349

Appendix - IntelliJ Hints and Tips **351**
Shortcut Keys 351
Code Completion 352
Navigating Source Code 352
Running a JUnit Test 353
Loading Project Source 353
Help Menu 353
Summary 354

Appendix - Exercise Answers **355**
Chapter Three - My First JUnit Test 355
Chapter Four - Work With Other Classes 357
Chapter Five - Work With Our Own Classes 358
Chapter Six - Java Classes Revisited: Constructors, Fields, Getter & Setter Methods 360
Chapter Eight - Selections and Decisions 362
Chapter Nine - Arrays and For Loop Iteration 369
Chapter Ten - Introducing Collections 374
Chapter Eleven - Introducing Exceptions 377

Chapter Twelve - Introducing Inheritance 382
Chapter Thirteen - More Exceptions 385
Chapter Fourteen - JUnit Explored 388
Chapter Fifteen - Strings Revisited 390
Chapter Sixteen - Random Data 398
Chapter Seventeen - Dates & Times 405
Chapter Eighteen - Properties and Property Files 409
Chapter Nineteen - Files 411
Chapter Twenty - Math and BigDecimal 418
Chapter Twenty One - Collections Revisited 419

Introduction

This is an introductory text. At times it takes a tutorial approach and adopts step by step instructions to coding. Some people more familiar with programming might find this slow. This book is not aimed at those people.

This book is aimed at people who are approaching Java for the first time, specifically with a view to adding automation to their test approach. I do not cover automation tools in this book.

I do cover the basic Java knowledge needed to write and structure code when automating.

I primarily wrote this book for software testers, and the approach to learning is oriented around writing automation code to support testing, rather than writing applications. As such it might be useful for anyone learning Java, who wants to learn from a "test first" perspective.

Automation to support testing is not limited to testers anymore, so this book is suitable for anyone wanting to improve their use of Java in automation: managers, business analysts, users, and of course, testers.

Testers use Java differently

I remember when I started learning Java from traditional books, and I remember that I was unnecessarily confused by some of the concepts that I rarely had to use e.g. creating manifest files, and compiling from the command line.

Testers use Java differently.

Most Java books start with a 'main' class and show how to compile code and write simple applications from the command line, then build up into more Java constructs and GUI applications. When I write Java, I rarely compile it to a standalone application, I spend a lot of time in the IDE, writing and running small checks and refactoring to abstraction layers.

By learning the basics of Java presented in this book, you will learn how to read and understand existing code bases, and write simple checks using JUnit quickly. You will not learn how to build and structure an application. That is useful knowledge, but it can be learned after you know how to contribute to the Java code base with JUnit tests.

My aim is to help you start writing automation code using Java, and have the basic knowledge you need to do that. This book focuses on core Java functionality rather than a lot of additional libraries, since once you have the basics, picking up a library and learning how to use it becomes a matter of reading the documentation and sample code.

Exclusions

This is not a 'comprehensive' introduction. This is a 'getting started' guide. Even though I concentrate on core Java, there are still aspects of Java that I haven't covered in detail, I have covered them 'just enough' to understand. e.g. inheritance, interfaces, enums, inner classes, etc.

Some people may look disparagingly on the text based on the exclusions. So consider this an opinionated introduction to Java because I know that I did not need to use many of those exclusions for the first few years of my automation programming.

I maintain that there is a core set of Java that you need in order to start writing automation code and start adding value to automation projects. I aim to cover that core in this book.

Essentially, I looked at the Java I needed when I started writing automation to support my testing, and used that as scope for this book. While knowledge of Interfaces, Inheritance, and enums, all help make my automation abstractions more readable and maintainable; I did not use those constructs with my early automation.

I also want to keep the book small, and approachable, so that people actually read it and work through it, rather than buying and leaving on their shelf because they were too intimidated to pick it up. And that means leaving out the parts of Java, which you can pick up yourself, once you have mastered the concepts in this book.

This book does not cover any Java 1.8 functionality. The highest version of Java required to work with this book is Java 1.7. The code in this book will work with Java 1.8, I simply don't cover any of the new functionality added in Java 1.8 because I want you to learn the basics, and start being productive quickly. After you complete this book, you should be able to pick up the new features in Java 1.8 when you need them.

Windows and Mac supported

The source code was primarily written on Windows 7 and 8, using IntelliJ 13 and 14. But has also been run on Mac using IntelliJ 14.

Instructions are provided for installation, and IntelliJ usage, on both Mac and Windows.

Supporting Source Code

You can download the source code for this book from github.com[1]. The source contains the examples and answers to exercises.

I suggest you work through the book and give it your best shot before consulting the source code.

- github.com/eviltester/javaForTestersCode[2]

The source code has been organized into two high level source folders: `main` and `test`. The full significance of these will be explained in later chapters. But for now, the `test` folder contains all the JUnit tests that you see in this book. Each chapter has a package and beneath that an `exercises` and an `examples` folder:

e.g.

- The main folder for Chapter 3 is:
  - `src\test\java\com\javafortesters\chap003myfirsttest`
- it contains an `examples` folder with all the code used in the main body of the text
- it contains an `exercises` folder with all the code for the answers I created for the exercises in Chapter 3

This should make it easier for you to navigate the code base. And if you experience difficulties typing in any of the code then you can compare it with the actual code to support the book.

To allow you to read the book without needing to have the source code open, I have added a lot of code in the body of the book and you can find much of the code for the `exercises` in the appendix.

The Appendix "IntelliJ Hints and Tips" has information on loading the source and offers a reference section for helping you navigate and work with the source code in IntelliJ.

[1]https://github.com

[2]https://github.com/eviltester/javaForTestersCode

About the Author

Alan Richardson has worked as a Software professional since 1995 (although it feels longer). Primarily working with Software Testing, although he has written commercial software in C++, and a variety of other languages.

Alan has a variety of on-line training courses, both free and commercial:

- "Selenium 2 WebDriver With Java"
- "Start Using Selenium WebDriver"
- "Technical Web Testing"

You can find details of his other books, training courses, conference papers and slides, and videos, on his main company web site:

- CompendiumDev.co.uk[3]

Alan maintains a number of web sites:

- SeleniumSimplified.com[4] : Web Automation using Selenium WebDriver
- EvilTester.com[5] : Technical testing
- JavaForTesters.com[6] : Java, aimed at software testers.
  - JavaForTesters.com also acts as the support site for this book.

Alan tweets using the handle @eviltester[7]

Acknowledgments

This book was created as a "work in progress" on leanpub.com[8]. My thanks go to everyone who bought the book in its early stages, this provided the continued motivation to create

[3]http://compendiumdev.co.uk
[4]http://seleniumsimplified.com
[5]http://eviltester.com
[6]http://javafortesters.com
[7]https://twitter.com/eviltester
[8]https://leanpub.com/javaForTesters

something that added value, and then spend the extra time needed to add polish and readability.

Special thanks go to the following people who provided early and helpful feedback during the writing process: Jay Gehlot, Faezeh Seyedarabi, Szymon Kazmierczak, Srinivas Kadiyala, Tony Bruce, James 'Drew' Cobb, Adrian Rapan, Ajay Bansode.

I am also grateful to every Java developer that I have worked with who took the time to explain their code. You helped me observe what a good developer does and how they work. The fact that you were good, forced me to 'up my game' and improve both my coding and testing skills.

All mistakes in this book are my fault. If you find any, please let me know via compendiumDev.co.uk/contact[9] or via any of the sites mentioned above.

---

[9]http://www.compendiumdev.co.uk/contact

Chapter One - Basics of Java Revealed

Chapter Summary

An overview of Java code to set the scene:

- `class` is the basic building block
- a `class` has methods
- method names start with lowercase letters
- `class` names start with uppercase letters
- a *JUnit test* is a method annotated with `@Test`
- *JUnit test* methods can be run without creating an application

In this first chapter I will show you Java code, and the language I use to describe it, with little explanation.

I do this to provide you with some context. I want to wrap you in the language typically used to describe Java code. And I want to show you small sections of code in context. I don't expect you to understand it yet. Just read the pages which follow, look at the code, soak it in, accept that it works, and is consistent.

Then in later pages, I will explain the code constructs in more detail, you will write some code, and I'll reinforce the explanations.

Java Example Code

Remember - just read the following section

Just read the following section, and don't worry if you don't understand it all immediately. I explain it in later pages. I have *emphasized* text which I will explain later. So if you don't understand what an *emphasized* word means, then don't worry, you will in a few pages time.

An empty class

A *class* is the basic building block that we use to build our Java code base.

All the code that we write to do stuff, we write inside a class. I have named this class `AnEmptyClass`.

```
package com.javafortesters.chap001basicsofjava.examples.classes;

public class AnEmptyClass {
}
```

Just like your name, class names start with an uppercase letter in Java. I'm using something called *Camel Case* to construct the names, instead of spaces to separate words, we write the first letter of each word in uppercase.

The first line is the *package* that I added the class to. A package is like a directory on the file system, this allows us to find, and use, the class in the rest of our code.

A class with a method

A class, on its own, doesn't do anything. We have to add *methods* to the class before we can do anything. *Methods* are the commands we can call, to make something happen.

In the following example I have created a new class called `AClassWithAMethod`, and this class has a method called `aMethodOnAClass` which, when called, prints out `"Hello World"` to the *console.*

```
package com.javafortesters.chap001basicsofjava.examples.classes;

public class AClassWithAMethod {

    public void aMethodOnAClass(){
        System.out.println("Hello World");
    }
}
```

Method names start with lowercase letters.

When we start learning Java we will call the methods of our classes from within *JUnit tests.*

A JUnit Test

For the code in this book we will use *JUnit*. JUnit is a commonly used library which makes it easy for us to write and run Java code with assertions.

A *JUnit test* is simply a method in a class which is *annotated* with `@Test` (i.e. we write `@Test` before the method declaration).

```
package com.javafortesters.chap001basicsofjava.examples.classes;

import org.junit.Test;

public class ASysOutJunitTest {

    @Test
    public void canOutputHelloWorldToConsole(){
        AClassWithAMethod myClass = new AClassWithAMethod();
        myClass.aMethodOnAClass();
    }
}
```

In the above code, I *instantiate* a *variable* of *type* `AClassWithAMethod` (which is the name I gave to the class earlier). I had to add this class to the *package*, and I had to *import* the `@Test` annotation before I could use it, and I did that as the first few lines in the file.

I can run this method from the IDE without creating a Java application because I have used JUnit and annotated the method with `@Test`.

When I run this method then I will see the following text printed out to the Java console in my IDE:

```
Hello World
```

Summary

I have thrown you into the deep end here; presenting you with a page of possible gobbledygook. And I did that to introduce you to a the Java Programming Language quickly.

Java Programming Language Concepts:

- Class

- Method
- JUnit
- Annotation
- Package
- Variables
- Instantiate variables
- Type
- Import

Programming Convention Concepts:

- Camel Case
- *JUnit Tests* are Java methods annotated with `@Test`

Integrated Development Environment Concepts:

- Console

Over the next few chapters, I'll start to explain these concepts in more detail.

Chapter Two - Install the Necessary Software

Chapter Summary

In this chapter you will learn the tools you need to program in Java, and how to install them. You will also find links to additional FAQs and Video tutorials, should you get stuck.

The tools you will install are:

- Java Development Kit
- Maven
- An Integrated Development Environment (IDE)

You will also learn how to create your first project.

When you finish this chapter you will be ready to start coding.

I suggest you first, read this whole chapter, and then work through the chapter from the beginning and follow the steps listed.

Introduction

Programming requires you to setup a bunch of tools to allow you to work.

For Java, this means you need to install:

- JDK - Java Development Kit
- IDE - Integrated Development Environment

For this book we are also going to install:

- Maven - a dependency management and build tool

Installing Maven adds an additional degree of complexity to the setup process, but trust me. It will make the whole process of building projects and taking your Java to the next level a lot easier.

I have created a support page for installation, with videos and links to troubleshooting guides.

- JavaForTesters.com/install[10]

If you experience any problems that are not covered in this chapter, or on the support pages, then please let me know so I can try to help, or amend this chapter, and possibly add new resources to the support page.

Do you already have JDK or Maven installed?

Some of you may already have these tools installed with your machine. The first thing we should do is learn how to check if they are installed or not.

Java JDK

Many of you will already have a JRE installed (Java Runtime Environment), but when developing with Java we need to use a JDK.

If you type `javac -version` at your command line and get an error saying that `javac can not be found` (or something similar). Then you need to install and configure a JDK.

If you see something similar to:

```
> javac -version
javac 1.7.0_10
```

Then you have a JDK installed. It is worth following the instructions below to check if your installed JDK is up to date, but if you have a 1.7.x JDK (or higher) installed then you have a good enough version to work through this book without amendment. If your JDK is version 1.6 then some of the code examples will not work.

[10]http://javafortesters.com/install

Java Has Multiple Versions

The Java language improves over time. With each new version adding new features. If you are unfortunate enough to not be allowed to install Java 1.7 at work (then I suggest you work through this book at home, or on a VM), then parts of the source code will not work and the code you download for this book will throw errors.

Specifically, we cover the following features introduced in Java 1.7:

- The Diamond operator <> in the Collections chapters
- Binary literals e.g. `0b1001`
- Underscores in literals e.g. `9_000_000_000L`
- `switch` statements using `Strings`
- `Paths` and `Path` from `java.nio.file`

The above statements may not make sense yet, but if you are using a version of Java lower than 1.7 then you can expect to see these concepts throw errors with JDK 1.6 or below.

Install Maven

Maven requires a version of Java installed, so if you checked for Java and it wasn't there, you will need to install Maven.

If you type `mvn -version` at your command line, and receive an error that `mvn can not be found` (or something similar). Then you need to install and configure Maven before you follow the text in this book.

If you see something similar to:

```
> mvn -version
Apache Maven 3.0.4 (r1232337; 2012-01-17 08:44:56+0000)
Maven home: C:\mvn\apache-maven-3.0.4
Java version: 1.7.0_10, vendor: Oracle Corporation
Java home: C:\Program Files\Java\jdk1.7.0_10\jre
Default locale: en_GB, platform encoding: Cp1252
OS name: "windows 8", version: "6.2", arch: "amd64", family: "windows"
```

Then you have Maven installed. This book doesn't require a specific version of Maven, but having a version of 3.x.x or above should be fine.

Install The Java JDK

The Java JDK can be downloaded from `oracle.com`. If you mistakenly download from `java.com` then you will be downloading the JRE, and for development work we need the JDK.

- oracle.com/technetwork/java/javase/downloads[11]

From the above site you should follow the installation instructions for your specific platform.

You can check the JDK is installed by opening a new command line and running the command:

```
javac -version
```

This should show you the version number which you downloaded and installed from `oracle.com`

Install Maven

Maven is a dependency management and build tool. We will use it to add JUnit to our project and write our code based on Maven folder conventions to make it easier for others to review and work with our code base.

The official Maven web site is maven.apache.org[12]. You can download Maven and find installation instructions on the official web site.

Download Maven by visiting the download page:

- maven.apache.org/download.cgi[13]

The installation instructions can also be found on the download page:

- maven.apache.org/download.cgi#Installation_Instructions[14]

---

[11]http://www.oracle.com/technetwork/java/javase/downloads/index.html
[12]http://maven.apache.org
[13]http://maven.apache.org/download.cgi
[14]http://maven.apache.org/download.cgi#Installation_Instructions

I summarize the instructions below:

For Windows:

- Unzip the distribution archive where you want to install Maven
- Create an `M2_HOME` user/environment variable that points to the above directory
- Create an `M2` user/environment variable that points to `M2_HOME\bin`
  - on Windows `%M2_HOME%\bin`
    * sometimes on Windows, I find I have to avoid re-using the `M2_HOME` variable and instead copy the path in again
  - on Unix `$M2_HOME/bin`
- Add the `M2` user/environment variable to your path
- Make sure you have a `JAVA_HOME` user/environment variable that points to your JDK root directory
- Add `JAVA_HOME` to your path

For Mac:

- Unzip the distribution archive
- if you don't have a `/usr/local` folder then create one with `sudo mkdir /usr/local` from a terminal
- extract the contents into an `/usr/local/apache-maven`
- edit `~/.bash_profile`
- add the following lines to your `.bash_profile` file
  - `export M2_HOME=/usr/local/apache-maven`
  - `export M2=$M2_HOME/bin`
  - `export PATH=$M2:$PATH`
  - `export JAVA_HOME="$(/usr/libexec/java_home)"`
- save your `.bash_profile` file
- from a terminal enter `source ~/.bash_profile`

You can check it is installed by opening up a new command line and running the command:

```
mvn -version
```

This should show you the version number that you just installed and the path for your JDK.

I recommend you take the time to read the "Maven in 5 Minutes" guide on the official Maven web site:

- maven.apache.org/guides/getting-started/maven-in-five-minutes.html[15]

Install The IDE

While the code in this book will work with any IDE, I recommend you install IntelliJ. I find that IntelliJ works well for beginners since it tends to pick up paths and default locations better than Eclipse.

For this book, I will use IntelliJ and any supporting videos I create for this book, or any short cut keys I mention relating to the IDE will assume you are using IntelliJ.

The official IntelliJ web site is jetbrains.com/idea[16]

IntelliJ comes in two versions a 'Community' edition which is free, and an 'Ultimate' edition which you have to pay for.

For the purposes of this book, and most of your automation development work, the 'Community' edition will meet your needs.

Download the Community Edition IDE from:

- jetbrains.com/idea/download[17]

The installation should use the standard installation approach for your platform.

When you are comfortable with the concepts in this book, you can experiment with other IDEs e.g. Eclipse[18] or Netbeans[19].

I suggest you stick with IntelliJ until you are more familiar with Java because then you minimize the risk of issues with the IDE confusing you into believing that you have a problem with your Java.

Create a Project using the IDE

To create your first project, use IntelliJ to do the hard work. The instructions below are for IntelliJ 14, but should be very similar for future versions of IntelliJ. Remember to check JavaForTesters.com/install[20] for updates and additional videos.

---

[15] http://maven.apache.org/guides/getting-started/maven-in-five-minutes.html
[16] http://www.jetbrains.com/idea
[17] http://www.jetbrains.com/idea/download
[18] http://www.eclipse.org
[19] https://netbeans.org
[20] http://javafortesters.com/install

- Start your installed IntelliJ
- Either use the "Create New Project" wizard that starts when you first run the application or, `File \ New Project`
- choose `Maven`
  - If maven hasn't filled in the Project SDK automatically then select `[New]` and choose the location of your JDK
- Press `[Next]`
- For GroupId and ArtifactId enter the name of your project, I used 'javaForTesters'
- Leave the version as the default '1.0-SNAPSHOT', and press [Next]
- Enter a project name, I used 'javaForTesters'
- Select a location to save the project source files
- select `Finish`
- select `OK`

You should be able to use all the default settings for the wizard.

About your new project

The `New Project` wizard should create a new folder with a structure something like the following:

```
+ javaForTesters
  + .idea
  + src
    + main
      + java
      + resources
    + test
      + java
  javaForTesters.iml
  pom.xml
```

In the above hierarchy,

- the `.idea` folder is where most of the IntelliJ configuration files will be stored,
- the `.iml` file has other IntelliJ configuration details,

- the `pom.xml` file is your Maven project configuration file.

If the wizard created any `.java` files in any of the directories then you can delete them as they are not important. You will be starting this project from scratch.

The above directory structure is a standard Maven structure. Maven expects certain files to be in certain directories to use the default Maven configuration. Since you are just starting you can leave the directory structure as it is.

Certain conventions that you will follow to make your life as a beginning developer easier:

- Add your JUnit Test Classes into the `src\test\java` folder hierarchy
- When you create a JUnit Test Class, make sure you append `Test` to the Class name

The `src\main\java` folder hierarchy is for Java code that is not used for asserting behaviour. Typically this is application code. We will use this for our abstraction layer code. We could add all the code we create in this book in the `src\test\java` hierarchy but where possible I split the abstraction code into a separate folder.

The above convention description may not make sense at the moment, but hopefully it will become clear as you work through the book. Don't worry about it now.

The `pom.xml` file will probably look like the following:

```
<?xml version="1.0" encoding="UTF-8"?>
<project xmlns="http://maven.apache.org/POM/4.0.0"
         xmlns:xsi="http://www.w3.org/2001/XMLSchema-instance"
         xsi:schemaLocation="http://maven.apache.org/POM/4.0.0
                             http://maven.apache.org/xsd/maven-4.0.0.xsd">
    <modelVersion>4.0.0</modelVersion>

    <groupId>javaForTesters</groupId>
    <artifactId>javaForTesters</artifactId>
    <version>1.0-SNAPSHOT</version>

</project>
```

This is the basics for a blank project file and defines the name of the project.

You can find information about the `pom.xml` file on the official Maven site.

- maven.apache.org/pom.html[21]

[21]http://maven.apache.org/pom.html

Add JUnit to the `pom.xml` file

We will use a library called JUnit to help us run our code.

- junit.org[22]

You can find installation instructions for using JUnit with Maven on the JUnit web site.

- github.com/junit-team/junit/wiki/Download-and-Install[23]

We basically edit the `pom.xml` file to include a dependency on JUnit. We do this by creating a `dependencies` XML element and a `dependency` XML element which defines the version of JUnit we want to use. At the time of writing it was version `4.11`

The `pom.xml` file that we will use for this book, only requires a dependency on JUnit, so it looks like this:

```
<?xml version="1.0" encoding="UTF-8"?>
 <project xmlns="http://maven.apache.org/POM/4.0.0"
 xmlns:xsi="http://www.w3.org/2001/XMLSchema-instance"
 xsi:schemaLocation="http://maven.apache.org/POM/4.0.0
                    http://maven.apache.org/xsd/maven-4.0.0.xsd">

    <modelVersion>4.0.0</modelVersion>

    <groupId>javaForTesters</groupId>
    <artifactId>javaForTesters</artifactId>
    <version>1.0-SNAPSHOT</version>
    <packaging>jar</packaging>

    <properties>
        <project.build.sourceEncoding>UTF-8</project.build.sourceEncoding>
    </properties>

    <dependencies>

        <dependency>
```

[22]http://junit.org

[23]https://github.com/junit-team/junit/wiki/Download-and-Install

```
            <groupId>junit</groupId>
            <artifactId>junit</artifactId>
            <version>4.11</version>
        </dependency>

    </dependencies>

    <build>
        <plugins>
            <plugin>
                <groupId>org.apache.maven.plugins</groupId>
                <artifactId>maven-compiler-plugin</artifactId>
                <version>3.1</version>
                <configuration>
                    <source>1.7</source>
                    <target>1.7</target>
                </configuration>
            </plugin>
        </plugins>
    </build>
</project>
```

You can see I also added a `build` section with a `maven-compiler-plugin`. This was mainly to cut down on warnings in the Maven output. If you really want to make the pom.xml file small you could get away with adding the `<dependencies>` XML element and all its containing information about JUnit.

Amend your `pom.xml` file to contain the `dependencies` and `build` elements above. IntelliJ should download the JUnit dependency ready for you to write your first *JUnit Test*, in the next chapter.

You can find more information about this plugin on the Maven site:

- maven.apache.org/plugins/maven-compiler-plugin[24]

Summary

If you followed the instructions in this chapter then you should now have:

[24]http://maven.apache.org/plugins/maven-compiler-plugin

- Maven installed - `mvn -version`
- JDK installed - `javac -version`
- IntelliJ IDE installed
- Created your first project
- A `pom.xml` file with JUnit as a dependency

I can't anticipate all the problems you might have installing the three tools listed in this chapter (JDK, Maven, IDE).

The installation should be simple, but things can go wrong.

I have created a few videos on the JavaForTesters.com/install[25] site which show how to install the various tools.

- JavaForTesters.com/install[26]

I added some Maven Troubleshooting Hints and Tips to the "Java For Testers" blog:

- javafortesters.blogspot.co.uk/2013/08/maven-troubleshooting-faqs-and-tips.html[27]

If you do get stuck then try and use your favourite search engine and copy and paste the exact error message you receive into the search engine and you'll probably find someone else has already managed to resolve your exact issue.

---

[25]http://javafortesters.com

[26]http://javafortesters.com/install

[27]http://javafortesters.blogspot.co.uk/2013/08/maven-troubleshooting-faqs-and-tips.html

Chapter Three - Writing Your First Java Code

Chapter Summary

In this tutorial chapter you will follow along with the text and create your first *JUnit test*. You will learn:

- How to organize your code and import other classes
- Creating classes and naming classes as *JUnit tests*
- Making Java methods run as *JUnit tests*
- Adding asserts to report errors during the execution
- How to run *JUnit tests* from the IDE and the command line
- How to write basic arithmetic statements in Java
- About Java comments

Follow along with the text, and use the example code as a guide. If you have issues then compare the code you have written carefully against the code in the book.

In this chapter we will take a slightly different approach. We will advance step-by-step through the chapter and we will write a simple method which we will run as a *JUnit test*.

My First JUnit Test

The code will calculate the answer to "2+2", and then *assert* that the answer is "4".

The code we write will be very simple, and will look like the following:

```
package com.javafortesters.chap003myfirsttest.examples;
import org.junit.Test;
import static org.junit.Assert.assertEquals;

public class MyFirstTest {

    @Test
    public void canAddTwoPlusTwo(){
        int answer = 2+2;
        assertEquals("2+2=4", 4, answer );
    }
}
```

I'm showing you this now, so you have an understanding of what we are working towards. If you get stuck, you can refer back to this final state and compare it with your current state to help resolve any problems.

Prerequisites

I'm assuming that you have followed the setup chapter and have the following in place:

- JDK Installed
- IDE Installed
- Maven Installed
- Created a project
- Added JUnit to the project `pom.xml`

We are going to add all the code we create in this book to the project you have created.

Create A JUnit Test Class

The first thing we have to do is create a class, to which we will add our JUnit test method.

A class is the basic building block for our Java code. So we want to create a class called `MyFirstTest`.

The name `MyFirstTest` has some very important features.

- It starts with an uppercase letter
- It has the word `Test` at the end
- It uses camel case

It starts with an uppercase letter because, by convention, Java classes start with an uppercase letter. *By convention* means that it doesn't have to. You won't see Java throw any errors if you name the class `myFirstTest` with a lowercase letter. When you run the code, Java won't complain.

But everyone that you work with will.

We expect Java classes to start with an uppercase letter because they are proper names.

Trust me.

Get in the habit of naming your classes with the first letter in uppercase. Then when you read code you can tell the difference between a class and a variable, and you'll expect the same from code that other people have written.

It has the word `Test` at the end. We can take advantage of the 'out of the box' Maven functionality to run our *JUnit tests* from the command line, instead of the IDE, by typing `mvn test`. This might not seem important now, but at some point we are going to want to run our code automatically as part of a build process. And we can make that easier if we add `Test` in the Class name, either as the start of the class name, or at the end. By naming our classes in this way, Maven will automatically run our *JUnit test* classes at the appropriate part of the build process.

Incorrectly Named Classes Will Run From the IDE

Very often we run our *JUnit test* code from the IDE. And the IDE will run the methods in *JUnit test* classes even if the classes are not named as Maven requires. If we do not name a class correctly then it will not run from the command line when we type `mvn test` but because we saw it run in the IDE, we believe it is running.

This leaves us thinking we have more coverage than we actually do.

It uses camel case where each 'word' in a string of concatenated words starts with an uppercase letter. This again is a Java convention, it is not enforced by the compiler. But people reading your code will expect to see it written like this.

Maven Projects need to be imported

As you code, if you see a little pop up in IntelliJ which says "Maven Projects need to be imported". Click the "Enable Auto-Import". This will make your life easier as it will automatically add import statements in your code and update when you change your `pom.xml` file.

If you miss this then you can set the option later using '`Maven. Importing`'[28] from `Settings`.

To create the class

In the IDE, open up the Project hierarchy so that you can see the `src\test\java` branch and the `src\main\java` branch. The Project hierarchy is shown be default as the tree structure on the left of the screen, and you can make if visible (if you close it) by selecting the `Project` button shown vertically on the left of the IntelliJ GUI.

My project hierarchy looks like this:

```
+ javaForTesters
  + .idea
  + src
    + main
      + java
      + resources
    + test
      + java
```

`.idea` is the IntelliJ folder, so I can ignore that.

I right click on the `java` folder under `test` and select the `New \ Java Class` menu item.

Or, I could click on the `java` folder under `test` and use the keyboard shortcut `alt + insert`, and select `Java Class` (on a Mac use `ctrl + n`)

Type in the name of the Java class that you want to create i.e. `MyFirstTest` and select `[OK]`

Don't worry about the package structure for now. We can easily manually move our code around later. Or have IntelliJ move it around for us using refactoring[29].

---

[28] https://www.jetbrains.com/idea/help/maven-importing.html

[29] http://refactoring.com/

Template code

You might find that you have a code block of comments which IntelliJ added automatically

```
/**
 * Created with IntelliJ IDEA.
 * User: Alan
 * Date: 24/04/13
 * Time: 11:48
 * To change this template use File | Settings | File Templates.
 */
```

You can ignore this code as it is a comment. You can delete all those lines if you want to.

Introduction to Comments In Java

Comments are explanatory text that is not executed.

You can use `// to comment out to the end of a line.`

You can comment out blocks of text by using `/*` and `*/`

Where `/*` delimits the start of the comment and `*/` delimits the end of the comment.

So `/* everything inside is a comment */`

```
/* Comments created with
forward slash asterisk
can span multiple lines */
```

Add the class to a package

IntelliJ will have created an empty class for us. e.g.

```
public class MyFirstTest {
}
```

And since we didn't specify a package, it will be at the root level of our `test\java` hierarchy.

We have two ways of creating a package and then moving the class into it:

- Manually create the package and drag and drop the class into it
- Add the `package` statement into our code and have IntelliJ move the class

Manually create the package and drag and drop the class into it by right clicking on the `java` folder under `test` and selecting `New \ Package`, then enter the package name you want to create.

For this book, I'm going to suggest that you use the top level package structure:

- `com.javafortesters`

And then name any sub structures as required. So for this class we could create a package called `com.javafortesters.chap003myfirsttest.examples`. You don't have to use the `chap003` prefix, but it might help you trace your code back to the chapter in the book. I use this convention to help you find the example and exercise source code in the source download.

Package Naming

In Java, package names tend to be all lowercase, and not use camelCase.

If we want to, we can **add the `package` statement into our code and have IntelliJ move the class**:

Add the following line as the first line in the class:

```
package com.javafortesters.chap003myfirsttest.examples;
```

The semi-colon at the end of the line is important because Java statements end with a semi-colon.

IntelliJ will highlight this line with a red underscore because our class is not in a folder structure that represents that package.

IntelliJ can do more than just tell us what our problems are, it can also fix this problem for us if we click the mouse in the underscored text, and then press the keys `alt + return`.

IntelliJ will show a pop up menu which will offer us the option to:

```
Move to package com.javafortesters.chap003myfirsttest.examples
```

Select this option and IntelliJ will automatically move the class to the correct location.

You could create the package first

Of course, I could have created the package first, but sometimes I like to create the classes, and concentrate on the code, before I concentrate on the ordering and categorization of the code.

You will develop your own style of coding as you become more experienced. I like to have the IDE do as much work for me as I can, while I remain in the 'flow' of coding.

The Empty Class Explained

```
package com.javafortesters.chap003myfirsttest.examples;


public class MyFirstTest {
}
```

If you've followed along then you will have an empty class, in the correct package and the Project window will show a directory structure that matches the package hierarchy you have created.

Package Statement

The `package` statement is a line of code which defines the package that this class belongs in.

```
package com.javafortesters.chap003myfirsttest.examples;
```

When we want to use this class in our later code then we would `import` the class from this package.

The `package` maps on to the physical folder structure beneath your `src\test` folder. So if you look in explorer under your project folder you will see that the package is actually a nested set of folders.

```
+ src
  + test
    + java
```

And underneath the `java` folder you will have a folder structure that represents the package structure.

```
+ com
  + javafortesters
    + chap003myfirsttest
      + examples
```

Java classes only have to be uniquely named within a package. So I could create another class called `MyFirstTest` and place it into a different package in my source tree and Java would not complain. I would simply have to `import` the correct package structure to get the correct version of the class.

Class Declaration

The following lines, are our *class declaration.*

```
public class MyFirstTest {
}
```

We have to declare a class before we use it. And when we do so, we are also defining the rules about how other classes can use it too.

Here the class has `public` scope. This means that any class, in any package, can use this class if they import it.

Java has more scope declarations

Java has other scope declarations, like `private` and `protected` but we don't have to concern ourselves with those yet.

When we create classes that will be used for *JUnit tests,* we need to make them `public` so that JUnit can use them.

The { and } are block markers. The opening brace { delimits the start of a block, and the closing brace } delimits the end of a block.

All the code that we write for a class has to go between the opening and closing block that represents the class body.

In this case the class body is empty, because we haven't written any code yet, but we still need to have the block markers, otherwise it will be invalid Java syntax and your IDE will flag the code as being in error.

Create a Method

We are going to create a method to add two numbers. Specifically `2+2`.

I create a new method by typing out the method declaration:

```
    public void canAddTwoPlusTwo(){
    }
```

Remember, the method declaration is enclosed inside the class body block:

```
public class MyFirstTest {

    public void canAddTwoPlusTwo(){
    }
}
```

- `public`

This method is declared as `public` meaning that any class that can use `MyFirstTest` can call the method.

When we use JUnit, any method that we want to use as a *JUnit test* should be declared as `public`.

- `void`

The `void` means that the method does not return a value when it is called. We will cover this in detail later, but as a general rule, if you are going to make a method a *JUnit test*, you probably want to declare it as `void`.

- `()`

Every method declaration has to define what parameters the method can be called with. At the moment we haven't explained what this means because our method doesn't take any parameters, and so after the method name we have "`()`", the open and close parentheses. If we did have any parameters they would be declared inside these parentheses.

- `{}`

In order to write code in a method we add it in the code block of the method body i.e. inside the opening and closing braces.

We haven't written any code in the method yet, so the code block is empty.

Naming JUnit Test Methods

A lot of people don't give enough thought to *JUnit test* method names. And use names like `addTest` or `addNumbers`. I try to write names that:

- explain the purpose of the method without writing additional comments
- describe the capability or function we want to check
- show the scope of what is being checked

Make the method a *JUnit test*

We can make the method a *JUnit test.* By annotating it with `@Test`.

In this book we will learn how to use annotations. We rarely have to create custom annotations when automating, so we won't cover how to create your own annotations in this book.

JUnit implements a few annotations that we will learn. The first, and most fundamental, is the `@Test` annotation. JUnit only runs the methods which are annotated with `@Test` as *JUnit tests.* We can have additional methods in our classes without the annotation, and JUnit will not try and run those.

Because the `@Test` annotation comes with JUnit we have to import it into our code.

When you type `@Test` on the line before the method declaration. The IDE will highlight it as an error.

```
@Test
public void canAddTwoPlusTwo(){
}
```

When we click on the line with the error and press the key combination `alt + return` then we will receive an option to:

`Import Class`

Choosing that option will result in IntelliJ adding the import statement into our class.

```
import org.junit.Test;
```

We have to make sure that we look at the list of import options carefully. Sometimes we will be offered multiple options, because there may be many classes with the same name, where the difference is the package they have been placed into.

If you select the wrong import

If you accidentally select the wrong import then simply delete the existing import statement from the code, and then use IntelliJ to `alt + return` and import the correct class and package.

Calculate the sum

To actually calculate the sum `2+2` I will need to create a variable, then I can store the result of the calculation in the variable.

```
    int answer = 2+2;
```

Variables are a symbol which represent some other value. In programming, we use them to store values: strings, integers etc. so that we can use them and amend them during the program code.

I will create a variable called `answer`.

I will make the variable an '`int`'. `int` declares the type of variable. `int` is short for integer and is a *primitive type*, so doesn't have a lot of functionality other than storing an integer value for us. An `int` is not a class so doesn't have any methods.

The symbol `2` in the code is called a *numeric literal*, or an *integer literal*.

An `int` has limits

An `int` can store values from -2,147,483,648 to 2,147,483,647. e.g.

```
int minimumInt = -2147483648;
int maximumInt = 2147483647;
```

When I create the variable I will set it to `2+2`.

Java will do the calculation for us because I have used the `+` operator. The `+` operator will act on two `int` operands and return a result. i.e. it will add `2` and `2` and return the value `4` which will be stored in the `int` variable `answer`.

Java Operators

Java has a few obvious basic operators we can use:

- `+` to add
- `-` to subtract
- `*` to multiply
- `/` to divide

There are more, but we will cover those later.

Assert the value

The next thing we have to do is *assert* the value.

```
assertEquals("2+2=4", 4, answer );
```

When we write `@Test` methods we have to make sure that we *assert* something because we want to make sure that our code reports failures to us automatically.

An assert is a special type of check:

- If the check fails then the assert throws an assertion error and our method will fail.
- If the check passes then the assert doesn't have any side-effects

The asserts we will initially use in our code come from the JUnit `Assert` package.

So when I type the assert, IntelliJ will show the statement as being in error, because I haven't imported the `assertEquals` method or `Assert` class from JUnit.

To fix the error I will `alt + return` on the `assertEquals` statement and choose to:

`static import method...`

from

`Assert.assertEquals` in the `org.junit` package

IntelliJ will then add the correct `import` statement into my code.

```
import static org.junit.Assert.assertEquals;
```

The `assertEquals` method is *polymorphic*. Which simply means that it can be used with different types of parameters.

I have chosen to use a form of:

```
        assertEquals("2+2=4", 4, answer );
```

Where:

- `assertEquals` is an assert that checks if two values are equal
- `"2+2=4"` is a message that is displayed if the assert fails.
- `4` is an `int` literal that represents the expected value, i.e. I expect `2+2` to equal `4`
- `answer` is the int variable which has the actual value I want to check against the expected value

I could have written the assert as:

```
        assertEquals(4, answer );
```

In this form, I have not added a message, so if the assert fails there are fewer clues telling me what should happen, and in some cases I might even have to add a comment in the code to explain what the assert does.

I try to remember to add a message when I use the JUnit assert methods because it makes the code easier to read and helps me when asserts do fail.

Note that in both forms, the **expected result** is the parameter, before the **actual result**.

If you get these the wrong way round then JUnit won't throw an error, since it doesn't know what you intended, but the output from a failed assert would mislead you. e.g. if I accidentally wrote `2+3` when initializing the `int answer`, and I put the **expected** and **actual** result the wrong way round, then the output would say something like:

```
java.lang.AssertionError: 2+2=4 expected:<5> but was:<4>
```

And that would confuse me, because I would expect `2+2` to equal `4`.

Assertion Tips

Try to remember to add a message in the assertion to make the output readable.

Make sure that you put the expected and actual parameters in the correct order.

Run the `@Test` method

Now that we have written the method, it is time to run the method and make sure it passes.

To do that either:

Run all the `@Test` annotated methods in the class

- right click on the class name in the Project Hierarchy and select:
  - `Run 'MyFirstTest'`
- click on the class in the Project Hierarchy and press the key combination:
  - `ctrl + shift + F10`
- right click on the class name in the code editor and select:
  - `Run 'MyFirstTest'`

Run a single `@Test` annotated method in the class

- right click on the method name in the code editor and select:
  - `Run 'canAddTwoPlusTwo()'`
- click on the method name in the code editor and press the key combination:
  - `ctrl + shift + F10`

Since we only have one `@Test` annotated method at the moment they will both achieve the same result, but when you have more than one `@Test` annotated method in the class then the ability to run individual methods, rather than all the methods in the class can come in very handy.

Run all the `@Test` annotated methods from the command line

If you know how to use the command line on your computer, and change directory then you can also run the `@Test` annotated methods from the command line using the command:

- `mvn test`

To do this:

- open a command prompt,
- ensure that you are in the same folder as the root of your project. i.e the same folder as your `pom.xml` file
- run the command `mvn test`

You should see the annotated methods run and the Maven output to the command line.

Summary

That was a fairly involved explanation of a very simple *JUnit test* class:

```
package com.javafortesters.chap003myfirsttest.examples;
import org.junit.Test;
import static org.junit.Assert.assertEquals;

public class MyFirstTest {

    @Test
    public void canAddTwoPlusTwo(){
        int answer = 2+2;
        assertEquals("2+2=4", 4, answer );
    }
}
```

Hopefully when you read the code now, it all makes sense, and you can feel confident that you can start creating your own simple self contained tests.

This book differs from normal presentations of Java, because they would start with creating simple applications which you run from the command line.

When we write automation code, we spend a lot of time working in the IDE and running the `@Test` annotated methods from the IDE, so we code and run Java slightly differently than if you were writing an application.

This also means that you will learn Java concepts in a slightly different order than other books, but everything you learn will be instantly usable, rather than learning things that you are not likely to use very often in the real world.

Although there is not a lot of code, we have covered the basics of a lot of important Java concepts.

- Ordering classes into packages
- Importing classes from packages to use them
- Creating and naming classes
- Creating methods
- Creating a *JUnit Test*
- Adding an assertion to a *JUnit test*
- Running `@Test` annotated methods from the IDE
- primitive types
- basic arithmetic operators
- an introduction to Java variables

- Java comments
- Java statements
- Java blocks

You also encountered the following IntelliJ shortcut keys:

Function	Windows	Mac
Create New	`alt + insert`	`ctrl + n`
Intention Actions	`alt + enter`	`alt + enter`
Intention Actions	`alt + return`	`alt + return`
Run JUnit Test	`ctrl + shift + F10`	`ctrl + shift + F10`

And now that you know the basics, we can proceed faster through the next sections.

Exercise: Check for 5 instead of 4

Amend the code so that the assertion makes a check for 5 as the expected value instead of 4:

- Run the method and see what happens.
- This will get you used to seeing the result of a failing method.

Exercise: Create additional `@Test` annotated methods to check:

- 2-2 = 0
- 4/2 = 2
- 2*2 = 4

Exercise: Check the naming of the *JUnit test* classes:

When you run *JUnit test* classes from the IDE they do not require 'Test' at the start or end of the name. But they do need that convention to run from Maven. Verify this.

Create a class with a method containing a failing assert e.g. `assertTrue(false);`

Rename the `class` to the different rules below, and run it from `mvn test` and from the IDE so you see the naming makes a difference.

- `Test` at the start e.g. `TestNameClass` runs in the IDE and from `mvn test`
- `Test` at the end e.g. `NameClassTest` runs in the IDE and from `mvn test`
- `Test` in the middle e.g. `NameTestClass` runs in the IDE but not from `mvn test`
- without `Test` e.g. `NameClass` runs in the IDE but not from `mvn test`

References and Recommended Reading

- CamelCase explanation on WikiPedia
  - en.wikipedia.org/wiki/CamelCase[30]
- Official Oracle Java Documentation
  - What is an Object?
    - docs.oracle.com/javase/tutorial/java/concepts/object.html[31]
  - What is a Class?
    - docs.oracle.com/javase/tutorial/java/concepts/class.html[32]
  - Java Tutorial on Package Naming conventions
    - docs.oracle.com/javase/tutorial/java/package/namingpkgs.html[33]
  - Java code blocks
    - docs.oracle.com/javase/tutorial/java/nutsandbolts/expressions.html[34]
  - Java Operators

[30]http://en.wikipedia.org/wiki/CamelCase

[31]http://docs.oracle.com/javase/tutorial/java/concepts/object.html

[32]http://docs.oracle.com/javase/tutorial/java/concepts/class.html

[33]http://docs.oracle.com/javase/tutorial/java/package/namingpkgs.html

[34]http://docs.oracle.com/javase/tutorial/java/nutsandbolts/expressions.html

        * docs.oracle.com/javase/tutorial/java/nutsandbolts/operators.html[35]

- JUnit
    - Home Page
        * junit.org[36]
    - Documentation
        * github.com/junit-team/junit/wiki[37]
    - API Documentation
        * junit.org/javadoc/latest[38]
    - @Test
        * junit.org/javadoc/latest/org/junit/Test.html[39]
- IntelliJ
    - IntelliJ Editor Auto Import Settings
        * jetbrains.com/idea/help/auto-import.html[40]
    - IntelliJ Maven Importing Settings
        * jetbrains.com/idea/help/maven-importing.html[41]

---

[35]http://docs.oracle.com/javase/tutorial/java/nutsandbolts/operators.html
[36]http://junit.org
[37]https://github.com/junit-team/junit/wiki
[38]http://junit.org/javadoc/latest
[39]http://junit.org/javadoc/latest/org/junit/Test.html
[40]https://www.jetbrains.com/idea/help/auto-import.html
[41]https://www.jetbrains.com/idea/help/maven-importing.html

Chapter Four - Work with Other Classes

Chapter Summary

In this chapter you will learn:

- How to use `static` methods of another class
- How to instantiate a class to an object variable
- How to access `static` fields and constants on a class
- The difference between `Integer` value and instantiation

In this chapter you are going to learn how to use other classes in your `@Test` method code. Eventually these will be classes that you write, but for the moment we will use other classes that are built in to Java.

You have already done this in the previous chapter. Because you used the JUnit `Assert` class to check conditions, but we imported it statically, so you might not have noticed. (I'll explain what static import means in the next chapter).

But first, some guidance on how to learn Java.

Use `@Test` methods to understand Java

When I work with people learning Java, I encourage them to write methods and assertions which help them understand the Java libraries they are using. And that is what we will do in this chapter.

For example, you have already seen a `primitive type` called an `int`.

Java also provides a class called `Integer`.

Because `Integer` is a class, it has methods that we can call, and we can instantiate an object variable as an `Integer`.

When I create an `int` variable, all I can do with it, is store a number in the variable, and retrieve the number.

If I create an `Integer` variable, I gain access to a lot of methods on the integer e.g.

- `compareTo` - compare it to another integer
- `intValue` - return an `int` primitive
- `longValue` - return a `long` primitive
- `shortValue` - return a `short` primitive

Explore the Integer class with `@Test` methods

In fact you can see for yourself the methods available to an integer.

- Create a new package:
  - `com.javafortesters.chap004testswithotherclasses.examples`
- Create a new class `IntegerExamplesTest`
- Create a method `integerExploration`
- Annotate the method with `@Test` so you can run it with JUnit

You should end up with something like the following:

```
package com.javafortesters.chap004testswithotherclasses.examples;


import org.junit.Test;

public class IntegerExamplesTest {

    @Test
    public void integerExploration(){
    }
}
```

We can use the `integerExploration` method to experiment with the Integer class.

Instantiate an Integer Class

The first thing we need to do is create a variable of type `Integer`.

```
Integer four = new Integer(4);
```

Because `Integer` is a class, this is called *instantiating a class* and the variable is an *object variable.*

- `int` was a *primitive type.*
- `Integer` is a class.
- To use a class we instantiate it with the `new` keyword
- The `new` keyword creates a new instance of a class
- The new instance is referred to as an *object* or *an instance of a class*

You can also see that I passed in the literal `4` as a parameter. I did this because the `Integer` class has a constructor method which takes an `int` as a parameter so the object has a value of `4`.

What is a Constructor?

A constructor is a method on a class which is called when a new instance of the class is created.

A constructor can take parameters, but never returns a value and is declared without a return type. e.g. `public Integer(int value){...}`

A constructor has the same name as the class including starting with an uppercase letter.

The `Integer` class actually has more than one constructor. You can see this for yourself.

- Type in the statement to instantiate a new `Integer` object with the value `4`
- Click inside the parentheses where the `4` is, as if you were about to type a new parameter,
- press the keys `ctrl + p` (`cmd + p` on a Mac)

You should see a pop-up showing you all the forms the constructor can take. In the case of an `Integer` it can accept an `int` or a `String`.

Check that `intValue` returns the correct `int`

We know that the `Integer` class has a method `intValue` which returns an `int`, so we can create an assertion to check the returned value.

After the statement which instantiates the `Integer`.

Add a new statement which asserts that `intValue` returns an `int` with the value `4`.

```
assertEquals("intValue returns int 4",
             4, four.intValue());
```

When you run this method it should pass.

Instantiate an Integer with a String

We saw that one of the constructors for `Integer` can take a `String`, so lets write some code to experiment with that.

- Instantiate a new `Integer` variable, calling the `Integer` constructor with the `String` `"5"`,
- Assert that `intValue` returns the `Integer` `5`

```
Integer five = new Integer("5");
assertEquals("intValue returns int 5",
             5, five.intValue());
```

Quick Summary

```
package com.javafortesters.chap004testswithotherclasses.examples;

import org.junit.Test;
import static org.junit.Assert.assertEquals;

public class IntegerExamplesTest {

    @Test
    public void integerExploration(){
        Integer four = new Integer(4);
        assertEquals("intValue returns int 4",
                     4, four.intValue());
        Integer five = new Integer("5");
        assertEquals("intValue returns int 5",
                     5, five.intValue());
        Integer six = 6;
        assertEquals("autoboxing assignment for 6",
                      6, six.intValue());
    }
}
```

It might not seem like it but we just covered some important things there.

- Did you notice that you didn't have to `import` the `Integer` class?
  - Because the `Integer` class is built in to the language, we can just use it. There are a few classes like that, `String` is another one. The classes do exist in a package structure, they are in `java.lang`, but you don't have to `import` them to use them.
- We just learned that to use an object of a class, that someone else has provided, or that we write, we have to instantiate the object variables using the `new` keyword.
- Use `ctrl + p` to have the IDE show you what parameters a method can take (`cmd + p` on a Mac).
- When we instantiate a class with the `new` keyword, a constructor method on the class is called automatically.

AutoBoxing

In the versions of Java that we will be using, we don't actually need to instantiate the `Integer` class with the `new` keyword.

We can take advantage of a Java feature called 'autoboxing' which was introduced in Java version 1.5. Autoboxing will automatically convert from a `primitive type` to the associated class automatically.

So we can instead simply assign an `int` to an `Integer` and autoboxing will take care of the conversion for us e.g.

```
Integer six = 6;
assertEquals("autoboxing assignment for 6",
              6, six.intValue());
```

Static methods on the Integer class

Another feature that classes provide are `static` methods.

You already used `static` methods on the `Assert` class from JUnit. i.e. `assertEquals`

A `static` method operates at the class level, rather than the instance or object level. Which means that we don't have to instantiate the class into a variable in order to call a `static` method.

e.g. `Integer` provides `static` methods like:

- `Integer.valueOf(String s)` - returns an `Integer` initialized with the value of the `String`
- `Integer.parseInt(String s)` - returns an `int` initialized with the value of the `String`

You can see all the `static` methods by looking at the documentation for `Integer`, or in your code write `Integer.` then immediately after typing the `.` the IDE should show you the code completion for all the `static` methods.

For each of these methods, if you press `ctrl + q` (`ctrl + j` on a Mac) you should see the help file information for that method.

Exercise: Convert an int to Hex:

`Integer` has a static method called `toHexString` which takes an `int` as parameter, this returns the `int` as a `String` formatted in hex.

Write an `@Test` annotated method which uses `toHexString` and asserts:

- that 11 becomes b
- that 10 becomes a
- that 3 becomes 3
- that 21 becomes 15

Public Constants on the Integer class

It is possible to create variables at a class level (these are called *fields*) which are also `static`. These field variables are available without instantiating the class. The `Integer` class exposes a few of these but the most important ones are `MIN_VALUE` and `MAX_VALUE`.

In addition to being `static` fields, these are also *constants*, in that you can't change them. (We'll cover how to do this in a later chapter). The naming convention for *constants* is to use only uppercase, with _ as the word delimiter.

`MIN_VALUE` and `MAX_VALUE` contain the minimum and maximum values that an `int` can support. It is worth using these values instead of `-2147483648` and `2147483647` to ensure future compatibility and cross platform compatibility.

To access a constant, you don't need to add parenthesis because you are accessing a variable, and not calling a method.

i.e. you write "`Integer.MAX_VALUE`" and not "`Integer.MAX_VALUE()`".

Exercise: Confirm MAX and MIN Integer sizes:

In the previous chapter we said that an `int` ranged from `-2147483648`, to `2147483647`. `Integer` has static constants `MIN_VALUE` and `MAX_VALUE`.

Write an `@Test` annotated method to assert that:

- `Integer.MIN_VALUE` equals `-2147483648`
- `Integer.MAX_VALUE` equals `2147483647`

Do this regularly

I encourage you to do the following regularly.

When you encounter:

- any Java library that you don't know how to use
- parts of Java that you are unsure of
- code on your team that you didn't write and don't understand

Then you can:

- read the documentation - `ctrl + q` (`ctrl + j` on Mac) or on-line web docs
- read the source - `ctrl` and click on the method, to see the source
- write some `@Test` annotated methods, with assertions, to help you explore the functionality of the library

When writing the `@Test` methods you need to keep the following in mind:

- write just enough code to trigger the functionality
- ensure you write assertion statements that cover the functionality well and are readable
- experiment with 'odd' circumstances

This will help you when you come to write assertions against your own code as well.

Warnings about `Integer`

I used `Integer` in this chapter because we used the `int` primitive in an earlier chapter and `Integer` is the related follow on class.

But... experienced developers will now be worried that you will start using `Integer` in your code, and worse, instantiating new integers in your code e.g. `new Integer(0)`

They worry because while an `int` equals an `int`, an `Integer` does not always equal an `Integer`.

I'm less worried because:

- I trust you,
- Automation code has slightly different usages than production code and you'll more than likely use the `Integer` `static` methods
- I'm using this as an example of instantiating a class and using static methods,
- This is only "Chapter 4" and we still have a way to go

I'll illustrate with a code example, why the experienced developers are concerned. You might not understand the next few paragraphs yet, but I just want to give you a little detail as to why one `Integer`, or one Object, does not always equal another Object.

e.g. if the following assertions were in an `@Test` method then they would pass:

```
assertEquals(4,4);
assertTrue(4==4);
```

Note that "==" is the Java operator for checking if one thing equals another.

If the following code was in an `@Test` method, then the second assertion would fail:

```
Integer firstFour = new Integer(4);
Integer secondFour = new Integer(4);

assertEquals(firstFour, secondFour);
assertTrue(firstFour==secondFour);
```

Specifically, the following assertion would fail:

```
assertTrue(firstFour==secondFour);
```

Why is this?

Well, primitives are simple and there is no difference between *value* and *identity* for primitives. Every `4` in the code refers to the same `4`.

Objects are different, we *instantiate* them, so the two `Integer` variables (`firstFour` and `secondFour`) both refer to different objects. Even though they have the same 'value', they are different objects.

When I do an `assertEquals`, JUnit uses the `equals` method on the object to compare the 'value' or the object (i.e. `4` in this case). But when I use the `"=="` operator, Java is checking if the two object variables refer to the same instantiation, and they don't, they refer to two independently instantiated objects.

So the `assertEquals` is actually equivalent to:

```
assertTrue(firstFour.equals(secondFour));
```

Don't worry if you don't understand this yet. It will make sense later.

For now, just recognize that:

- you can create object instances of a class with the `new` keyword, and use the non-static methods on the class e.g. `anInteger.intValue()`
- you can access the `static` methods on the class without instantiating the class as an object e.g. `Integer.equals(..)`.

Summary

You learned that in IntelliJ you can press `ctrl` and then the left mouse button to click on a method name and IntelliJ will jump to the source of that method.

You learned the following shortcut keys:

Function	Windows	Mac
Show Parameters	`ctrl + p`	`cmd + p`
Show JavaDoc	`ctrl + q`	`ctrl + j`

You also learned about static methods and the difference between object *value* and object *identity*.

Whatever you learn in this book, make sure you continue to experiment with writing assertions around code that you use or want to understand.

You also learned how to instantiate a new object and what a constructor does.

References and Recommended Reading

- Creating Objects
  - docs.oracle.com/javase/tutorial/java/javaOO/objectcreation.html[42]
- Autoboxing
  - docs.oracle.com/javase/tutorial/java/data/autoboxing.html[43]

[42]http://docs.oracle.com/javase/tutorial/java/javaOO/objectcreation.html
[43]http://docs.oracle.com/javase/tutorial/java/data/autoboxing.html

- Integer
  - docs.oracle.com/javase/7/docs/api/java/lang/Integer.html[44]

---

[44]http://docs.oracle.com/javase/7/docs/api/java/lang/Integer.html

Chapter Five - Working with Our Own Classes

Chapter Summary

In this chapter you will learn how to:

- Write your own class
- Write `@Test` annotated methods to help check your class method functionality
- Call the methods on the class
- Create static methods and static constants
- See the difference between static and non-static
- Use the IDE to write much of your code for you

And you will learn how to do all of this using Test Driven Development.

When we write code using TDD (Test Driven Development[45]) we write `@Test` methods and assertions first, and then write the code to make the assertions pass.

I like to do this when I'm writing code because I can use the IDE's features to help me type less and write code with fewer errors.

Context

Throughout this book I want to use examples and code which prepare you for using Java in the real world when writing automation code to support testing. As such we are going to be building different types of examples than we would in a normal Java book.

We are going to start small, and I want to introduce you to the concept of a 'domain' object. A 'domain' object is an object instantiated from a Class which represents *something* in the

[45]http://en.wikipedia.org/wiki/Test-driven_development

'domain' you are working in e.g. if you work on a banking application then you might have 'domain' objects such as: account, balance, transaction, etc.

When we build automation code we need to build a library of supporting objects to help us. We do this so that:

- our code is maintainable,
- our code becomes more readable,
- our code is faster to write, because we have higher level abstractions to help,
- we avoid repeating code.

All of the above are normal coding process goodness. Because when we write automation code for a production application, we are writing production code, and it must stand up to the same scrutiny that we apply to the live production code.

We have a number of possible object groupings when writing automation code, the following is one I use a lot:

- Physical
  - Application
    - e.g. login page, navigation menu
  - Environmental
    - e.g. installed URI, port
- Logical
  - Domain Entities
    - e.g. user, account

Essentially you can build as many categorizations and modeling levels as you need, in order to effectively model your system. I recommend the book 'Domain Driven Design'[46] by Eric Evans, if you want to learn more about domain modeling.

For the examples in this chapter we are going to look at an environmental domain object called `TestAppEnv` which represents the test environment we run our automation and assertions against.

Imagine that you have an application under test, that you have installed it on a number of test environments, and you want to run your automation code on any of those environments (and possibly on live).

[46]http://domainlanguage.com/ddd/

You don't want to have to change your automation code every time you use a different environment, so you want to abstract away the actual environment configuration behind an object that will handle that for you.

So instead of writing an `@Test` method like the following:

```
@Test
public void checkTitleCorrectOnApp(){

    FirefoxDriver driver = new FirefoxDriver();
    driver.get("http://192.123.0.3:67");

    assertEquals("Title should match",
            "Test App", driver.getTitle());
}
```

Note: the above sample code above uses the WebDriver[47] API, so it won't work if you type it in. What it says is: start Firefox browser, open the URL `"http://192.123.0.3:67"` and check the page title is `"Test App"`.

You could instead abstract away the application connection details into an environment domain object, e.g. `TestAppEnv`:

```
@Test
public void checkTitleCorrectOnAppWithDomainObject(){

    FirefoxDriver driver = new FirefoxDriver();
    driver.get(TestAppEnv.getUrl());

    assertEquals("Title should match",
            "Test App", driver.getTitle());
}
```

By doing this, instead of having a hard coded `String` literal `"http://192.123.0.3:67"` in all your `@Test` methods, you make a call to an object `TestAppEnv.getUrl()`.

By following along with the text in this chapter, you are going to build the `TestAppEnv` class, with its associated `@Test` methods and assertions.

[47]http://seleniumhq.org

First create an `@Test` method

The first thing we want to do, is create an `@Test` method.

To do that, we need a `Class` to put the method in.

- `@Test` methods reside in the `test` folder hierarchy of your project.
- I'm going to create a package called
  - `com.javafortesters.chap005testwithourownclasses.domainobject.examples`
- And in that package, create a class called `TestAppEnvironmentTest`.

Reminder on package and *JUnit test* class creation

Use the Project Tree to create packages. Click on the parent package, in the appropriate `src` folder branch e.g. `src\test\java` then right click and select `New \ Package`. Then enter the package name.

If you mess it up you can delete it and start again, or just drag it into the correct place using the Project Tree.

Use the Project Tree to create classes. Repeat the above but choose `New \ Java Class` in the package you want to create the class.

```
package com.javafortesters.chap005testwithourownclasses.domainobject.examples;

public class TestAppEnvironmentTest {
}
```

Then add an `@Test` method. I'm going to create one called `canGetUrlStatically` because I have decided that I want to be able to retrieve the URL from the `TestAppEnv` class statically, rather than instantiate a new instance of `TestAppEnv` every time I want to use it.

```
    @Test
    public void canGetUrlStatically(){
    }
```

Reminder on @Test method creation

Create the method code inside the body of the class, between the start { and end } code block braces.

Remember to add `import org.junit.Test;` to import the `@Test` annotation if the IDE does not add it automatically.

Write code that doesn't exist

Since I haven't created the `TestAppEnv` class yet, any code that I write using it, isn't going to work.

The natural tendency then, would be to go off an create the `TestAppEnv` class, write the code, and then come back to our *JUnit test* class and write methods and assertions to check it.

We are not going to do that. We are going to drive our code creation by writing automation code.

So in the `canGetUrlStatically` `@Test` method we are going to write the code that we want to see exist.

In effect we are designing the code by seeing it in a usage context.

So in my method `canGetUrlStatically` I write the line:

```
TestAppEnv.getUrl()
```

We can automatically add the import for `assertEquals` from the JUnit `Assert` package. But the IDE will complain that it `cannot resolve symbol TestAppEnv`. No surprise there, since we haven't written it yet.

We are going to let the IDE do the hard lifting here, and have it create the class for us.

Create a Class

Click on `TestAppEnv` and press the keys `alt + enter` (IntelliJ's *Intention Actions*[48] shortcut key) and you should see a small pop up menu of quick fix options. Something like:

[48]http://www.jetbrains.com/idea/webhelp/intention-actions.html

- `Create local variable 'TestAppEnv'`
- `Create class 'TestAppEnv'`
- `Create field 'TestAppEnv'`
- `Create inner class 'TestAppEnv'`
- `Create parameter 'TestAppEnv'`
- etc.

The important one for us is `Create class 'TestAppEnv'`

Select `Create class 'TestAppEnv'` then we need to tell the IDE where we want to create it.

We are going to use a different package.

We use packages to organize our code, and just because our `@Test` method code has been organized into a package for this chapter, it doesn't mean that our domain object needs to be in the same package.

I'm going to use a package:

```
package com.javafortesters.domainobject;
```

Since this is `class` is part of my abstraction layer, I don't want it it in the `src\test\java` folder structure, I want it in my main code `src\main\java`. Make sure you change the `Target destination folder` and create it in the main code base.

Don't worry if you mess it up

It is important that we try to choose good package names, but it is also important that we don't get too hung up on it, because re-organizing the code into different packages is pretty easy once the code is working, and the IDE has a lot of automated refactoring tools to make that simple.

Same with the target destination. If you mess it up, just delete it and try again, or drag drop the files in the Project tree to get it the way you want.

With the domain object class created, jump back to your *JUnit test* class, and see what new error exists in the code.

Create a method

Now the IDE should have highlighted `getUrl()` as having a problem because it `Cannot resolve method 'getUrl()'`

Again, because we haven't created that method. And we can use the IDE quick fix functionality to help us.

Click on the `getUrl` code and press the keys `alt + enter` and select `Create method 'getUrl'`

The IDE will create the method and may even add a `return null;` in there for us too, to make the code valid.

```
package com.javafortesters.domainobject;

public class TestAppEnv {

    public static String getUrl() {
        return null;
    }
}
```

Add the code to make the `@Test` method pass

Since our `@Test` method is being written to match our fictional environment. We need the `getUrl` method to return `"http://192.123.0.3:67"`.

All we do then, is replace `null` in the method body code block, with the `String` we want to return.

```
public class TestAppEnv {

    public static String getUrl() {
        return "http://192.123.0.3:67";
    }
}
```

If we jump back to our `@Test` method now.

We should have no syntax errors and we can run the `@Test` method.

A quick explanation of the code

There are no new concepts in the `@Test` method you have written, we are using the same concepts that we used in the previous chapter.

The `TestAppEnv` class, allows us to revisit a few concepts in more detail.

The method `getURL` was declared as `public static String`

- `public` this method is accessible to any class that imports `TestAppEnv`
- `static` this method can be used and called, without instantiating a `TestAppEnv` object
- `String` this method returns a string, to the calling code

Because the method needs to return a `String` we add a `return` statement.

```
return "http://192.123.0.3:67";
```

This particular `return` statement passes back a `String` literal. Which is then used in the `assertEquals` statement in the method.

Exercise: Experiment with the code

- Replace the `String` with an `int`. What happens?
- Replace the `String` literal `"http://192.123.0.3:67"` with `null` and run the `@Test` method. What happens?

What we just learned

Again, we have condensed a whole bunch of concepts into a fairly small piece of working code.

You learned:

- How to use IntelliJ Quick Fix functionality "Intention Actions" (`alt + enter`) to write code
- The basics of TDD:

  - write a failing `@Test` method,
  - run it,
  - watch it fail,
  - write just enough code to make it pass,
  - run it,
  - watch it pass,
  - repeat.
- How to create a `static` method
- How to declare a method that returns a value
- How to return a value from a method
- How to call a `static` method on a `Class`
- How to use a method's returned value in an assert statement

New Requirements

Now that we have a working `@Test` method, we can start to refactor the object and make it more suitable for our needs.

Immediately though, if we had used the `String` `"http://192.123.0.3:67"` anywhere in our code, we could replace it with `TestAppEnv.getUrl()` and gain the benefits of abstraction and maintenance.

I'm going to add a few more requirements so that we can learn a little more Java and amend our class.

Sometimes in our automation code we don't always want to get the full URL, sometimes we want, just the Domain or just the Port.

My initial idea is that we want to be able to do the following:

```
@Test
public void canGetDomainAndPortStatically(){

    assertEquals("Just the Domain",
            "192.123.0.3",
            TestAppEnv.DOMAIN);

    assertEquals("Just the port",
            "67",
            TestAppEnv.PORT);
}
```

Notice, that again, I'm thinking through the usage and the code with an `@Test` method. By writing the code I want to see, I can experiment with different concepts before actually writing any implementation code to make the `@Test` method pass.

All we have to do now is implement the two new *Constant Fields* `DOMAIN` and `PORT`.

Type in the new `@Test` method code, and use the IntelliJ Quick fix function to create these *Constant Fields*.

Fields

A *field* is a Java variable that exists at the class level rather than local to a method.

Constant means that the variable won't change once a value has been assigned.

Fields are located within the `Class` code block. And, by convention, before any methods.

You should end up with code like the following in your `TestAppEnv` object.

```
public static final String DOMAIN = "192.123.0.3";
public static final String PORT = "67";
```

- `public` - the field can be accessed by any code that imports the `TestAppEnv` class
- `static` - `TestAppEnv` does not need to be instantiated with `new` before usage
- `final` - the variable can not change once a value has been assigned
- `String` - declares the variable as a `String` object
- `DOMAIN`, `PORT` - by convention constants are written in uppercase, with multiple words delimited by _ underscore

I set the constants to the the string values that we passed back originally in the `getUrl` method.

If we run our `@Test` methods, they should pass.

Now Refactor

An important element of TDD, and all programming, is to refactor.

This means going back. Looking at our code. Identifying waste and improvements. And changing the code, such that the `@Test` annotated methods continue to pass, and no external interface to the code is amended.

In our case, this means that we can change any of the code in our `TestAppEnv` so long as we still have two fields named `DOMAIN` and `PORT` and a method `getUrl` which returns the same `String` object as that checked by the assertions.

The obvious thing to change is that we have repeated `String` literals in our domain object since our `DOMAIN` string and `PORT` string are repeated as part of the hard coded `String` in `getUrl`. i.e. the following line

```
return "http://192.123.0.3:67";
```

A little string concatenation

Since the values of the `DOMAIN` *constant* and the `PORT` *constant* are part of the hard coded `String` in `getUrl` we really want to build the `String` passed back from `getUrl` using the `DOMAIN` and `PORT` constants, that way if the environment details change then we only have to amend the fields, and not the `String` in the methods.

String concatenation is something we do a lot when building automation code e.g.:

- creating messages to send to systems
- generating input data
- creating log messages
- etc.

I'm going to quickly show the simplest way of concatenating Strings. And in fact you've already seen the code we need to use.

+

Yes, the 'plus' sign can join the values of `String` objects together.

I can amend the `getUrl` method so that it uses `DOMAIN` and `PORT`

```
return "http://" + DOMAIN + ":" + PORT;
```

By doing this, I have reduced the duplicated code and only have to change a single line of code in the abstraction layer if I want to change the environment details used by the `@Test` methods.

Run the *JUnit test* class and make sure that the `@Test` methods still pass.

There is more that I could do to this class, but for now it is good enough, and we will revisit it later.

The `TestAppEnv` code

I've included the source code we built in this chapter so you can check your results. Later chapters will not include the full source code since I recommend that you download and view the full source used for the book:

- github.com/eviltester/javaForTestersCode[49]

After all the changes, your TestAppEnv class should look like the following:

```
package com.javafortesters.domainobject;

public class TestAppEnv {

    public static final String DOMAIN = "192.123.0.3";
    public static final String PORT = "67";

    public static String getUrl() {
        return "http://" + DOMAIN + ":" + PORT;
    }
}
```

Since it is a very simple class, we have not needed to add any additional imports.

The code for the `TestAppEnvironmentTest` class which we used to create `TestAppEnv` is shown below:

[49]https://github.com/eviltester/javaForTestersCode

```
package com.javafortesters.chap005testwithourownclasses.domainobject.examples;

import com.javafortesters.domainobject.TestAppEnv;
import org.junit.Test;
import static org.junit.Assert.assertEquals;

public class TestAppEnvironmentTest {

    @Test
    public void canGetUrlStatically(){

        assertEquals("Returns Hard Coded URL",
                "http://192.123.0.3:67",
                TestAppEnv.getUrl()
                );
    }

    @Test
    public void canGetDomainAndPortStatically(){

        assertEquals("Just the Domain",
                "192.123.0.3",
                TestAppEnv.DOMAIN);

        assertEquals("Just the port",
                "67",
                TestAppEnv.PORT);
    }
}
```

Static Usage versus Static Import

One thing to point out, now that we have examples, is the difference between 'Static Usage' and 'Static Import'.

You can see examples of both in the `TestAppEnvironmentTest` code.

Static Usage

We use the `static` constants from `TestAppEnv`. So we `import` the `TestAppEnv` class:

```
import com.javafortesters.domainobject.TestAppEnv;
```

Every time we want to use the `static` constants `DOMAIN` or `PORT`, we prefix them with the class that they are from, i.e. `TestAppEnv`, as shown in the code below:

```
        assertEquals("Just the Domain",
                "192.123.0.3",
                TestAppEnv.DOMAIN);
```

Static Import

We statically import the `assertEquals` from JUnit.

```
import static org.junit.Assert.assertEquals;
```

This means that we can type `assertEquals` in our code without having to prefix it with `Assert` in the same way that we do for the `DOMAIN` and `PORT` constants from `TestAppEnv` e.g.

```
                TestAppEnv.getUrl()
```

The only difference is the `import`

Both the `assertEquals` method, and the *constants* `DOMAIN` and `PORT`, are declared as `static` and `public`, in their respective classes.

The only difference in our *JUnit test* code, is how we imported them.

Had I imported the `JUnit` assert in a non-static manner i.e. the same way I imported `TestAppEnv`:

```
import org.junit.Assert;
```

Then I would not have been able to write `assertEquals` in my code, I would have to prefix it with `Assert` e.g.

```
Assert.assertEquals("Returns Hard Coded URL",
        "http://192.123.0.3:67",
        TestAppEnv.getUrl());
```

Similarly, I could have imported the `TestAppEnv` constants `DOMAIN` and `PORT` statically, and then avoided the prefix `TestAppEnv` on each usage.

I could either `import static` the `DOMAIN` and `PORT` as separate imports, or just import everything from `TestAppEnv`, and then I wouldn't have to prefix calls to `getUrl` e.g.

```
import static com.javafortesters.domainobject.TestAppEnv.*;
```

Exercise: Convert from Static Usage to Static Import

Experiment with the `static` import in your `TestAppEnvironmentTest`.

- Convert the `assertEquals` `import static` to an `import` of just the `Assert` and amend the `@Test` methods accordingly so you prefix each usage of `assertEquals` with `Assert`.
- Convert the `import` of `TestAppEnv` to an import static of the `DOMAIN` and the `PORT`, and convert the `@Test` methods so you use them without the prefix.
- Convert the `import` of `TestAppEnv` to an import static of everything in `TestAppEnv` and convert the `@Test` methods so the constants have no prefix.

As you make the changes, reflect on: how does the automation code look? is it maintainable? etc.

How to decide what to `static import`

Deciding what to import statically might be made for you through organizational coding standards. i.e. some teams always write `Assert.assertEquals`

I usually make the decision based on my standards of readability, so I generally `import static` the assert methods I use. But I probably would not `import static` the `TestAppEnv` constants since I don't think that seeing `DOMAIN` or `PORT` in the `@Test` methods really gives me enough information and I'd wonder "which domain?" and "which port?", but I rarely wonder "which assertEquals?".

Overuse of `import static` can make your code less readable because people might confuse your statically imported method, or constant, as one which is locally defined.

The important point at the moment is to know that you:

- have a choice over how you statically import.
- decide which approach to use on a case by case basis (or follow your organizational standards).
- can make code less readable and maintainable if you `import static` too many methods and constants, so use this power sparingly.

Summary

Again, I've tried to condense a bunch of learning into a single chapter. I hope you managed to follow along. If not, go back through this chapter and try again, or compare your code to the main Github source (or included above).

We covered a lot of fundamental concepts, and having actually done the work, by typing it into your IDE, you will have learned more than you may realize:

- We managed to make it easier to amend the environment location.
- We abstracted the change away from the `@Test` methods so that our abstraction code can change without requiring any other code changes in the `test` branch.
- We now know how to create `static` methods.
- We now know how to create `static` *constant* fields.
- We now know a little refactoring.
- We know a little `String` concatenation.
- We know to keep our abstractions in `src\main\java` and our `@Test` methods in `src\test\java`.
- We know that we can use classes from other packages.
- We know that we can organize our `@Test` method code differently from our abstraction code.

Our next few chapters are going to concentrate on learning some of the Java Concepts and libraries that we need to understand to help us write automation code.

Chapter Six - Java Classes Revisited: Constructors, Fields, Getter & Setter Methods

Chapter Summary

In this chapter you will learn how to:

- Understand what a *Constructor* is
- Create a *default constructor*
- Create a *constructor* with parameters
- Call one *constructor* from another
- Create *getter* and *setter* methods

The first few chapters have been 'throw in the deep end' and 'tutorials'.

Now we are going to step through Java concepts in more detail.

We can do that because you already know how to:

- create classes,
- create methods,
- annotate methods with `@Test` to run them as *JUnit tests*

Context

When modeling applications, one of the Domain Entities I often end up creating is `User`. Typically someone with an account on the system who can login with a 'username' and 'password'. A `User` may have a few other details as well.

For the examples in this chapter we should imagine that we want to build a `User` object for use in our *JUnit tests.*

We need to follow the normal process to get us started:

- create a package `'com.javafortesters.domainentities'`
- create it under `src.main.java` since it is an abstraction, not a *JUnit test* class
- in the package create a `class User`

```
package com.javafortesters.domainentities;

public class User {
}
```

Next create a *JUnit test* class to allow us to construct the class using TDD.

- create a package `'com.javafortesters.chap006domainentities.examples'`
- remember to create it under `src.test.java`
- in the package create a `class UserTest`

```
package com.javafortesters.chap006domainentities.examples;

public class UserTest {
}
```

Constructor

What is a Constructor?

A constructor is a special method that is called when a class is instantiated with the `new` keyword.

Write an `@Test` method which instantiates a new user:

```
@Test
public void canConstructANewUser(){
    User user = new User();
}
```

Hopefully no syntax errors - remember to import `org.junit.Test`.

You would also have to import the `User` class.

Sharing the same package

If the `User` class and the `UserTest` class were in the same package then you would be able to use the `User` class without importing it.

The classes would be in different folder structures, but if they were in the same package then you could use any public classes in the same package without importing them.

Experiment with the package structure

Move the `UserTest` to a different package, either above or in a sibling to `.domainentities`. Can you use the `User` class without importing it?

Watch out - depending on how you moved it, your IDE might have added the import for you automatically.

Package Scoping

If you declare a field or method with no modifier i.e. miss out the `public`, then only classes in the same `package` can use it, not every class that imports it.

Default Constructor

If you run the `@Test` method - what does it do?

Well, nothing really.

It creates a new instance of the class `User` and stores it in the variable `user`. But we did not create a constructor on the `User` class, therefore no code in the `User` class is executed when the object is instantiated.

Now we shall add some code that executes when the class is instantiated. By writing a constructor, that doesn't take any arguments, in the `User` class. Known as a *no-argument constructor.*

Default Constructor

If you don't write a constructor, then Java automatically creates one which sets all your fields to their default values and calls the default constructor for any superclass. (we haven't covered *superclass* yet, so this will make sense later)

No-argument Constructor

If we have particular defaults in mind for *fields* on the class then a good place to initialize them is in a no-argument constructor.

I want to have a `username` field and a `password` field and have them default to `"username"` and `"password"`.

I could just go in to the `User` class and create code to set this up, but I want to get in the habit of creating `@Test` methods first.

To help me maintain that habit, I'm going to create an `@Test` method which creates a `User` object and then *gets* the `username` and `password` and *asserts* they have been *set* to my desired default values.

I do this by creating an `@Test` method which looks like this:

```
@Test
public void userHasDefaultUsernameAndPassword(){

    User user = new User();

    assertEquals("default username expected",
            "username",
            user.getUsername());

    assertEquals("default password expected",
```

```
                "password",
                user.getPassword());
    }
```

The `getUsername` and `getPassword` methods don't exist so I have to create them.

My IDE can create the basic methods for me, but I don't have any `username` or `password` to return. Which means it is now time to add `username` and `password` as *fields* in my `User` class.

I create a constructor in `User` that takes no arguments. And assign default values to the fields `username` and `password`. Demonstrated by the following code:

```
    private String username;
    private String password;

    public User(){
        username = "username";
        password = "password";
    }
```

In the code snippet, you can see that I created a `String` variable `username` and a `String` variable `password`. Because these variables are declared in the body of the *class*, rather than in a *method*, they are known as *fields* or *field variables.*

I have declared them `private` so that they are only accessible to methods in the `User` class itself, and not from any classes that `import` the `User` class.

The constructor I have written takes no arguments. You know it is a constructor because it does not have a return type in the declaration and the name is exactly the same as that of the class, complete with uppercase letter.

I assign default values to the `username` and `password` in the body of the *constructor*. Any method in a class can amend, and access, the *field variables* declared in that class.

I can then write the methods that return the `username` and `password`, so that the `@Test` method can pass.

```
public String getUsername() {
    return username;
}

public String getPassword() {
    return password;
}
```

The code should pass now. Write the code, and run the `@Test` method to see this for yourself.

A few notes on the `User` class

The `getUsername` and `getPassword` methods are known as *accessor* or *getter* methods because they allow us to 'access', or 'get' the value of a *field*. They take no parameters, and return the values of the *field variables*.

The combination of the field `username`, and the getter method `getUsername`, is sometimes known as a 'property'.

Because we declared the *field variables* as `private`, we need to create methods which allow other classes to access the values of those variables.

I could have made the field variables `public`, and then I would not have needed to create an *accessor* method, but then I reduce the amount of control that we have over the values because other classes could amend the values of those fields at any point.

Experiment with private and public fields

Try it for yourself. Make the fields `public` and in an `@Test` method, set `username` and `password` to a new value, and *get* the value just by accessing the field.

e.g.

```
User auser = new User();
auser.username = "bob";
assertEquals("not default username", "bob", auser.username);
```

A Constructor with arguments

At the moment we have no way of changing the `username` and `password` on a `User`. So we will write a *constructor* which allows us to create a `User` object and *set* the `username` and `password` at the same time.

As demonstrated in the following code, you can see that I create a `User` with a `username` of `"admin"` and a `password` of `"pA55w0rD"`:

```
@Test
public void canConstructWithUsernameAndPassword(){

    User user = new User("admin", "pA55w0rD");

    assertEquals("given username expected",
            "admin",
            user.getUsername());

    assertEquals("given password expected",
            "pA55w0rD",
            user.getPassword());
}
```

To make this `@Test` method pass, we have to create a new *constructor* in `User`, this time a *constructor* which takes two parameters, the `username` and `password` we want to assign to the `User`. This *constructor* is shown below:

```
public User(String username, String password) {
    this.username = username;
    this.password = password;
}
```

Note that the *constructor* now has two parameters: `String username` and `String password`.

Because these parameters have the same name as the fields, I have to use the `this` keyword in the method, when I want to access the `username` and `password` field on the current object. If I did not add `this.` then Java would not be able to distinguish between the *field* and the *parameter*.

I could have renamed the parameters `aUsername` and `aPassword` to avoid a naming clash. But I want to minimize the documentation I have to produce, and keeping the parameter names self-documenting helps long term maintenance. Also this gives us the opportunity to introduce you to the `this` keyword.

Experiment with the field and parameter names

Write the constructor code, as shown in the text which uses the `this` keyword.

Remove the `this.` from the *constructor*, and what happens?

Change the *constructor parameter* names so that the `@Test` method passes and you do not use the `this` keyword. When would you do this?

`this`

The `this` keyword refers to the current object.

You can use any method or field in the object with the `this` keyword.

The `this` keyword helps you distinguish between local variables with the same name as fields.

You can also use the `this` keyword to call methods or constructors.

Explicit Constructor Invocation

If you followed the previous sections then you will notice that you have duplicated code in the `User` class, since the *no-argument constructor* has code to assign values to the *fields*, as does the *constructor* which does take arguments.

```
public class User {

    private String username;
    private String password;

    public User(){
        username = "username";
        password = "password";
    }

    public User(String username, String password) {
        this.username = username;
        this.password = password;
    }
```

We can call one *constructor* from another

Using the `this` keyword we can call the *argument constructor* from the *no-argument constructor*, e.g:

```
public User(){
    this("username", "password");
}
```

By refactoring to this code, we:

- only have one place where the `username` and `password` fields are assigned values,
- still retain the ability to call the default *constructor* and assign defaults to the fields.

i.e.

```
public User(){
    this("username", "password");
}

public User(String username, String password) {
    this.username = username;
    this.password = password;
}
```

Getters and Setters

Getters

You have already seen two *getter* (or *accessor*) methods in the `User` class i.e. `getUsername` and `getPassword`.

```
public String getUsername() {
    return username;
}

public String getPassword() {
    return password;
}
```

Setters

We also want the ability to amend or *set* field values in a class. We do this through *setter* methods.

For our code we want to have the ability to amend the `password` but not the `username`.

Once our `username` has been *set* via a *constructor* invocation, we never want to allow any calling classes to amend the `username`, but we do want to allow amending the `password`.

To amend the `password` we will write a *setter* method (`setPassword`), which we use as specified in this code:

```
@Test
public void canSetPasswordAfterConstructed(){

    User user = new User();

    user.setPassword("PaZZwor6");

    assertEquals("setter password expected",
            "PaZZwor6",
            user.getPassword());
}
```

And the actual *setter* method in the `User` class looks like this:

```
public void setPassword(String password) {
    this.password = password;
}
```

Again you can see the use of the `this` keyword to distinguish between the *field* and the *local variable* defined by the `String password` parameter.

Write the code, and run the `@Test` methods to make sure all our assertions still pass.

Why Setters and Getters?

By creating a *setter* method we gain the ability to control the values that are assigned to the fields e.g.

- we could add code for validation and make sure we can't assign incorrect passwords
- if a password had to be minimum length we could write code to pad it to the correct length if we needed to

We can use *getter* methods to hide the implementation, e.g. we might 'calculate' the return value, rather than always return something which has been *set*.

There are occasionally times where we want to loosen up control over the object fields and make them public, so people can amend them and access them whenever, and however they want. But we are much more likely to use *setter* and *getter* methods to control access and allow us the flexibility in the future to change implementation details.

Summary

You should now know how to:

- create a *no-argument constructor* by creating a `public` scope method with no return type which has the same name as the class
- create a *constructor* that takes parameters
- have *parameters* named the same as *fields*, and use them in the same method body
- use the `this` keyword to distinguish between object fields and method parameters
- call a *constructor* from another *constructor*
- create *getter* methods which return values
- create *setter* methods to amend *field variables*

And you should also understand:

- the basics of *field* and *method* scoping `public`, `private` and with no explicit scope (`package`).

`User` class code

For your reference and comparison, we created the following `User` class, in this chapter:

```
package com.javafortesters.domainentities;

public class User {

    private String username;
    private String password;

    public User(){
        this("username", "password");
    }

    public User(String username, String password) {
        this.username = username;
        this.password = password;
    }

    public String getUsername() {
        return username;
    }

    public String getPassword() {
        return password;
    }

    public void setPassword(String password) {
        this.password = password;
    }

}
```

References and Recommended Reading

- Access Control
  - docs.oracle.com/javase/tutorial/java/javaOO/accesscontrol.html[50]
- Default Constructor
  - docs.oracle.com/javase/specs/jls/se7/html/jls-8.html#jls-8.8.9[51]
- Constructors
  - docs.oracle.com/javase/tutorial/java/javaOO/constructors.html[52]

[50]http://docs.oracle.com/javase/tutorial/java/javaOO/accesscontrol.html
[51]http://docs.oracle.com/javase/specs/jls/se7/html/jls-8.html#jls-8.8.9
[52]http://docs.oracle.com/javase/tutorial/java/javaOO/constructors.html

- Java 'this' keyword
  - docs.oracle.com/javase/tutorial/java/javaOO/thiskey.html[53]

[53]http://docs.oracle.com/javase/tutorial/java/javaOO/thiskey.html

Chapter Seven - Basics of Java Revisited

Chapter Summary

In this chapter you will receive an overview of:

- Java Comments
- Java naming conventions
- Working with packages
- Scope of fields, methods and classes
- the `final` keyword
- Data Types: boolean, integer, floating point, character and their wrapper classes
- `BigDecimal`
- Operators: Arithmetic, Assignment, Boolean, Conditional, Ternary and Bitwise
- Operator Precedence
- String concatenation and static methods

This chapter will quickly reinforce the topics covered in the previous tutorial chapters. You will also see reference to concepts you have not yet covered e.g. `BigDecimal`, we mention these because it makes sense in context, but we will cover the details later.

There are no specific exercises in this chapter, although you should read through the example code to make sure you understand it. I also recommend that you write `@Test` methods to experiment with your own examples and verify the statements made in this chapter.

You can use this as a reference chapter for later study. Rest assured that we continue to build on this information in later chapters, so don't worry if you don't absorb it all on first reading.

Comments

Comments are non-executable statements in the code.

There are 3 types of comments:

- comments that run to the end of the line `//`
- comments that mark out blocks starting `/*` and ending `*/`
- JavaDoc comments starting with `/**` and ending `*/`

When we want small comments we can add them after statements and anything after `//` will be treated as a comment. These comments are useful for quick explanations.

```
assertTrue(truthy); // comment till end of line
```

To comment out a block of code, or have a larger descriptive text we use a block comment which starts with `/*` and ends with `*/`. These comments can span lines and start and end in the middle of lines.

```
/*
  This code checks that the true
  value that truthy was set to
  is true. Pretty obvious really.
 */
boolean truthy = true;
assertTrue(truthy);
```

Block Comments do not nest

You cannot nest block comments, i.e. if you try and comment out a block of text which already contains a block comment then you will get a syntax error.

You can comment out a block comment by putting `//` at the start of each line.

JavaDoc comments help with communication because you can use the IDE to show you the JavaDoc on methods and classes i.e. if I press `ctrl + q` (`ctrl + j` on Mac) on the `addTwoNumbers` method call in `aJavaDocComment` I will see the JavaDoc documentation from the comment.

This is a very useful commenting style to use on abstraction layer classes and methods. e.g.

```
@Test
public void aJavaDocComment(){
    assertTrue(addTwoNumbers(4,3)==7);
}

/**
 * Add two integers and return an int.
 *
 * There is a risk of overflow since two big
 * integers would max out the return int.
 *
 * @param a is the first number to add
 * @param b is the second number to add
 * @return a+b as an int
 */
public int addTwoNumbers(int a, int b){
    return a+b;
}
```

We won't cover JavaDoc in detail in this book, but you can read the references to find out more.

Statement

A Java statement is the smallest chunk of executable Java code. We end a Java statement with `;` e.g.

```
assertEquals(4, 2+2);
```

Java statements can span lines. This is useful to make your code more readable and line up arguments on method calls. e.g.

```
assertEquals("2+2 always = 4",
             4,
             2+2);
```

Packages

Java allows us to group our *Classes* into *packages*. Each `class` has to be uniquely named within a *package*. We can have multiple *classes* with the same name, provided they are all in different packages.

```
package com.javafortesters.chap007basicsofjavarevisited.examples;
```

To add a class to a package you write a package declaration statement like the above, very often the first line in the `class`, and certainly before the code that declares the class.

Java Classes

All of our Java code will involve *classes* in some form. Either using *classes* that others have written, writing abstraction layers as *classes*, or creating *JUnit tests* (which are actually methods in a `class` annotated with `@Test`).

```
public class AnEmptyClass {
}
```

This example class shows many features of a class:

```
package com.javafortesters.chap007basicsofjavarevisited.examples;

 public class ClassExample {

    public static final String CONSTANT = "a constant string";
    public static String aClassField = "a class field";
    protected static String proField = "a class field";
    public String pubField = "a public field";
    private String privField = "a private field";
    private String name;

    public ClassExample(String name){
        this.name = name;
    }

    public String getName(){
        return this.name;
    }

    public void setName(String name){
        this.name = name;
    }
}
```

The first line of the `class` has the package declaration. This doesn't need to be the first line, it just needs to come before the `class` declaration.

```
package com.javafortesters.chap007basicsofjavarevisited.examples;
```

Here, the `class` is declared with the name `ClassExample` and declared as `public`.

```
public class ClassExample {
```

Because the `class` is public, it can be used by another `class`, so long as they import it, or if they are in the same *package*. If I didn't add the `public` then the `class` would have `package` scope[54] and only be available to other classes in the same *package*.

Static methods and fields

A *class* can expose `static` *methods* and *fields*, which allow you to use them without instantiating a new *instance object* of the *class*.

You have seen this when using any of the asserts in JUnit, these are all `static` *methods* on the `Assert` *class*.

Instantiating Classes

Most *classes* need to be *instantiated* before they can be used.

```
        ClassExample instance = new ClassExample("bob");
```

When we *instantiate* a class, we use the `new` keyword, and call one of the *class*'s *constructors*.

Field and Method Scope

The scope of a field or method is defined by `public`, `protected`, `private` or *package-private* (no modifier).

- `public` accessible to any *class* that imports the parent *class*

[54]http://docs.oracle.com/javase/tutorial/java/javaOO/accesscontrol.html

- `protected` accessible to any *class* in the same *package*, or any *subclass*
- `private` accessible to *methods* in the *class*
- **package-private** - when no modifier is used then the *field* or *method* is accessible to the *class* and any *class* in the same *package* (this is the default)

Additional *field* and *method* modifiers:

- `static` - the *field* or *method* exists at the *class* level, not the *instance level*, so is shared by all instances and can be accessed without needing to have an instantiated class variable.

Fields & Variables

Fields are variables that are accessible by any method in the *class* and, depending on the scope, possibly to other classes.

Field refers to variables declared at the *class* level and *local variable* refers to variables created in a *method*.

Additional modifiers are:

- `final` - once the *field*, or variable, has a value it cannot be changed

Examples of combinations and nuances of scope and modifiers are explained below.

Naming

A *field* or *variable* name must begin with a *letter*, which is any Unicode character that represents a letter: to play it safe, and keep code readable, we normally stick to 'A' to 'Z', 'a' to 'z', although some people also use the symbols '_' and '$' (and even ' £').

After this first letter, the variable name can contain any of the letters, or digits.

Case is significant so `aMount` is not the same as `Amount`.

Names tend to use camel case and start with a lowercase letter. *Constants* tend to be all uppercase, with '_' to delimit words.

A variable name can be very long, and you can use a wide range of characters in the name, but do try and keep the names readable, and capable of being read aloud.

```
@Test
public void variableNaming(){
    String $aString="bob";
    float £owed=10F;
    int aMount=4;
    long Amount=5;
    String A0123456789bCd$f="ugh";

    assertEquals(4,aMount);
    assertEquals(5, Amount);
    assertEquals(10.0F, £owed, 0);
    assertEquals("bob", $aString);
    assertEquals("ugh", A0123456789bCd$f);
}
```

Public Static Final

`public static final` fields are often known as *constants*, because once assigned a value, the value can not be changed. This makes them useful for exposing constant values to other classes.

```
public static final String CONSTANT = "a constant string";
```

Typically you will see the value assignment in the declaration as a constant, as shown in the example above, but it could also be set from a method call, which allows you to read constants from files or property values.

Final

Note that final does not have to have `public static` scope. Any of the scoping keywords can be used with `final` e.g. `private final`

`final` simply means that once assigned a value, it can't be changed. But it is so often used as `public static final` that I included it in this section.

Public Static

```
public static String aClassField = "a class field";
```

A `public static` field is available to any class which imports the `ClassExample` class. And because it is static, the field is available without having to instantiate the class into an instance variable. These `static` fields are often known as *class fields* e.g.

```
assertEquals(ClassExample.aClassField,
             "a class field");
```

You can access *class fields* from instance objects, but the IDE may warn you, or the field may not show up in code completion.

```
instance.aClassField = "changed";
```

Unlike *constants* these *fields* can have their values changed by other classes. This can make your code error prone - so be careful if you do this.

Public

```
public String pubField = "a public field";
```

A `public` *field* is accessible to all classes which instantiate a new instance variable of the class.

```
assertEquals(instance.pubField, "a public field");
instance.pubField = "amended public field";
assertEquals(instance.pubField, "amended public field");
```

Because these fields can be changed by other classes, you should consider if you need to make them public, or if it should be a private field, and the class should offer *setter* and *getter* methods instead.

Protected

`protected` means that the field can be used by any class in the same package, or any class which extends this class. (You will learn about `extends` later in this book)

Package-Private (default)

When no modifier is added to the *field* definition then it is only accessible by methods in the *class* or any classes in the same *package.*

Importing Classes

A *class* can use any *classes* in the same package. And any *class* declared as `public` in other packages, when we `import` that *class.*

We can `import` specific classes by specifying the `class` name in the the `import` statement.

```
import com.javafortesters.domainentities.User;
```

We can also use wildcard to `import` *all* the classes from a package e.g.

```
import com.javafortesters.chap001basicsofjava.examples.classes.*;
```

Note that you don't *have* to import. You can use classes without importing them, by prefixing the *class* name with the *package* path. But your code quickly becomes verbose and harder to maintain. e.g.

```
@org.junit.Test
public void nonImportTest(){
    org.junit.Assert.assertEquals(3, 2 + 1);
}
```

This can be helpful if you are trying to use two classes with the same name in your code. If they are in different packages then prefix the class's name with the full package when you declare and initialise it.

Static Imports

You can import specific methods and fields, as well as classes. You have already seen this with the JUnit imports. e.g.

```
import org.junit.Assert;
import static org.junit.Assert.assertEquals;
```

Above you can see two imports. A `static` import for the `assertEquals` method and an import for the `Assert` class.

When I use the `static` import of `assertEquals`, I can use the `assertEquals` method directly in my code e.g.

```
        assertEquals(6,3+3);
```

When I do not use the `static` import, I have to access the `static` method from the class itself e.g.

```
        Assert.assertEquals(5,3+2);
```

Data Types

Every variable in Java must have a type declared, either as a *primitive*, or an *object class*.

Boolean Type

A `boolean` has two constants `true` and `false`.

There is also an associated `Boolean` object.

```
    @Test
    public void BooleanType(){
        boolean truthy = true;
        boolean falsey = false;

        assertTrue(truthy);
        assertFalse(falsey);

        truthy = Boolean.TRUE;
        falsey = Boolean.FALSE;

        assertTrue(truthy);
        assertFalse(falsey);
    }
```

Integer Types

- `byte` range: -128 to 127
- `short` range: -32768 to 32767
- `int` range: -2147483648 to 2147483647
- `long` range: -9223372036854775808 to 9223372036854775807

Each *primitive* has an associated *Class* e.g. `Byte`, `Short`, `Integer`, `Long`. These can be used for conversions and have other support methods. They also have the `MIN_VALUE` and `MAX_VALUE` constants for each *primitive*.

Various Java syntax exists for representing *literals* as specific *primitives*:

- represent an integer literal as a `long` by adding the suffix `L`
- represent a hex value with the prefix `0x` (zero x)
- represent an octal value with the prefix `0` (zero)
- represent a binary value with the prefix `0b` (zero b) (Java 1.7)
- make numbers readable by adding _ e.g. `9_000_000` (underscore) (Java 1.7)

Examples of the above, can be seen below:

```
@Test
public void IntegerTypes(){
    byte aByteHas1Byte;
    short aShortHas2Bytes;
    int anIntHas4Bytes;
    long aLongHas8Bytes;

    System.out.println(
            "* `byte` range: " +
            Byte.MIN_VALUE + " to " +
            Byte.MAX_VALUE);

    System.out.println( "* `short` range: " +
            Short.MIN_VALUE + " to " +
            Short.MAX_VALUE);

    System.out.println( "* `int` range: " +
            Integer.MIN_VALUE + " to " +
```

```
                Integer.MAX_VALUE);

        System.out.println( "* `long` range: " +
                Long.MIN_VALUE + " to " +
                Long.MAX_VALUE);

        aLongHas8Bytes = 0L; //add suffix L for long
        assertEquals(0, aLongHas8Bytes);

        aByteHas1Byte = 0xA; //add prefix 0x for Hex
        assertEquals(10,aByteHas1Byte);

        anIntHas4Bytes = 010; //add 'zero' prefix for Octal
        assertEquals(8, anIntHas4Bytes);

        aByteHas1Byte = 0b0010; // Java 1.7 added 0b 'zero b' for binary
        assertEquals(aByteHas1Byte, 2);

        // Java 1.7 allows underscores for readability
        aLongHas8Bytes = 9_000_000_000L; // 9 000 million
        assertEquals(9000000000L, aLongHas8Bytes);
    }
```

Floating-point Types

Floating point types have two different precisions, which controls the size of value they can store:

- `float` : single precision 32 bit number
- `double` : double precision 64 bit number

Ranges:

- `float` range: 1.4E-45 to 3.4028235E38
- `double` range: 4.9E-324 to 1.7976931348623157E308

Suffixes:

- represent a `float` with the suffix `F`

- represent a `double` with the suffix `D`, or if you use a decimal point e.g. `20.0` then the number will default to a `double`

The official documents recommend the use of the `java.math.BigDecimal` class if you want precise values e.g. currency. `BigDecimal` helps avoid rounding errors.

These *primitive* types also have an associated *Class* e.g. `Float` and `Double`

```
@Test
public void FloatingPointType(){
    float singlePrecision32bit;
    double doublePrecision64bit;

    System.out.println("* `float` range: " +
                    Float.MIN_VALUE + " to " +
                    Float.MAX_VALUE);

    System.out.println( "* `double` range: " +
                    Double.MIN_VALUE + " to " +
                   Double.MAX_VALUE);

    singlePrecision32bit = 10.0F; // suffix F to get a float
    assertEquals(10F, singlePrecision32bit, 0);

    doublePrecision64bit = 20.0;  // default to double
    assertEquals(20D, doublePrecision64bit, 0);
}
```

Character Type

The `char` data type is used to represent an individual character e.g. `'a'`, it is a 16 bit Unicode character.

A `char` is not a `String`.

You can represent a unicode character as `\u0026` i.e. `\u` followed by the 4 character hex value of the Unicode character. e.g. `\u0026` is `&`

Java also has some *special characters* represented by *escape sequences* e.g.

- `\t` - a tab character

- `\b` - backspace
- `\n` - a new line
- `\r` - a carriage return
- `\'` - a single quote
- `\"` - a double quote
- `\\` - a backslash

All of these special characters are also available for use in `String`.

Java also has an associated `Character` class with *static* methods to help when working with `char` variables.

```
@Test
public void CharacterType(){
    char aChar = '\u0026';
    assertEquals(aChar, '&');
}
```

Operators

Traditional

Java has the traditional arithmetic operators that you would expect:

- `+` for addition
- `-` for subtraction
- `*` for multiplication
- `/` for division

All of the above can be used for *Integer* and *Floating point* numbers. Although you may not get the result you expect with *Floating point* numbers (due to rounding) - which is why `BigDecimal` is often recommended.

- `+` can also be used for `String` concatenation
- `%` for *integer* remainder calculations (i.e. *modulus*) e.g. `9%2` returns `1`

```
@Test
public void traditionalOperatorsExplored(){
    assertEquals(4, 2+2);
    assertEquals(5L, 10L - 5L);
    assertEquals(25.0F, 12.5F * 2F, 0);
    assertEquals(30.2D, 120.8D / 4D, 0);
    assertEquals("abcd", "ab" + "cd");
    assertEquals(1, 9%2);
}
```

Assignment

Operators are also used for assignment, as you have seen when you instantiate a variable.

- `=` to assign the value to the variable

The traditional operators can also be used during assignment:

- `+=` to increment the variable by value e.g. `+= 2` would add two
- `-=` to decrement the variable by value e.g. `-= 2` would subtract two
- `*=` to multiply the variable by value e.g. `*= 2` would multiply by two
- `/=` to divide the variable by value e.g. `/= 2` would divide by two
- `%=` to calculate and assign the modulus by value e.g. `%= 3` would assign the variable modulus the value

```
@Test
public void assignmentOperatorsExplored(){
    String ab = "ab";
    assertEquals("ab", ab);

    int num = 10;
    assertEquals(10, num);

    num += 2;
    assertEquals("+= increments by", 12, num);

    num -= 4;
    assertEquals("-= decrements by", 8, num);
```

```
        num *= 2;
        assertEquals("*= multiplies by", 16, num);

        num /= 4;
        assertEquals("/= divides by", 4, num);

        num %=3;
        assertEquals("%= modulus of", 1, num);
    }
```

Increment and Decrement

You can increment and decrement a variable using `++` and `--` e.g. `++num` would return `num` incremented by `1`

You can put `++` and `--` before or after the variable.

- Putting `++` or `--` before the variable means that you want to amend it before using it. (*prefix*)
- Putting `++` or `--` after the variable means that you want to use it and then amend it. (*postfix*)

e.g.

```
    @Test
    public void incrementDecrementOperatorsExplored(){
        int num = 10;
        assertEquals(11, ++num);
        assertEquals(10, --num);
        assertEquals(10, num++);
        assertEquals(11, num);
        assertEquals(11, num--);
        assertEquals(10, num);
    }
```

Boolean Operators

Java has a range of operators which compare two operands and return `true` or `false`.

- `==` test for equality
- `!=` test for inequality
- `>` greater than
- `<` less than
- `<=` less than or equal to
- `>=` greater than or equal to

You can also negate a boolean with `!` (known as *logical complement*);

```
@Test
public void booleanOperatorsExplored(){
    assertTrue( 4 == 4 );
    assertTrue(4 != 5);
    assertTrue(3 < 4);
    assertTrue(5 > 4);
    assertTrue( 6 >= 6);
    assertTrue( 7 >= 6);
    assertTrue( 8 <= 8);
    assertTrue( 8 <= 9);

    assertTrue(!false);

    boolean truthy = true;
    assertFalse(!truthy);
}
```

Conditional Operators

You can create complex boolean statements by using `&&` and `||`

- `&&` a logical *and*
- `||` a logical *or*

e.g.

```
@Test
public void conditionalOperatorsExplored(){
    assertTrue( true && true);
    assertTrue( true || false);
    assertTrue( false || true);
    assertFalse( false || false);
    assertFalse( false && true);
}
```

Note that these logical conditional operators *short cut*, so they only evaluate the second operand if required. e.g. `true || false` would only need to check the first `true` value, but `false || true` would have to evaluate both.

Ternary Operator

Java supports a *ternary* operator which performs a check on a condition and:

- if `true`, returns the value of the first operand, and
- if `false`, returns the value of the second operand.

condition ? *operand1* : *operand2*;

Note that you only need the ; on the end, if the ternary operator is on the right of a statement, if it is evaluated within a statement then you don't add the ;

e.g.

```
@Test
public void ternaryOperatorsExplored(){
    int x;
    x = 4>3 ? 2 : 1;
    assertEquals(2, x);

    assertTrue( 5>=4 ? true : false );
}
```

Bitwise Operators

You can perform binary based bitwise operations on integer `int` data types.

- & and
- | or
- ^ xor
- ~ bitwise two's complement (invert the bits)

```
@Test
public void bitwiseOperatorsExplored(){
    assertEquals(0b0001,
                 0b1001 & 0b0101);

    assertEquals(0b1101,
                 0b1001 | 0b0101);

    assertEquals(0b1100,
                 0b1001 ^ 0b0101);

    int x = 0b0001;
    assertEquals("11111111111111111111111111111110",
                 Integer.toBinaryString(~x));
}
```

The bitwise operators can also be used during an assignment.

```
@Test
public void bitwiseAssignmentOperatorsExplored(){
    byte x = 0b0001;

    x &= 0b1011;
    assertEquals(0b0001, x);

    x |= 0b1001;
    assertEquals(0b1001, x);

    x ^= 0b1110;
    assertEquals(0b0111, x);
}
```

Bit Shift Operators

You can perform binary arithmetic and shift operations on integer `int` data types.

- `<<` shift to the left e.g. `<<3` shift 3 to the left
- `>>` signed shift to the right
- `>>>` unsigned right shift (shift a zero into leftmost position)

The shift operators can also be used on assignment.

```
@Test
public void bitwiseShiftOperatorsExplored(){
    int x = 56;

    assertEquals(x*2, x<<1);
    assertEquals(x*4, x<<2);
    assertEquals(x*8, x<<3);

    x <<=3;
    assertEquals(56*8, x);

    x = Integer.MAX_VALUE;
    assertEquals(Integer.MAX_VALUE/2, x>>1);
    assertEquals(Integer.MAX_VALUE/4, x>>2);
    assertEquals(Integer.MAX_VALUE/8, x>>3);

    x = Integer.MIN_VALUE; // -ve
    assertEquals((Integer.MAX_VALUE/2)+1, x>>>1);
}
```

Operator precedence

The operator precedence is listed on the Java documentation page:

- docs.oracle.com/javase/tutorial/java/nutsandbolts/operators.html[55]

While it is worth understanding the precedence order, it is generally easier to read the intent behind a complex statement if the order of precedence is made clear by using parenthesis, `()` since nested operations are executed first.

e.g. compare the asserts below, which is easier to understand?

[55]http://docs.oracle.com/javase/tutorial/java/nutsandbolts/operators.html

```
@Test
public void operatorPrecedence(){
    assertEquals(8, 4+2*6/3 );
    assertEquals(12, (((4+2)*6)/3) );
}
```

Therefore try and use parenthesis, `()`, to control the order of precedence, as it will make the code easier to read and maintain.

The basic rules for precedence are:

- The operators with highest precedence are evaluated first.
- Operators with equal precedence are evaluated in left to right order
- Assignment operators are evaluated right to left

In the table below, operators are listed in precedence order, and where more than one operator is on the same row, they are of equal precedence.

<table>
<tr><th>Operator</th></tr>
<tr><td>x++ x--</td></tr>
<tr><td>++x --x +x -x ~ !</td></tr>
<tr><td>* / %</td></tr>
<tr><td>+ -</td></tr>
<tr><td><< >> >>></td></tr>
<tr><td>< > <= >=</td></tr>
<tr><td>== !=</td></tr>
<tr><td>&</td></tr>
<tr><td>^</td></tr>
<tr><td>|</td></tr>
<tr><td>&&</td></tr>
<tr><td>||</td></tr>
<tr><td>?:</td></tr>
<tr><td>= += -= *= /= %= &= ^= |= <<= >>= >>>=</td></tr>
</table>

Strings

A `String` is a *class* in `java.lang` so you don't need to import it to use it.

Strings are *immutable* so they can't change. All commands that look like they *change* the values of *strings*, actually return a new `String` with all the amendments.

String Concatenation

Strings can be concatenated using the + operator.

```
@Test
public void stringsConcatenated(){
    assertEquals("123456", "12" + "34" + "56");
}
```

String methods

The `String` *class* provides `static` methods that can be used without instantiating a `String` object variable:

- `length` the number of characters in the string
- `charAt` returns the character at a specific index
- `contains` returns true if a substring is contained
- etc.

```
@Test
public void someStringMethods(){
    String aString = "abcdef";

    assertEquals(6, aString.length());
    assertTrue(aString.compareToIgnoreCase("ABCDEF")==0);
    assertTrue(aString.contains("bcde"));
    assertTrue(aString.startsWith("abc"));

    // string indexing starts at 0
    assertEquals('c', aString.charAt(2));
    assertEquals("ef", aString.substring(4));
}
```

For methods which use indexes e.g. `substring` or `charAt` the *index* starts at `0` so the first character is at index `0`

Strings will be explored in more detail later in the book.

Summary

This was intended to be a fairly heavy chapter, but I interspersed it with a lot of code examples.

Make sure you work through the examples and understand them.

Recreate them in your own code and experiment with them if you want to deepen your knowledge.

Don't worry if you didn't understand it all. Since this is the first time you have seen some of the topics here, we will cover them in more detail later.

References and Recommended Reading

- JavaDoc Comments Documentation
  - oracle.com/technetwork/java/javase/documentation/index-137868.html[56]
- Wikipedia JavaDoc
  - en.wikipedia.org/wiki/Javadoc[57]
- Method Scope: public, private, protected, package
  - docs.oracle.com/javase/tutorial/java/javaOO/accesscontrol.html[58]
- Java Primitive Data Types
  - docs.oracle.com/javase/tutorial/java/nutsandbolts/datatypes.html[59]
- Unicode characters
  - en.wikipedia.org/wiki/List_of_Unicode_characters[60]
- Java characters
  - docs.oracle.com/javase/tutorial/java/data/characters.html[61]
- Two's Complement
  - en.wikipedia.org/wiki/Two%27s_complement[62]
- Operators and Precedence
  - docs.oracle.com/javase/tutorial/java/nutsandbolts/operators.html[63]

---

[56]http://www.oracle.com/technetwork/java/javase/documentation/index-137868.html

[57]http://en.wikipedia.org/wiki/Javadoc

[58]http://docs.oracle.com/javase/tutorial/java/javaOO/accesscontrol.html

[59]http://docs.oracle.com/javase/tutorial/java/nutsandbolts/datatypes.html

[60]http://en.wikipedia.org/wiki/List_of_Unicode_characters

[61]http://docs.oracle.com/javase/tutorial/java/data/characters.html

[62]http://en.wikipedia.org/wiki/Two%27s_complement

[63]http://docs.oracle.com/javase/tutorial/java/nutsandbolts/operators.html

Chapter Eight - Selections and Decisions

Chapter Summary

In this chapter you will learn, how to use selections and conditions in your code:

- How to use the ternary operator
- `if/else` statements
- The `switch` statement

When I was learning to program, a long time ago. I was taught that programming was made up of:

- Sequence
- Selection
- Iteration

Sequence, is what we've been doing: one statement, following another statement.

Selection, is making decisions, and choosing to do one thing, or another, depending on a particular condition.

Iteration, where we repeat actions until we have done what we needed.

This chapter is going to look at *Selection*. Or *Conditional Statements*

Ternary Operators

You have already seen the Ternary operator.

```
x = 4>3 ? 2 : 1;
```

x is set to 2, if 4 is greater than 3, otherwise x is set to 1

In the ternary operator, the condition is evaluated and:

- if the condition is `true`, the value of the first operand is returned,
- if the condition is `false` the value of the second operand is returned.

e.g.

```
@Test
public void moreTernary(){
    String url = "www.eviltester.com";

    url = url.startsWith("http") ? url : addHttp(url);

    assertTrue(url.startsWith("http://"));
    assertEquals("http://www.eviltester.com", url);
}

private String addHttp(String url) {
    return "http://" + url;
}
```

People often use this for simple, in-line, decision making or quick checks. I personally find it harder to read, so when I code I generally write `if` statements.

Exercise: Cat or Cats? Ternary Operator

Write an `@Test` method that uses a ternary operator to return `"cat"` if a `numberOfCats` equals `1`. And return `"cats"` if the `numberOfCats` is not `1`

Rewrite your code so that the ternary operator is used in a method which returns `"cat"` or `"cats"` depending on the `numberOfCats` parameter it is called with. e.g.

```
assertEquals("2 == cats", "cats", catOrCats(2));
```

`if` statement

The `if` statement takes the forms:

`if (`*condition*`)` *statement*`;`

or

`if (`*condition*`){`
statement1`;`
statement2`;`
`}`

- When only one statement is used in the `if` then you don't need to add the `{}` block delimiters.
- When multiple statements are used then you need to add the statements in the code block delimited with `{}`.

The statements are only executed when the condition evaluates to `true`

Coding Style

I tend to add `{}` regardless of the number of statements.

I think it makes the code easier to read. And I'm less likely to forget to add the block delimiters in later, when I add more statements to the `if` clause.

But these are personal style issues and are likely to be dictated by your personal style, or the style of coding enforced in your work place.

Example:

```
@Test
public void ifAddHttp(){
    String url = "www.seleniumsimplified.com";
    if(!url.startsWith("http")){
        url = addHttp(url);
    }
    assertTrue(url.startsWith("http://"));
    assertEquals("http://www.seleniumsimplified.com", url);
}
```

Exercise: AssertTrue if true

Given a variable:

```
boolean truthy=true;
```

Write an `@Test` method that uses an `if` statement without a set of braces `{}` to `assertTrue` on `truthy`, if `truthy` is `true`.

Write an `@Test` method that uses an `if` statement that when `truthy` is true, `assertsTrue` on `truthy`, and `assertsFalse` on `!truthy`

`else` statement

Since the statement block after the `if` only executes when the condition evaluates to `true`, we also need the ability to execute code if the condition evaluates to `false`.

And this is where the `else` keyword comes in.

`if (`*condition*`)`
statement;
`else`
statement;

or

`if (`*condition*`){`
statement1;
statement2;
`}else{`
statement3;

statement4;
}

Again you can see that when there is no delimited block then the `else` executes a single statement, but when the `else` has a delimited block then all the statements in that block will execute.

Example:

```
@Test
public void ifElseAddHttp(){
    String url = "www.seleniumsimplified.com";
    if(url.startsWith("http")){
        // do nothing the url is fine
    }else{
        url = addHttp(url);
    }
    assertTrue(url.startsWith("http://"));
    assertEquals("http://www.seleniumsimplified.com", url);
}
```

Compound Statement

A set of statements in a block is often called a 'compound statement'.

And a single statement is referred to as a 'simple' statement.

Exercise: AssertTrue else AssertFalse

Given a variable: `boolean truthy=true;`

Write an `@Test` method that uses an `if` statement without a set of braces `{}` to `assertTrue` on `truthy`, if `truthy` is `true`, otherwise it uses `assertFalse` on `truthy`.

Write an `@Test` method that uses an `if` statement that if `truthy` is true, `assertsTrue` on `truthy`, and `assertsFalse` on `!truthy`, otherwise it uses `assertFalse` on `truthy`

Make sure you run the methods with `truthy=false`, so you see the effect with both values.

Nested `if else`

Because `if` and `else` are statements they can be nested in the `if` and `else` statement block like any other statement.

e.g.

```
@Test
public void ifElseNestedAddHttp(){
    String url = "seleniumsimplified.com";
    if(url.startsWith("http")){
        // do nothing the url is fine
    }else{
        if(!url.startsWith("www")){
            url = "www." + url;
        }
        url = addHttp(url);
    }
    assertTrue(url.startsWith("http://"));
    assertEquals("http://www.seleniumsimplified.com", url);
}
```

Code formatting becomes very important when using nested `if` and `else`:

- indent your code
- line up statements
- line up braces {}

Also note that the coding style I adopt has the opening brace `{` at the end of the `if` or `else` statement on the same line, other people prefer to put the opening brace under the `if` or `else` but in line with it.

e.g.

```
if(url.startsWith("http"))
{
    // do nothing the url is fine
}else
{
    if(!url.startsWith("www"))
    {
        url = "www." + url;
    }
    url = addHttp(url);
}
```

I personally think that the above style takes up too much space, and that the opening brace { adds no information, but the closing brace } does add information about scope when I read the code.

Experiment and decide on a style that suits you. Look at the code in use in your organization and adopt the in house style.

Exercise: Nested If Else Horror

Write the following pseudo code as Java in an `@Test` method:

Given a variable `truthy` which is set to `true` and a variable `falsey` which is set to false:

- If truthy then
  - If !falsey then
    - If truthy and !falsey then
      - If falsey or truthy then
      - ....assert truthy is true, and
      - ....assert falsey is false
  - Else
    - assert truthy is true
    - assert falsey is true
- Else
  - If !truthy then
    - if falsey then
      - assert falsey is true
      - assert truthy is false
    - else
      - assert falsey is false
      - assert truthy is false

Try it with different combinations of values on `truthy` and `falsey` to make sure you have covered all paths.

`switch` statement

When your code has a lot of `if else` statements then it might be appropriate to use a `switch` statement instead.

The `switch` statement allows you to have a number of *cases* for a single condition check.

```
@Test
public void switchExample(){
    assertEquals("M", likelyGenderIs("sir"));
    assertEquals("M", likelyGenderIs("mr"));
    assertEquals("M", likelyGenderIs("master"));
    assertEquals("F", likelyGenderIs("miss"));
    assertEquals("F", likelyGenderIs("mrs"));
    assertEquals("F", likelyGenderIs("ms"));
    assertEquals("F", likelyGenderIs("lady"));
    assertEquals("F", likelyGenderIs("madam"));
}

public String likelyGenderIs(String title){
    String likelyGender;

    switch(title.toLowerCase()){
        case "sir":
            likelyGender = "M";
            break;
        case "mr":
            likelyGender = "M";
            break;
        case "master":
            likelyGender = "M";
            break;
        default:
            likelyGender = "F";
            break;
    }
    return likelyGender;
}
```

- The `switch` statement takes an expression to check.
- The `switch` block has a series of `case` statements.
- The `break` statement is important to end each `case`.
- The last `case` should be a `default` which is executed if no other case matches.
- `default` does not require a `break`, but I usually add one

Note: you need to use Java 1.7 or above if you want to have string literals in your `case` statements.

Be Careful. If you forget the `break` then the case will fall through to the next one. e.g.

I could have written the switch like this:

```
switch(title.toLowerCase()){
    case "sir":
    case "mr":
    case "master":
        likelyGender = "M";
        break;
    default:
        likelyGender = "F";
        break;
}
```

When written deliberately, the fall through can make code easy to read. Beware however that it is a simple mistake to make and forget the `break` statement and it can easily introduce bugs into your code.

Exercise: Switch on Short Code

Create a method which uses a `switch` statement to return a `String` depending on the `shortCode` passed in as a parameter to the method:

- given "UK" return "United Kingdom"
- given "US" return "United States"
- given "USA" return "United States"
- given "FR" return "France"
- given "SE" return "Sweden"
- given any other value, return "Rest Of World"

For bonus points, make the short code case insensitive i.e. "uK", "UK", "Uk", "uk" should all return "United Kingdom"

Exercise: Switch on `int`

Create a method which uses a `switch` statement to return a `String` representing the `int` passed in as a parameter to the method:

- given `1` return `"One"`
- given `2` return `"Two"`
- given `3` return `"Three"`
- given `4` return `"Four"`
- given an integer `> 4`, return `"Too big"`
- given an integer `< 1`, return `"Too small"`

As an experiment, also write the method such that every `case` in the `switch` is implemented as a `return` so no variables or `break` statements are used.

Summary

You have seen that you can write code without all the `{}` and `break` statements. But I find that adding them *all* the time, makes my code more readable and maintainable.

I tend not to use ternary operators very much, but some people use them all the time. So it is important to be able to read them.

Even though this was a short chapter. You do need to master conditional flows in your code and make decisions about which conditional operator you use.

References and Recommended Reading

- if-then-else Java tutorial
  - docs.oracle.com/javase/tutorial/java/nutsandbolts/if.html[64]
- switch Java tutorial
  - docs.oracle.com/javase/tutorial/java/nutsandbolts/switch.html[65]

[64] http://docs.oracle.com/javase/tutorial/java/nutsandbolts/if.html

[65] http://docs.oracle.com/javase/tutorial/java/nutsandbolts/switch.html

Chapter Nine - Arrays and For Loop Iteration

Chapter Summary

In this chapter you will learn, a simple way of collecting things, accessing them, and looping over them using:

- *Arrays* - a fixed size collection of 'things'
- *Array indexing* - access individual items in an array
- *For Each Loop* - iterate over each individual item in the array
- *For Loop* - iterate through a loop using indexes
- *Arrays of Arrays* - Arrays can contain other arrays
- *Ragged Arrays* - An array of arrays with different sizes
- `java.utils.Arrays` - A utility class for working with Arrays e.g. `fill`, `sort`, *copy*

In previous chapters you have seen how to create individual *variables* to store *objects* and *strings.*

If you wanted to create a collection of Domain Objects at the moment, then you would have to create an individual variable for each one: e.g. `user1`, `user2`, `user3`, etc.

Ideally, we want some sort of object that collects all these together and allows us to access each item individually. We also want to loop through them to process each in different ways.

Arrays, provide us with a simple way of doing exactly this.

Arrays

Arrays are the first collection data type we are going to learn.

An *array* represents a collection of items, all of the same type.

Arrays are fixed size. In future chapters we will learn about collections that can adjust their size dynamically as we add more items. But, because *arrays* are a fixed size, it makes them simple to understand.

As a quick example:

```
@Test
public void simpleArrayExample(){
    String[] numbers0123 = {"zero", "one", "two", "three"};

    for(String numberText : numbers0123){
        System.out.println(numberText);
    }

    assertEquals("zero", numbers0123[0]);
    assertEquals("three", numbers0123[3]);
}
```

The above code:

- creates an array called `numbers0123` which will hold `String` objects
- creates the array with four strings `"zero"`, `"one"`, `"two"`, and `"three"`
- iterates over the array printing out each string in the array so the console would display

```
zero
one
two
three
```

- asserts that the first value in the array equals `"zero"`
- asserts that the last value in the array equals `"three"`

The rest of this chapter will explain arrays in more detail and you will write your own code using arrays.

Create an Array

There are a number of ways to create a new *array*:

- Declare and create an array of fixed size
- Declare and create array with actual values
- Declare an empty array
- Declare an array for later initialization

Declare and Create an Array of Fixed Size

You can declare an *array* of a fixed size:

```
int[] integers = new int[10];
int []moreInts = new int[10];
int evenMore[] = new int[10];
```

You can see the type declaration (`int`), which means that this *array* can only store `int` values. You can also see that the `[]` can be before or after the variable name.

I prefer to put the `[]` after the type declaration, as in the first `int` example above. I think it is faster to read the declaration and see that it is an array.

I create the array with the code:

- `new int[10]`

This creates an `int` array of size `10`, so it can store `10 int` values.

I can create and declare an array of different types, so the following code shows the creation of a `String` array of size `10`, to hold `10 String` values.

```
String strings[] = new String[10];
```

Declare and Create an Array with Actual Values

You can also declare an array with the values in the declaration:

```
int[] ints1to10 = {1, 2, 3, 4, 5, 6, 7, 8, 9, 10};
```

Declare an Empty Array

You can declare an array of zero length, using the syntax presented below:

```
int[] zeroLength = {};
int[] moreZeroLength = new int[0];
```

Declare an Array for Later Initialization

If you want to, you can declare an array and initialize it later. For example, this code declares an array but does not initialize it.

```
int[] uninitializedArray;
```

I prefer to initialize it at declaration, or initialize it as an empty array.

If you want to allocate a new array to an existing array variable then you can use the syntax you saw in the declaration i.e.

```
uninitializedArray = new int[10];
```

Or you can also use the following syntax, which creates an anonymous array and allocates it to an existing variable:

```
uninitializedArray = new int[] {100, 200, 300};
```

Access items in an array

You can access the items in an array by using the `[i]` notation, where `i` is the index you want to access.

Arrays are indexed starting at `0` so the first item in an array is at `[0]`.

```
String[] workdays = {"Monday", "Tuesday", "Wednesday",
                     "Thursday", "Friday"};
```

```
    assertEquals("Monday", workdays[0]);
    assertEquals("Friday", workdays[4]);
```

Exercise: Create an Array of Users

Using the `User` domain object that you created previously.

Create an array containing 3 `User` objects.

Iterate through an array

We can iterate through an array with a *for each* loop and a *for* loop.

The iteration examples below, all use the following `workdays` array:

```
String[] workdays = {"Monday", "Tuesday", "Wednesday",
                     "Thursday", "Friday"};
```

For Each loop

A *for each* loop, iterates through each item in the array.

```
for ( variable : collection ){
   // do something
}
```

The *variable* is automatically assigned the next item from the *collection*, and iterates over each item in the array automatically.

e.g.

```
String days="";

for(String workday : workdays){
    days = days + "|" + workday;
}

assertEquals("|Monday|Tuesday|Wednesday|Thursday|Friday",days);
```

- `for` - create a for loop with a *variable declaration* : *array*
  - in this case the variable is a `String` called `workday`
  - the collection is the *array* `workdays`
- the code iterates through the array, and each item in the array is assigned to the *variable* `workday`
- so the first time through the loop the variable `workday` is assigned the `[0]` indexed value from the array `workdays` which is `"Monday"`
- the second time through the loop the variable `workday` is assigned the `[1]` indexed value from the array `workdays` which is `"Tuesday"`, etc.
- the loop iterates over every item in the array
- the loop stops when there are no more items in the array to iterate over

This looping construct means that we can iterate over every item in the array and not miss any. Thereby avoiding the *off by one* errors that traditional boundary value analysis is so fond of trying to detect.

Exercise: Iterate over the Array of Users

Using your array of three `User` objects created in the previous exercise.

Iterate over the array and `System.out.println` the name of each `User`.

For loop

The `for` loop gives us more control over the looping. We setup the initial variable we want to use for looping, then have a condition which decides if we end the `for` loop, then we have a statement which sets up the next iteration of the loop.

```
for ( variable ; loop_condition ; iterator ){
   // do something
}
```

e.g. the traditional use of a `for` loop

```
String days="";

for(int i=0; i<5; i++){
    days = days + "|" + workdays[i];
}

assertEquals("|Monday|Tuesday|Wednesday|Thursday|Friday",days);
```

- `for` creates a *for* loop
- `int i=0` declares an index variable with an initial value of `0`
- `i<5` the loop will continue while the loop condition is met, in this case while we are still accessing an item in the array - there are 5 items in the array. Remember array indexes start at 0 so the last item is 4. Index 5 would be out of bounds, so we use `<5`.
- `i++` increment the value of the index

The more generic explanation of a for loop is actually:

`for (` *initialize statement executed once*`;` *loop condition*`;` *executed after each loop*`){`
`// do something`
`}`

So I could have written the loop:

```
int i=0;
for(; i<5; i++){
    days = days + "|" + workdays[i];
}
```

Where the variable is initialized outside the loop and my *initialize statement* is empty.

Also:

```
int i=0;
for(; i<5; ){
    days = days + "|" + workdays[i];
    i++;
}
```

And even:

```
int i=0;
for(; ; ){
    days = days + "|" + workdays[i];
    i++;
    if(i>=5) break;
}
```

In the above code I'm using the `break` statement which we saw in the `switch` section, to `break` out of the loop.

break

`break` is a generic keyword to end control statement execution. `break` can exit an `if`, `switch`, `for` and later iteration constructs `while`, `do...while`

Generally, keeping to the traditional example shown at the start of this section makes your code more readable and maintainable. e.g.

```
for(int i=0; i<5; i++){
    days = days + "|" + workdays[i];
}
```

You can see from each of the variants that even when one of the statements in the `for(...)` are missing, you still need to have the `;` in place.

Using `for` to iterate through an array, can leave you open to *off by one* errors, so be careful. But it does mean that you have an index count easily available to use in the loop.

e.g. in the following example I add the loop index to the output `String`

```
@Test
public void forLoopUsingIndexFixedCondition(){
    String days="";

    for(int i=0; i<5; i++){
        days = days + "|" + i + "-" + workdays[i];
    }

    assertEquals(
        "|0-Monday|1-Tuesday|2-Wednesday|3-Thursday|4-Friday",
        days);
}
```

Index in a *for each* loop

If you want an index inside a *for each* loop then you can do it easily enough by creating a variable outside the loop, and incrementing the variable value within the loop. e.g. in the following example I use `dayindex` as the index variable:

```
int dayindex =0;
for(String workday : workdays){
    days = days + "|" + workday;
    System.out.println("found " + workday +
                       " at position " + dayindex);
    dayindex++;
}
```

Which would output:

```
found Monday at position 0
found Tuesday at position 1
found Wednesday at position 2
found Thursday at position 3
found Friday at position 4
```

Exercise: Create an array of 100 users

Create an array which can hold 100 `User` objects. Use a `for` loop to fill the array with `User` objects having the following `username`, `password` combinations:

- user1, password1
- user2, password2
- etc.

Find a way to check the array was created.

For bonus points, write some code to assert that the array was filled properly.

Calculate Size of an Array with the `length` method

- `length` - returns the length of the array

Once declared, you can find the size of an *array* using the `length` method:

```
assertEquals(5, workdays.length);
```

The typical use for the `length` method is in a `for` *loop condition* e.g.

```
for(int i=0; i<workdays.length; i++){
    days = days + "|" + workdays[i];
}
```

Since the `length` of an array is always the index of the next item to add in the array, we make sure that we use `<` *array.length* in the loop condition.

Useful methods in the `Arrays` class

Java provides an `Arrays` class in `java.utils`.

In order to use `Arrays`, you need to import it.

```
import java.util.Arrays;
```

The `Arrays` class provides a number of useful static methods.

We will cover a subset of the methods here. You can see the full range of methods in the official documentation.

- `copyOf` - create a copy of an array, and resize if desired
- `copyOfRange` - create a copy of part of the array
- `fill` - fill the array, or part of the array with a single value
- `sort` - sort the array

The sections below refer to the `workdays` array:

```
String[] workdays = {"Monday", "Tuesday", "Wednesday",
                     "Thursday", "Friday"};
```

Use `copyOf` to copy and resize an Array

```
String[] weekDays;
weekDays = Arrays.copyOf(workdays, 7);
```

Using the static method `copyOf` on `Array` we can create a copy of an array, and optionally resize it.

The `copyOf` method takes two arguments:

`Arrays.copyOf(`*arrayToCopy*`,` *length*`);`

This is typically used to create a copy and increase the size. When we increase the size, the values in the array, which were not in the original array, are set to the default value for that data type e.g. `0` for *integer* and `null` for `String`.

In our example if we create a copy of `workdays` and resize it from `5` to `7` then the last two indexes will contain `null`.

```
assertEquals(null, weekDays[5]);
assertEquals(null, weekDays[6]);
```

Therefore we should set the values on the new array if we want to control the contents.

```
weekDays[5] = "Saturday";
weekDays[6] = "Sunday";
```

We can also use `copyOf` to truncate the array and make it shorter:

```
String[] weekDays;
weekDays = Arrays.copyOf(workdays, 3);

assertEquals(3, weekDays.length);
assertEquals("Monday", weekDays[0]);
assertEquals("Tuesday", weekDays[1]);
assertEquals("Wednesday", weekDays[2]);
```

Use `copyOfRange` to copy a subset of an Array

The `copyOfRange` copies a subset of an array into a new array of the size of the subset.

`Assert.copyOfRange(`*arrayToCopy*`, `*startIndex*`, `*endItemCount*`);`

The *startIndex* is the first item in the array that you want to copy.

The *endItemCount* is the `index + 1` that you want to copy.

e.g. if I want to copy items 3 to 5 inclusive ("Wednesday", "Thursday", "Friday"), then I would start the copy from `2` (the index of the third item), and end the copy on `5` (even though the index of the fifth item is `4`).

Example code might help:

```
String[] weekDays = Arrays.copyOfRange(workdays, 2, 5);

assertEquals(3, weekDays.length);
assertEquals("Wednesday", weekDays[0]);
assertEquals("Thursday", weekDays[1]);
assertEquals("Friday", weekDays[2]);

assertEquals(weekDays[0], workdays[2]);
assertEquals(weekDays[1], workdays[3]);
assertEquals(weekDays[2], workdays[4]);
```

We can also use `copyOfRange` to increase the size of the array, much like we did with `copyOf`. To do this we just use an *endItemCount* greater than the array size. e.g.

```
String[] weekDays = Arrays.copyOfRange(workdays, 2, 7);

assertEquals(5, weekDays.length);
assertEquals("Wednesday", weekDays[0]);
assertEquals("Thursday", weekDays[1]);
assertEquals("Friday", weekDays[2]);
assertEquals(null, weekDays[3]);
assertEquals(null, weekDays[4]);
```

Use `fill` to populate an Array with data

Arrays provides a static method called `fill` which we can use to fill an array with a specific value, or fill a range of indexes in the array.

To fill every item in the array with the same value we make a simple call to `fill`

`Arrays.fill(`*array*, *value*`);`

e.g. to fill an array of integers with the value minus one (`-1`), I can do the following:

```
int[] minusOne = new int[30];
Arrays.fill(minusOne,-1);
```

I might choose to fill part of an array - possibly if I have just done a `copy`, or `copyOf` and resized the array larger.

`Arrays.fill(`*array*, *startIndex*, *endItemCount*, *value*`);`

Again, the start of the range is the index number of the item we want to start at, and the end of the range is the `index + 1` e.g. if we wanted to stop on the 10th item in an array, which is at index '9' we would use the value '10':

```
int[] tenItems = {0,0,0,0,0,1,1,1,1,1};

// fill cells 5 - 9 with '2'
Arrays.fill(tenItems,5,10,2);

// 0 - 4 are untouched
assertEquals(0, tenItems[0]);
assertEquals(0, tenItems[4]);

// 5 - 9 now equal 2
```

```
assertEquals(2, tenItems[5]);
assertEquals(2, tenItems[6]);
assertEquals(2, tenItems[7]);
assertEquals(2, tenItems[8]);
assertEquals(2, tenItems[9]);
```

Use `sort` to *QuickSort* an Array

Java provides an implementation of QuickSort[66]. To quickly sort an array.

`Arrays.sort(`*array*`);`

e.g. If I have an array of integers in the wrong order, then I can quickly sort them.

```
int[] outOfOrder = {2,4,3,1,5,0};

Arrays.sort(outOfOrder);

assertEquals(0, outOfOrder[0]);
assertEquals(1, outOfOrder[1]);
assertEquals(2, outOfOrder[2]);
assertEquals(3, outOfOrder[3]);
assertEquals(4, outOfOrder[4]);
assertEquals(5, outOfOrder[5]);
```

You can also sort `String`, or other objects. Although with *strings* remember that uppercase letters have lower Unicode values than lowercase letters, so you might want to make the strings consistent with case usage before you sort them.

[66]http://en.wikipedia.org/wiki/Quicksort

Exercise: Sort Workdays Array and Assert Result

Create an `@Test` method which instantiates a `workdays` array, as shown in the examples previously.

```
String[] workdays = {"Monday", "Tuesday", "Wednesday", "Thursday",
"Friday"};
```

Then sort it using `Arrays.sort`

Assert that the order of values in the array are as you expect.

Create another `@Test` method so that the workdays have mixed case, and assert the result i.e.

```
{"monday", "Tuesday", "Wednesday", "thursday", "Friday"}
```

Arrays of Arrays

Regular Multidimensional Arrays

A multidimensional *array* is an *array of arrays.*

A regular multidimensional *array* has all the *nested arrays* of equal length.

So I could define a 2 dimensional `int` multidimensional array as:

```
int[][] multi = new int[4][4];
```

This creates a multidimensional array called `multi`. Which is 4 by 4, and since I haven't initialized it, all the values are default of 0.

```
0,0,0,0,
0,0,0,0,
0,0,0,0,
0,0,0,0,
```

Where each item in `multi` is an *array* of length 4. e.g. `multi[0]`

```
assertEquals(4, multi[0].length);
```

And I can access the values in that array by adding another index e.g. access the first value in `multi[0]` with `multi[0][0]`

```
assertEquals(0, multi[0][1]);
```

As with the one dimensional arrays, I can declare and initialize an array in a single statement:

```
int[][] multi = {{1,2,3,4},
                 {5,6,7,8},
                 {9,10,11,12},
                 {13,14,15,16}};
```

The above array would be populated as follows:

```
1,2,3,4,
5,6,7,8,
9,10,11,12,
13,14,15,16,
```

And we would access the values with the `[0][0]` multi index notation:

```
assertEquals(1, multi[0][0]);
assertEquals(7, multi[1][2]);
assertEquals(12, multi[2][3]);
assertEquals(14, multi[3][1]);
```

I could create additional dimensions if I wanted e.g. a 3 dimensional array of 3 by 4 by 5

```
int[][][] multi3d = new int[3][4][5];
```

- Where `multi3d` is an array of length 3,
  - and each item is an array of length 4,
    - where each item is an array of length 5
      - where each item is an `int`

```
assertEquals(3, multi3d.length);
assertEquals(4, multi3d[0].length);
assertEquals(4, multi3d[1].length);
assertEquals(4, multi3d[2].length);
assertEquals(5, multi3d[0][1].length);
assertEquals(5, multi3d[0][2].length);
assertEquals(5, multi3d[1][3].length);
```

And we can access individual `int` items using the full `[0][0][0]` multi index notation:

```
assertEquals(0, multi3d[0][0][0]);
```

Ragged Arrays

Since we know that a multidimensional array is actually an *array, of arrays, of…*

We can see how easy it is to create ragged arrays, where each array has different lengths:

```
int[][] ragged2d = {{1,2,3,4},
                    {5,6},
                    {7,8,9}
                    };
```

Which would create the following array:

```
1,2,3,4,
5,6,
7,8,9,
```

Each of the arrays has a different length:

```
assertEquals(4, ragged2d[0].length);
assertEquals(2, ragged2d[1].length);
assertEquals(3, ragged2d[2].length);
```

And we would access the array values using the normal notation:

```
assertEquals(4, ragged2d[0][3]);
assertEquals(6, ragged2d[1][1]);
assertEquals(7, ragged2d[2][0]);
```

We can define ragged arrays dynamically, by leaving the ragged dimensions blank when we create it:

```
int[][] ragged2d= new int[10][];
```

The above code creates a 2 dimensional array of *10 x undefined*, where we haven't defined the length of each of the 10 arrays, we would do that when we initialize them e.g.

```
ragged2d[0] = new int[10];
ragged2d[1] = new int[3];
```

The above code initializes the first 2 items in `ragged2d` as an array with 10 items, and an array with 3 items, all the remaining items in `ragged2d` will remain on their default of `null`. e.g.

```
0,0,0,0,0,0,0,0,0,0,
0,0,0,
null
null
null
null
null
null
null
null
```

Exercises

Understand how `print2DIntArray` method works

I used The following code when writing the book to printout the 2D arrays you've seen in this chapter.

Have a look through the code and make sure you understand it.

```
public void print2DIntArray(int [][]multi){
    for(int[] outer : multi){
        if(outer==null){
            System.out.print("null");
        }else{
            for(int inner : outer){
                System.out.print(inner + ",");
            }
        }
        System.out.println("");
    }
}
```

Create a Triangle

Create a ragged array, such that when you pass the array to `print2DIntArray` as an argument you output a triangle to the console that looks like the following:

```
0,
0,1,
0,1,2,
0,1,2,3,
0,1,2,3,4,
0,1,2,3,4,5,
0,1,2,3,4,5,6,
0,1,2,3,4,5,6,7,
0,1,2,3,4,5,6,7,8,
0,1,2,3,4,5,6,7,8,9,
0,1,2,3,4,5,6,7,8,9,10,
0,1,2,3,4,5,6,7,8,9,10,11,
0,1,2,3,4,5,6,7,8,9,10,11,12,
0,1,2,3,4,5,6,7,8,9,10,11,12,13,
0,1,2,3,4,5,6,7,8,9,10,11,12,13,14,
0,1,2,3,4,5,6,7,8,9,10,11,12,13,14,15,
```

Summary

Arrays are a fast and easy way of collecting objects.

They require a little work to define the size of the array in advance, but you've seen that you can use the *copy* utility methods in `java.util.Array` to help resize an array.

Remember to be careful when iterating through arrays so that you don't introduce *off by one* errors. If you are in any doubt then using the *for each* form of a `for` loop can help avoid introducing this error.

References and Recommended Reading

- Java For Loop
  - docs.oracle.com/javase/tutorial/java/nutsandbolts/for.html[67]
- Branch statement
  - docs.oracle.com/javase/tutorial/java/nutsandbolts/branch.html[68]
- Java Arrays
  - docs.oracle.com/javase/tutorial/java/nutsandbolts/arrays.html[69]
- Java 1.7 Arrays documentation
  - docs.oracle.com/javase/7/docs/api/java/util/Arrays.html[70]

---

[67] http://docs.oracle.com/javase/tutorial/java/nutsandbolts/for.html

[68] http://docs.oracle.com/javase/tutorial/java/nutsandbolts/branch.html

[69] http://docs.oracle.com/javase/tutorial/java/nutsandbolts/arrays.html

[70] http://docs.oracle.com/javase/7/docs/api/java/util/Arrays.html

Chapter Ten - Introducing Collections

We have already seen the basic collection concept in action with Arrays. I presented Arrays first so that you would understand the concept and the basics of iterating over a collection.

Collections are a good place to consider other looping constructs like `while`, `do while`. And we will also introduce the concept of *Interfaces*.

Chapter Summary

In this chapter you will learn the main collection classes. These offer more flexibility and power to you in your development work.

- *For Each* Loop - iterate over each individual element in a collection
- *Conversion* - converting collections to arrays and arrays to collections
- `while` *and* `do...while` - additional looping constructs you can use
- *Interfaces* - Collections are organized by interfaces and each interface has multiple implementations
- *Generics* - you will learn the basics of Generics to help you declare collections
- *Core Collections* - Core collection interfaces: `List`, `Set`, `Map`
- *Core Implementations* - Core collection implementations: `ArrayList`, `HashSet`, `HashMap`

This is one of the longest chapters in this book. And I know it can seem overwhelming. So I will start the chapter with a simple introduction, comparing arrays to a specific type of collection called a `List`, then cover looping over collections, and then the different interfaces and implementations for collections.

A Simple Introduction

To introduce collections, I will show you a simple example comparing use of a `Collection` to use of an Array.

```
@Test
public void simpleArrayExample(){
    String[] numbers0123 = {"zero", "one", "two", "three"};

    for(String numberText : numbers0123){
        System.out.println(numberText);
    }

    assertEquals("zero", numbers0123[0]);
    assertEquals("three", numbers0123[3]);
}
```

The above is array code you have seen before.

The following is the above code, rewritten to use a `Collection`.

```
@Test
public void simpleCollectionExample(){
    String[] numbers0123Array = {"zero", "one", "two", "three"};
    List<String> numbers0123 = Arrays.asList(numbers0123Array);

    for(String numberText : numbers0123){
        System.out.println(numberText);
    }

    assertEquals("zero", numbers0123.get(0));
    assertEquals("three", numbers0123.get(3));
}
```

In the above code you can see that I converted the array to a `List` using the `asList` method on the `java.util.Arrays` class.

I iterate over the `List` in the same way that I iterate over the array.

I access specific elements in the `List` using the same index numbering scheme as an array, i.e. `0` is the first element in the `List`, `3` is the fourth element in the `List`.

I declare the `List` using a different syntax. i.e. `List<String>`. This uses 'Generics' notation, which I will explain in this chapter, but essentially I'm saying "a `List` of `Strings`".

Collections are dynamic

One advantage collections have, over arrays, is that they are dynamic, so we don't have to declare their size in advance.

I can rewrite the example you have seen such that I build the `List` dynamically.

```
@Test
public void simpleDynamicCollectionExample(){
    List<String> numbers0123 = new ArrayList<String>();

    numbers0123.add("zero");
    numbers0123.add("one");
    numbers0123.add("two");
    numbers0123.add("three");

    for(String numberText : numbers0123){
        System.out.println(numberText);
    }

    assertEquals("zero", numbers0123.get(0));
    assertEquals("three", numbers0123.get(3));
}
```

In the above example, you can see that I have a new declaration syntax. And I `add` the `String` values into the `List` without worrying about the size of the `List` because I know that the `List` will resize.

```
    List<String> numbers0123 = new ArrayList<String>();
```

In the above declaration `List` is an *interface* which declares the *type* of `Collection` I am using.

`ArrayList` is the specific implementation of `List` that I am using.

I will explain *interface* in more detail in this chapter. But for the moment, an *interface* is a type of class which specifies the methods that an object will implement. So when I declare my `numbers0123` to be a `List` I know that I have access to the `get` method, and that the elements in the `List` will be added in order.

So a `List` is equivalent to the behaviour of an array, but is dynamic. Indeed an `ArrayList` is a type of `List` which is implemented using an *Array*.

Iterating with `while` and `do...while`

In addition to the `for` loop, Java also provides the `while` loop. This allows us to loop 'while' a particular condition is met.

I tend to use the `for` loop for iterating around a collection. But sometimes we don't want to process every element or want to iterate until a particular condition is met.

There are two forms:

- `while(condition){...}`
- `do{...}while(condition)`

With a `while` loop, the body of the loop might never be executed, because the condition may not be satisfied.

With a `do...while` loop, the body of the loop is always executed at least once.

As an example comparison I will create a simple list of days.

```
String[] someDays = {"Tuesday","Thursday",
                     "Wednesday","Monday",
                     "Saturday","Sunday",
                     "Friday"};

List<String> days = Arrays.asList(someDays);
```

I will write some simple code using each of the loop constructs:

- `for each`
- `for`
- `do while`
- `while`

And we will see the different approaches I take for finding the position of `"Monday"` in the `List`.

With the `for each` loop, I can iterate over every element in the `List` and when I find `"Monday"` I will have to `break` out of the loop.

```
int forCount=0;
for(String day : days){
    if(day.equals("Monday")){
        break;
    }
    forCount++;
}
assertEquals("Monday is at position 3", 3, forCount);
```

With the `for` loop, I will iterate over the size of the `List` and `break` when I find `"Monday"`:

```
int loopCount;
for(loopCount=0; loopCount <= days.size(); loopCount++ ){
    if(days.get(loopCount).equals("Monday")){
        break;
    }
}
assertEquals("Monday is at position 3", 3, loopCount);
```

With the `while` loop, I can make the check for `"Monday"` the loop exit condition, so I only 'do' the body of the loop, 'while' I have not found `"Monday"`:

```
int count=0;
while(!days.get(count).equals("Monday") ){
   count++;
}
assertEquals("Monday is at position 3", 3, count);
```

With the `do...while` loop, I need to set the index outside the valid boundary of the list because I increment it in the body of the loop, and again I only 'do' the body of the loop 'while' I have not found `"Monday"`:

```
int docount=-1;
do{
    docount++;
}while(!days.get(docount).equals("Monday"));
assertEquals("Monday is at position 3", 3, docount);
```

The `for each` loop is an excellent choice when you want to loop around every element in a collection. You don't have to worry about off by one index errors or out of bounds exceptions. But you have to `break` to finish the loop early.

The `for` loop, is a very powerful construct, but can become hard to read if the condition is long, or the setup or end of loop actions are complicated.

The `while` and `do...while` loop are an excellent choice if the loop needs to terminate based on an arbitrary or complex condition. Choosing between `while` and `do...while` is done on the basis of:

- use `do...while` if you want the loop to run 1 or more times
- use `while` if you want the loop to run 0 or more times

Exercise: Use a `for` loop instead of a `while` loop

Use the code above to create the days of the week Array, convert it to a list, and iterate over it with a `while loop`. Then convert the `while` loop into a `for` loop. Hint: Use the condition in the `while` loop as a `for` loop condition statement and demonstrate that the `for` loop can be used as a `while` loop.

e.g. `for(...;` *add while condition here* `; ...)`

Interfaces

Arrays are a simple collection mechanism but they don't offer the same interface as collections.

Java has a concept of an *interface*. By interface, I mean the methods they expose and the API that we use to work with the classes, i.e. an interface defines what you can do.

A class can implement a number of interfaces, in which case it must implement the methods that are defined in all of those interfaces.

Java provides a number of interfaces for collections:

- `Collection` - a generic collection that you can `add` objects to

- `Set` - a collection that does not allow duplicates
- `List` - a collection you can access and add elements at specific index positions
- `Map` - a "key, value" pair where you store an object in the collection, but can access it with a unique key

The Collection interfaces are all in `java.util`

Important Interfaces

I have only listed above, what I consider the *most important* interfaces above, i.e. the ones that I use most often.

This demonstrates my biases, and the needs of the code I write.

Over time you will identify the interfaces, and implementation that you use a lot. Learn those in detail so that you understand them well. But make sure that you learn the capabilities of the other interfaces and implementations so that you know when to use them, and don't try and use a single collection type, when another would fit your needs better.

Declare as Interfaces, Instantiate Implementations

An Interface on its own cannot be used to do anything. Other classes implement interfaces and so we declare variables as the interface but have to instantiate them with implementations. e.g.

```
Collection workdays;
workdays = new ArrayList();
```

Here I have declared a variable called `workdays` as a `Collection` because I only need to use the methods that the `Collection` interface provides. But I have to instantiate it as an `ArrayList` which is a class that implements the `Collection` interface.

The `ArrayList` class exposes many more methods than the `Collection` interface. Had I declared the variable `workdays` as an `ArrayList` I would gain access to methods like `indexOf`, `trimToSize`, and `get`.

When I only need access to the methods on `Collection` then I should declare my variables at the minimum level of functionality needed.

By coding to interfaces like this, we have the ability to swap in and out the implementation class; if we discover that one implementation is faster than another, or takes less memory. But we don't have to change the body of the method code when we swap a different one in.

e.g. I could use `ArrayList`[71] or `LinkedList`[72] or `HashSet`[73] as my implementation for Collection because each implement the `Collection` interface. But I need to understand the implementation in case one of them imposes constraints on my code that I don't want, for example a `HashSet` does not allow duplicate elements, but an `ArrayList` does.

This may not make sense yet, but it is an important concept and I will try to illustrate it through all the examples in this chapter.

Core Collection Interfaces

The official documentation lists the following as the Core Collection interfaces:

- `Collection`
  - `List`
  - `Set`
    - `SortedSet`
  - `Queue`
  - `Deque`
- `Map`
  - `SortedMap`

In this chapter we will cover `List`, `Set` and `Map` and leave the other collections until later in the book.

Inheritance Hierarchy

This is an inheritance hierarchy; so a *Set* is a *Collection*, a *List* is a *Collection*, but both *Set* and *List* have nuances that make them unique.

There are two main collection concepts: `Collection` and `Map`

`Collection` provides a way of grouping objects. `Map` provides a way of associating objects with a 'key' for later retrieval and accessing.

The following table provides a summary of the main methods on the Interfaces:

[71]http://docs.oracle.com/javase/7/docs/api/java/util/ArrayList.html

[72]http://docs.oracle.com/javase/7/docs/api/java/util/LinkedList.html

[73]http://docs.oracle.com/javase/7/docs/api/java/util/HashSet.html

Collection	List	Set	Map
`add(e)`	`get(i)`	*All in Collection*	`put(k,v)`
`remove(e)`	`remove(i)`		`remove(k)`
`removeAll(c)`	`add(i,e)`		`entrySet`
`retainAll(c)`	`addAll(i,c)`		`get(k)`
`clear`	`indexOf(e)`		`clear`
`contains(e)`	`lastIndexOf(e)`		`containsKey(k)`
`containsAll(c)`	`set(i,e)`		`containsValue(v)`
`size`	`subList(i1,i2)`		`size`
`isEmpty`			`isEmpty`
`toArray`	*All in Collection*		`values`
`toArray(a)`			`keySet`
`addAll(c)`			`putAll(m)`

where: e == element, c == collection, a == array, i == index, k == key, v == value, m == map

Collection Interface

A `Collection` is a group of objects. Where each object is referred to as an element. The `Collection` interface provides the basic superset of methods.

- `add` - to add an element to a collection
- `remove` - to remove an element from a collection
- `size` - to return the number of elements in the collection
- `isEmpty` - check if a collection is empty
- `addAll` - to add every element of another collection into the collection
- `removeAll` - remove every element of another collection from the collection
- `retainAll` - remove every element in the collection which is not in another collection
- `clear` - to remove all the elements from the collection
- `contains` - to check if an object is in the collection
- `containsAll` - to check that one collection contains all the elements of another
- `toArray` - to convert a collection to an array

Instantiating a collection

We cannot instantiate a `Collection` because a `Collection` is an interface. There are classes which implement the interface, e.g. `ArrayList`. So we declare our variables as `Collection` and instantiate them as class which implements the interface.

```
Collection workdays;
workdays = new ArrayList();
```

In the above code we have a usable variable called `workdays`. But a collection can contain any `object`, and since we didn't specify what the collection will contain it defaults to `object`. This will become an annoyance later when we try and iterate through the collection and have to *cast* the elements from *object* to *String*.

As a recommendation, when you work with a collection, and the objects to be stored in the collection are all of the same type then declare the collection as a *collection of type* e.g.

```
Collection<String> weekendDays = new <String>ArrayList();
Collection<String> daysOfWeek = new <String>ArrayList();
```

In the above code I declare the `Collection` as a collection of `<String>`. Which I instantiate with an `ArrayList` that will only contain `<String>`.

This provides a number of benefits:

- It makes the code clear as to the contents of the collection
- It makes the collections strongly typed which helps with code completion later

Try to get in the habit of declaring the type of the contents of the collection when you know that the collection will only contain one type of element.

Generics

The `<String>` notation, is a usage of *Java Generics* which is a way of declaring classes to use a particular type of object, but only defining the type at compile time.

A full discussion of generics is beyond the scope of this book, but it is important to recognize the usage of it, and know how to take advantage of it with the classes you use. At the moment you have only seen *Generics* in the context of collections.

Read the references on generics if you want to self-study generics in more detail.

For now, understand that `<String>` declares the type of elements in the `Collection` and implementation Class.

Generic Syntax

In most of the examples in this book I will use syntax like the following:

```
Collection<String> weekendDays = new <String>ArrayList();
```

It is also possible to leave out the `<String>` on the ArrayList and use `<>` and the Java compiler will use the *Generic* value from the interface declaration e.g.

```
Collection<String> weekendDays = new ArrayList<>();
```

The newer syntax is shorter and sometimes your IDE will code complete in the above format for you.

The reason I don't use it, is simply because I'm not used to using it, I think it only arrived in Java 1.7

The following syntax for using Generics are equivalent:

```
Collection<String> cola = new ArrayList<String>();
Collection<String> colb = new <String>ArrayList();
Collection<String> colc = new ArrayList<>();
```

adding elements to a collection: `add`, `addAll`, `size`, `containsAll`

We can add elements to a collection with the `add` method.

```
workdays.add("Monday");
workdays.add("Tuesday");
workdays.add("Wednesday");
workdays.add("Thursday");
workdays.add("Friday");

assertEquals(5, workdays.size());
```

We can use the `size` method to count the number of elements in the `Collection`.

And we can use the `addAll` method to add all the elements from one `Collection` into another:

```
daysOfWeek.addAll(workdays);

assertEquals( workdays.size(), daysOfWeek.size() );
assertTrue( daysOfWeek.containsAll(workdays ));
```

In the above code we add all the elements in `workdays` to an empty collection `daysOfWeek`.

The `containsAll` method can help us check if a `Collection` contains all the elements of another collection. The `Collection` that we call the `containsAll` method on (i.e. `daysOfWeek`) can contain more elements than the argument `Collection` (i.e. `workdays`), but in order for `containsAll` to return true, all of the elements of the argument collection, must be present.

removing individual elements: `remove`, `contains`

If I add some elements to `weekendDays`.

```
weekendDays.add("Saturday");
weekendDays.add("Funday");
```

Then you can see that I made a mistake by spelling *Sunday* incorrectly as *Funday*.

I can fix that error by removing *Funday* with the `remove` method:

```
weekendDays.remove("Funday");
```

I can use the `contains` method to check if a `Collection` contains a specific element. If I check for *Funday* `contains` should return false:

```
assertFalse(weekendDays.contains("Funday"));
```

Of course I can `add` the correct value into the `Collection`, and check its presence.

```
weekendDays.add("Sunday");

assertEquals(2, weekendDays.size());
assertTrue("Bug Fixed, Sunday is in the collection now",
        weekendDays.contains("Sunday"));
```

Iterate over a collection

A `Collection` actually implements the `Iterable` interface. Which forms the backbone of the *for each* functionality that we saw earlier.

So, assuming that I have added all the `workdays` and `weekendDays` into `daysOfWeek`, I can iterate over it with the *for each* construct.

```
for(String dayOfWeek : daysOfWeek){
    System.out.println(dayOfWeek);
}
```

To generate the following output to the console:

```
Monday
Tuesday
Wednesday
Thursday
Friday
Saturday
Sunday
```

Iterating over the `Collection` provides a good illustration of why we want to declare the type of element that the collection holds. For the declaration of `workdays` that we presented earlier:

```
Collection workdays;
workdays = new ArrayList();
```

When I iterate over this, I get an `Object` rather than a specific type:

```
for(Object workday : workdays){
    String outputDay = (String)workday;
    System.out.println(outputDay);
}
```

In the above code I had to declare `workday` as an `Object` and when I used it within the loop, I had to cast it to `String` using the `(String)` notation.

When we want to refine the type of an object then we can cast it to a specific type. We can do that when the object supports the interface for that type, or *is* of that type.

We used to have to cast objects a lot in Java, but now that the collections support *Generics* we can specify the type in the declaration and avoid casting later.

Empty a Collection: `clear, isEmpty`

The `clear` method allows us to empty a collection.

```
Collection<String> daysOfWeek = new <String>ArrayList();

daysOfWeek.addAll(workdays);
daysOfWeek.addAll(weekendDays);

assertEquals(7, daysOfWeek.size());

daysOfWeek.clear();

assertEquals(0, daysOfWeek.size());
assertTrue(daysOfWeek.isEmpty());
```

We can use `size` and `isEmpty` to verify that it has no elements.

Removing All of one collection from another: `removeAll`

Assuming that my `daysOfWeek` `Collection` contains all the `weekendDays` and `workdays`.

I can remove the contents of the `weekendDays` `Collection` from `daysOfWeek` with the `removeAll` method:

```
Collection<String> daysOfWeek = new <String>ArrayList();

daysOfWeek.addAll(workdays);
daysOfWeek.addAll(weekendDays);

assertEquals(7, daysOfWeek.size());

daysOfWeek.removeAll(weekendDays);

assertTrue(daysOfWeek.containsAll(workdays));
assertEquals(5, daysOfWeek.size());
assertFalse(daysOfWeek.containsAll(weekendDays));
```

I can use the `containsAll` method to check that the removal took place.

Remove all but one collection from another: `retainAll`

So to retain only the `weekendDays` in `daysOfWeek` I would do the following:

```
daysOfWeek.retainAll(weekendDays);
```

Use the `retainAll` method to *remove all but* one collection from another. Or in other words, retain only the elements from the argument collection, in the collection I call the method on.

```
Collection<String> daysOfWeek = new <String>ArrayList();

daysOfWeek.addAll(workdays);
daysOfWeek.addAll(weekendDays);

assertTrue(daysOfWeek.containsAll(workdays));
assertTrue(daysOfWeek.containsAll(weekendDays));

daysOfWeek.retainAll(weekendDays);

assertEquals("only weekend days now", 2, daysOfWeek.size());
assertTrue(daysOfWeek.containsAll(weekendDays));
assertFalse(daysOfWeek.containsAll(workdays));
```

Convert a collection to an array

Use the `toArray` method to convert a `Collection` to an array.

This method can be used in two forms.

- `toArray()`
- `toArray(anArray)`

When we call `toArray` without an argument, it will return an array of `Object`

```
Object[] daysOfWeekArray = daysOfWeek.toArray();
assertEquals(7, daysOfWeekArray.length);
```

If we subsequently wanted to use elements from the array we would have to cast them as String. i.e. `(String)`:

```
assertEquals("Monday".length(),
            ((String)daysOfWeekArray[0]).length());
```

The `toArray(anArray)` call, where we pass as argument an initialized array, avoids these problems:

```
String[] anotherArray = new String[daysOfWeek.size()];
daysOfWeek.toArray(anotherArray);
assertEquals("Monday".length(),
            anotherArray[0].length());
```

In the above code I declare a `String` array, and initialize the array at the correct size to hold the collection contents. Then call the `toArray` method with that array as the argument.

Collection Documentation

You can find the details of `Collection` on the official documentation site.

Interface:

- docs.oracle.com/javase/tutorial/collections/interfaces/collection.html[74]

Implementations:

- docs.oracle.com/javase/tutorial/collections/implementations[75]

I typically use a *List* implementation when I want just a generic `Collection`, but we will cover other implementations later in this chapter.

Exercise: Create and manipulate a `Collection` of Users

- Create a Collection of `Users`
- Assert that the `size()==0` and `isEmpty()==true`
- Create two `User` objects
- Add the `User` objects to the collection
- Assert that the `size()==2` and `isEmpty()==false`
- Create a second collection with two different users
- `addAll` the second collection to the first collection
- check that the first collection now `contains` objects from the second collection
- `removeAll` the `User` objects from the second collection
- `clear` the first collection

Ensure you assert after each step

List

A `List` builds on the `Collection`, so all `Collection` methods are available.

A List:

- allows storing of duplicate elements,
- retains elements in the order added.

[74]http://docs.oracle.com/javase/tutorial/collections/interfaces/collection.html
[75]http://docs.oracle.com/javase/tutorial/collections/implementations

- allows adding elements in specific places in the list

I tend to use a *List* in preference to an Array. Arrays are clearly at a lower level and faster. But I only use an Array when I'm working with a fixed set of objects that I know are never going to change.

If my code needs to be particularly fast then I might optimize down to an Array. But if I'm working on any code dynamically, then a *List* will often be my first choice as it is a very simple collection.

A `List` offers all the methods from `Collection` and adds:

- `get(i)` to retrieve an element from a specific index
- `remove(i)` to remove the element at an index
- `add(i,e)` to add at a specific index, an element
- `addAll(i,c)` to add, at a specific index, all elements in a collection
- `indexOf(e)` to return the index of an element
- `lastIndexOf(e)` to return the last index of an element
- `set(i,e)` to set the element at a particular index
- `subList(i1,i2)` to return a sublist from index1 to index2

In all of the examples I will declare a `List` that will contain `String`, and will instantiate as an `ArrayList`, which you also saw in the `Collection` `@Test` methods. I tend to default to `ArrayList` for both `Collection` and `List`. e.g.

```
List<String> days = new ArrayList<String>();
```

`get` an element at index

A `List` exposes an array style interface where each element in the list has a positional index, which like an array starts at `0`.

```
@Test
public void getAnElementAtAnIndex(){
    List<String> days = new ArrayList<String>();

    days.add("Monday");
    days.add("Tuesday");
    days.add("Wednesday");

    assertEquals("Monday", days.get(0));
    assertEquals("Tuesday", days.get(1));
    assertEquals("Wednesday", days.get(2));
}
```

In the above code, the `List` guarantees that the elements I add will be accessible in the order that I add them so that the first element added can be accessed with index `0`, the second element added can be accessed with index `1` etc.

`remove` an element at index

In addition to having the ability to `remove` an element, we can also remove elements based on their index.

```
@Test
public void removeAnElementAtAnIndex(){
    List<String> days = new ArrayList<String>();

    days.add("Monday");
    days.add("Tuesday");
    days.add("Wednesday");

    days.remove(1);

    assertEquals(2, days.size());
    assertEquals("Monday", days.get(0));
    assertEquals("Wednesday", days.get(1));
}
```

When I `remove` an element based on its index, the list resizes and elements after the one removed have their indexes adjusted. So if I remove the element at index `1`, the element that was at index `2` can now be found at index `1`.

`add` an element at a specific index

With a `Collection` we can add elements, but they are just *in* the collection, they could be anywhere, we don't care.

With an array, we have to resize the array if we want to add new elements.

With a `List` we can add elements at specific points in the `List`.

In this example, I start with a partial list of days.

```
List<String> days = new ArrayList<String>();

days.add("Tuesday");
days.add("Thursday");
days.add("Saturday");
```

I need to add a few days to this list:

```
days.add(0, "Monday");
days.add(2, "Wednesday");
days.add(4, "Friday");
days.add(6, "Sunday");
```

I add "Monday" to the start of the list, then "Wednesday" and "Friday" into the middle of the list, and "Sunday" at the end of the list.

You can see that when I `add` an element in the middle or the start, that it doesn't overwrite the element that is already there, it *inserts* the element and moves everything else in the list to a new index.

Adding to the end

When adding to the end of the `List` you can only add to the end, you can't add way beyond the size of the `List` and expect it to resize.

i.e. if I have `3` elements in my `List` then I can add another one at index `3`. Index `3` doesn't exist until I add it (I can't `get(3)`), but I can increase the size of the list by adding to the end. I cannot add an element to index `20`, Java would throw an IndexOutOfBoundsException.

I could also use the `add(e)` method, because adding an element to a `List` adds it to the end of the `List`.

`addAll` elements in a collection at a specific index

With a `Collection` the `addAll` adds the elements somewhere in the collection. With a `List` we can control exactly where we *insert* the elements in the collection.

For example, if I created a `List` for days:

```
days.add("Monday");
days.add("Friday");
```

I could create another collection with the `missingDays` and insert them, into the middle of the `days` collection.

```
days.addAll(1, missingDays);
```

This would insert the collection at index `1`, and move "Friday" to position `4`. It would not overwrite the element existing at index `1`, the `addAll` at an index performs an *insert*

```
List<String> days = new ArrayList<String>();
List<String> missingDays = new ArrayList<String>();

days.add("Monday");
days.add("Friday");

missingDays.add("Tuesday");
missingDays.add("Wednesday");
missingDays.add("Thursday");

days.addAll(1, missingDays);

assertEquals(5, days.size());
assertEquals("Monday", days.get(0));
assertEquals("Tuesday", days.get(1));
assertEquals("Wednesday", days.get(2));
assertEquals("Thursday", days.get(3));
assertEquals("Friday", days.get(4));
```

Can Insert at Start and End

As with `add` the `addAll(i,c)` method can *insert* the collection at the start of the `List` by using index `0`, or at the end of the `List` by using the 'next index' or the 'size'.

Adding to the end of the `List` with an index is equivalent to using the `add` or `addAll` method without an index. Since the add methods on a `List` add to the end of the `List`.

`indexOf` find the index of an element

When we have a `List` and we don't know the index of the element in the list then we can use the `indexOf` method to tell us where in the `List` the element can be found.

```
List<String> days = new ArrayList<String>();

days.add("Tuesday");
days.add("Thursday");
days.add("Saturday");

assertEquals(1, days.indexOf("Thursday"));
```

If `indexOf` is used on a `List` with duplicates then it will return the first index of the element.

`lastIndexOf` the the last index of an element

A `List` allows duplicate elements, so we may want to find the position of the last of the duplicates. In which case we would use the `lastIndexOf` method to do this.

```
List<String> days = new ArrayList<String>();

days.add("Tuesday");
days.add("Thursday");
days.add("Saturday");
days.add("Thursday");
days.add("Thursday");
days.add("Sunday");

assertEquals(4, days.lastIndexOf("Thursday"));
```

If `lastIndexOf` is used on a `List` with no duplicates then it returns the same as `indexOf`.

`set` the element at an index

When using an array, the `array[1]="New Element"` would overwrite the existing contents at index `1`. We can do the same thing with `set` which allows us to `set` the value of a particular index.

For example:

```
List<String> days = new ArrayList<String>();

days.add("Monday");
days.add("Thursday");
days.add("Wednesday");

days.set(1, "Tuesday");

assertEquals("Tuesday", days.get(1));
```

In the above code, I originally `add` `"Thursday"` into index `1`, but then overwrite it to `"Tuesday"` with the `set` method.

```
days.set(1, "Tuesday");
```

And because `set` performs an overwrite, the size of the `List` does not change and no re-ordering takes place.

```
assertEquals(3, days.size());
assertEquals("Monday", days.get(0));
assertEquals("Tuesday", days.get(1));
assertEquals("Wednesday", days.get(2));
```

`subList` to create a portion of the list

To create a new `List` with a selection of elements from a parent `List` we use the `subList` method.

`subList` takes two arguments, the `fromIndex`, and the `toIndex`. The `toIndex` is 1 more than the index you want.

For example, if I create a list of days and want a `subList` of just the work days `"Monday"` through `"Friday"`. `"Monday"` will be at index `0`, and `"Friday"` is at index `4`, but if I want to include `"Friday"` in the new *sub-list* then I have to use `5` as my `toIndex`:

```
List<String> days = new ArrayList<String>();

days.add("Monday");
days.add("Tuesday");
days.add("Wednesday");
days.add("Thursday");
days.add("Friday");
days.add("Saturday");
days.add("Sunday");

List<String> workdays = days.subList(0,5);

assertEquals(5, workdays.size());
assertEquals("Monday", workdays.get(0));
assertEquals("Tuesday", workdays.get(1));
assertEquals("Wednesday", workdays.get(2));
assertEquals("Thursday", workdays.get(3));
assertEquals("Friday", workdays.get(4));
```

List Documentation

You can find the details of `List` on the official documentation site.

Interface:

- docs.oracle.com/javase/tutorial/collections/interfaces/list.html[76]

Implementation:

- docs.oracle.com/javase/tutorial/collections/implementations/list.html[77]

Exercise: Create and manipulate a `List` of `Users`

Write an `@Test` annotated method, and create a `List` of `User` objects.

- Create the `List`
- Create two `User` objects
- Add a `User` to the list
- Add a `User` to the front of the list
- Assert on the `indexOf` positions of the `User` objects
- `remove` the first `User` object

Remember to assert after each action on the `List`

Set

A `Set` builds on the `Collection`, so all `Collection` methods are available.

A Set:

- does not allow storing duplicates, adding a duplicate is ignored.
- ordering is not guaranteed, if you iterate through a set it may not bring back the elements in the order you expect

[76]http://docs.oracle.com/javase/tutorial/collections/interfaces/list.html

[77]http://docs.oracle.com/javase/tutorial/collections/implementations/list.html

```
@Test
public void setDoesNotAllowDuplicateElements(){
    Set workdays = new HashSet();

    workdays.add("Monday");
    workdays.add("Monday");
    workdays.add("Monday");
    workdays.add("Monday");
    workdays.add("Monday");

    assertEquals(1, workdays.size());
}
```

I tend to use a `HashSet` from `java.util` as my default `Set` implementation.

Sets of Custom Objects

Be careful if you want to create a `Set` of your own objects and have Java identify the duplicated elements. The duplication check is based on a *hash* and you need to implement your own `hashCode` method which generates a unique hash for each unique object.

You should also implement your own `equals` method.

I have decided to make this out of scope for this book because I think most of you are unlikely to experience this. I'm assuming that you are mainly likely to create a `Set` containing built in classes.

I very often avoid this problem by creating sets of 'keys' for objects stored in a `Map` and the keys tend to be `String`.

However if you do need to create a `Set` of custom objects then the references in the "Next Steps" chapter, or at the end of this chapter, should help.

Set Documentation

You can find the details of `Set` on the official documentation site.

Interface:

- docs.oracle.com/javase/tutorial/collections/interfaces/set.html[78]

[78]http://docs.oracle.com/javase/tutorial/collections/interfaces/set.html

Implementation:

- docs.oracle.com/javase/tutorial/collections/implementations/set.html[79]

Exercise: Create and manipulate a `Set` of `Users`

Write an `@Test` annotated method, and create a `Set` of `User` objects.

- Create a `User`
- Add the `User` to the `Set`
- Add the `User` to the `Set` again
- Check that the `User` has only been added to the `Set` once

Map

A `Map` is a collection where each *element* is a *value*, and the *element* is stored with an associated *key*.

The `Map` is a collection of *key value* pairs.

Each *key* must be unique. And each *key* maps to only one *value*.

`Map` has some methods in common with `Collection`:

- size
- clear
- isEmpty

Which means you already know what those methods do.

And some methods that have a very similar counterpart: `containsKey` and `containsValue` are similar to the `Collection` method `contains`.

- `put(k,v)` to add "key, value" pairs to the map

[79]http://docs.oracle.com/javase/tutorial/collections/implementations/set.html

- `remove(k)` to remove the element with that key
- `entrySet` to return a `Set` of all elements as `Map.Entry` objects
- `get(k)` to return the element based on the key
- `containsKey(k)` returns true if the key is in the `Map`
- `containsValue(v)` returns true if the value is in the `Map`
- `values` returns a `Collection` of all the values
- `keySet` returns a `Set` of all the keys
- `putAll(m)` adds a `Map` (m) to the `Map` object

I tend to use `HashMap` as my default implementation. And below you can see examples of the declaration and initialization code:

```
Map<String,User> mapa = new HashMap<>();
Map<String,User> mapb = new HashMap<String,User>();
Map<String,User> mapc = new <String,User>HashMap();
```

In the above code you can see that a `Map` is declared with two values `Map<Key,Value>` so in the above code I declare the `Map` variables as having a `String` key, and a `User` value. So I would use the `Map` to store `User` objects.

put(k,v)

Add "key, value" pairs to a `Map` with the `put` method.

```
Map<String,String> map = new HashMap<>();

map.put("key1", "value1");
map.put("key2", "value2");
map.put("key3", "value3");

assertEquals(3, map.size());
```

The key can be an object, as can the value. The declaration of the `Map` determines what objects we can `put` into the `Map`.

If I `put` a "key, value" pair, where the key already exists in the `Map` then the old value will be overwritten with the new value:

```
map.put("key1", "newvalue1");
assertEquals("newvalue1", map.get("key1"));
```

`get(k)` to retrieve a value from the Map

I can `get` values from the `Map` using the key that I `put` the value into the `Map` with.

```
assertEquals("value1", map.get("key1"));
assertEquals("value2", map.get("key2"));
assertEquals("value3", map.get("key3"));
```

If I attempt to `get` a value with a key that does not exist then `null` will be returned.

```
assertEquals(null, map.get("key4"));
```

`remove(k)` to remove a "key, value" pair

I can remove a value from a `Map` by calling the `remove` method with an existing key.

```
map.remove("key1");

assertEquals(2, map.size());
```

If the key does not exist then no exception is thrown and nothing happens to the `Map`, the method call has no impact.

Empty a Map with `clear`, check with `size`, `isEmpty`

Just as we could with the `Collection`, we can empty the `Map` by calling the `clear` method.

```
map.clear();
assertEquals(0, map.size());
assertTrue(map.isEmpty());
```

I can check that the `Map` is empty using the `size` and the `isEmpty` methods.

Check contents of `Map` with `containsKey(k)` and `containsValue(v)`

The `containsKey` method returns `true` or `false`. `true` when something with the key has been put in the `Map` and `false` when nothing using that key has been put in the `Map`

```
Map<String,String> map = new HashMap<>();

map.put("key1", "value1");
map.put("key2", "value2");
map.put("key3", "value3");

assertTrue(map.containsKey("key1"));
assertFalse(map.containsKey("key23"));

assertTrue(map.containsValue("value2"));
assertFalse(map.containsValue("value23"));
```

`putAll(m)` to add a `Map` to the `Map`

I can put one `Map` inside another `Map` with the `putAll` method:

```
map.putAll(mapToAdd);
```

If I try and add a `Map` that contains a key duplicating an existing key, then the value from the new `Map` will be used: e.g. in the following code the key "key1" is duplicated across both `Map` objects:

```
map.put("key1", "value1");
map.put("key2", "value2");
map.put("key3", "value3");

mapToAdd.put("key1", "keyvalue1");
mapToAdd.put("key4", "value4");
```

When I put `mapToAdd` into `map`:

```
map.putAll(mapToAdd);
```

The existing value for "key1" is overwritten with the value from `mapToAdd`:

```
assertEquals(4, map.size());
assertEquals("keyvalue1", map.get("key1"));
```

`values`

`values` returns a `Collection` containing all the values in the `Map`:

```
Collection<String> values = map.values();
```

Each value will be of the type declared for the `Map`

`keySet`

`keySet` returns a `Set` where each element is a key from the `Map`:

```
Set<String> keys = map.keySet();
```

`entrySet` to work with "key, value" pairs

`entrySet` returns a `Set` of `Entry` objects from `java.util.Map`.

An `Entry` is the "key, value" pair.

Entry exposes the methods:

- `getValue` to return the value
- `getKey` to return the key
- `setValue` to set the value

The following code iterates through the entries in the `Map` and sets all the values to `"bob"`:

```
Set<Map.Entry<String,String>> entries = map.entrySet();

for( Map.Entry<String,String> entry : entries){
    entry.setValue("bob");
}
```

Map Documentation

You can find the details of `Map` on the official documentation site.

Interface:

- docs.oracle.com/javase/tutorial/collections/interfaces/map.html[80]

[80]http://docs.oracle.com/javase/tutorial/collections/interfaces/map.html

Implementation:

- docs.oracle.com/javase/tutorial/collections/implementations/map.html[81]

Exercise: Create and manipulate a `Map` of `User` objects

Write an `@Test` annotated method, and create a `Map` of `User` objects.

- Create a `Map` of `User` objects
- Create two `User` objects
- Add both `User` objects to the `Map` using the same key
- Check that only one `User` object has been added

Summary

In this chapter you learned the basics of Collections.

A `Collection` is the most generic collection interface which supports adding, removing and iterating over a collection of objects.

Collections use the *Generics* syntax to define the type of object in the collection e.g. `List<String>` to create a `List` of `String` objects.

The basic `Collection` interfaces are:

- `Collection` - a basic container
- `List` - to allow accessing by index
- `Set` - to avoid duplicates
- `Map` - to store "key, value" pairs

Each *interface* can have multiple implementations, the implementations we used in this chapter were:

[81]http://docs.oracle.com/javase/tutorial/collections/implementations/map.html

- **Collection** & **List**:
  - ArrayList
- **Set**:
  - HashSet
- **Map**:
  - HashMap

Collections offer us the ability to create dynamic and re-sizable containers, rather than fixed size *array* containers.

References and Recommended Reading

- Program to an interface, not an implementation
  - artima.com/lejava/articles/designprinciplesP.html[82]
- Java Interface Tutorial
  - docs.oracle.com/javase/tutorial/java/concepts/interface.html[83]
- Java Collections Tutorials
  - docs.oracle.com/javase/tutorial/collections[84]
- Java Collection Interfaces
  - docs.oracle.com/javase/tutorial/collections/interfaces/index.html[85]
- Java Generics
  - docs.oracle.com/javase/tutorial/java/generics[86]
- Java Collection Implementations
  - docs.oracle.com/javase/tutorial/collections/implementations[87]
- HashCode
  - docs.oracle.com/javase/6/docs/api/java/lang/Object.html#hashCode%28%29[88]
- List
  - Interface
    - docs.oracle.com/javase/tutorial/collections/interfaces/list.html[89]

[82]http://www.artima.com/lejava/articles/designprinciplesP.html

[83]http://docs.oracle.com/javase/tutorial/java/concepts/interface.html

[84]http://docs.oracle.com/javase/tutorial/collections/

[85]http://docs.oracle.com/javase/tutorial/collections/interfaces/index.html

[86]http://docs.oracle.com/javase/tutorial/java/generics/

[87]http://docs.oracle.com/javase/tutorial/collections/implementations/

[88]http://docs.oracle.com/javase/6/docs/api/java/lang/Object.html#hashCode%28%29

[89]http://docs.oracle.com/javase/tutorial/collections/interfaces/list.html

  - Implementations
    * docs.oracle.com/javase/tutorial/collections/implementations/list.html[90]
- Set
  - Interface
    * docs.oracle.com/javase/tutorial/collections/interfaces/set.html[91]
  - Implementations
    * docs.oracle.com/javase/tutorial/collections/implementations/set.html[92]
- Map
  - Interface
    * docs.oracle.com/javase/tutorial/collections/interfaces/map.html[93]
  - Implementations
    * docs.oracle.com/javase/tutorial/collections/implementations/map.html[94]

---

[90]http://docs.oracle.com/javase/tutorial/collections/implementations/list.html
[91]http://docs.oracle.com/javase/tutorial/collections/interfaces/set.html
[92]http://docs.oracle.com/javase/tutorial/collections/implementations/set.html
[93]http://docs.oracle.com/javase/tutorial/collections/interfaces/map.html
[94]http://docs.oracle.com/javase/tutorial/collections/implementations/map.html

Chapter Eleven - Introducing Exceptions

Chapter Summary

In this chapter you will learn about exceptions:

- an exception is an unexpected event which can interrupt our code execution
- understand the stack trace on an exception
- how to handle an exception using `try` and `catch` and `finally`
- trigger a `NullPointerException` and how to catch them
- throwing exceptions from your own code
- using methods on the exception e.g. `getMessage`, `getStackTrace`
- catching multiple exceptions
- JUnit's `expected` parameter on `@Test`

An exception is something that happens to you when you least expect it. Often because you have written code which compiles, but has an error at runtime e.g. you try to access a file that does not exist, or access a variable that has not been set. And sometimes because something untoward happened on the machine your code was executing e.g. the system runs out of memory.

A very important part of learning to write automation involves handling and processing exceptions.

What is An exception?

An exception is an object raised which interrupts the flow of execution in an application.

Because we are using automation to support our testing, we should expect our automation code to trigger anomalous and exceptional behaviour. Our automation code will encounter bugs and unexpected situations and we have to be able to handle them.

We also use exceptions in our abstractions to let the calling automation code know that something unexpected has happened.

Automation code is very different from application code in that we often want exceptions to show themselves and cause our `@Test` methods to fail.

In application code we rarely want exceptions to manifest because they slow the whole system down and create a poor user experience.

What is an exception?

Normally Java code proceeds from one statement to the next e.g.

```
String ageAsString = age.toString();

String yourAge =
        "You are " + ageAsString + " years old";
```

In the above code Java would:

- call the method `toString` on the age variable
- assign the return value from `toString` to the `ageAsString` variable
- build a `String` from the constant `"You are "`, the variable `ageAsString`, and the constant `"years old"`
- assign that `String` to the `yourAge` variable

All of the above code would execute in sequence.

An exception is a way of interrupting the normal flow of execution when something goes wrong.

When an exception occurs the current statement is terminated and the execution flow stops. If there is no program code to catch and handle the exception anywhere in the sequence of calling code then the exception will terminate the program.

What does an exception look like?

The simplest way of understanding an exception is to see one in action.

I have created a package in `src\test\java` called:

```
package com.javafortesters.chap011exceptions.examples;
```

And added a *JUnit test* `class` called `ExceptionsExampleTest`.

I will add all my `@Test` annotated methods into this class.

The following code, when annotated with `@Test`, will cause a `NullPointerException` to be thrown.

Run it and see:

```
public void throwANullPointerException(){
    Integer age=null;

    String ageAsString = age.toString();

    String yourAge =
            "You are " + ageAsString + " years old";

    assertEquals("You are 18 years old", yourAge);
}
```

In the above code, you can see that I forgot to assign a value to the `Integer age`, and it is set to `null`. So when I try to call the `toString()` method on `age`, Java throws a `NullPointerException`.

In this case the thrown exception is good for us, because we see that we made a mistake in our coding, and we can fix it by assigning a value, i.e. `18`, to the `age` variable.

The exception report is written to the console:

```
java.lang.NullPointerException
    at com.javafortesters.exceptions.ExceptionsExampleTest.
    throwANullPointerException(ExceptionsExampleTest.java:15)
    at sun.reflect.NativeMethodAccessorImpl.invoke0(Native Method)
    ...
    at org.junit.runners.ParentRunner.run(ParentRunner.java:309)
    at org.junit.runner.JUnitCore.run(JUnitCore.java:160)
    at com.intellij.junit4.JUnit4IdeaTestRunner.startRunnerWithArgs
       (JUnit4IdeaTestRunner.java:77)
    at com.intellij.rt.execution.junit.JUnitStarter.prepareStreamsAndStart
       (JUnitStarter.java:195)
```

```
12      at com.intellij.rt.execution.junit.JUnitStarter.main
13         (JUnitStarter.java:63)
14      at sun.reflect.NativeMethodAccessorImpl.invoke0(Native Method)
15      at sun.reflect.NativeMethodAccessorImpl.invoke
16         (NativeMethodAccessorImpl.java:57)
17      at com.intellij.rt.execution.application.AppMain.main(AppMain.java:120)
```

In the above exception message you can see the *call stack trace.* I removed a few lines to avoid cluttering the page (represented by `...` in the listing).

Each of the `at` lines represents a *call* and is a nested step in the execution of the code. The most recent call is at the top (lines 2 and 3 in the listing). These lines tell us that a NullPointerException was thrown on line 15 of `ExceptionsExampleTest.java`.

```
throwANullPointerException(ExceptionsExampleTest.java:15)
```

Then each of the lower `at` lines is another level where the code was executed. Because we are using JUnit and I ran the code from the IDE, there are a lot of steps involved.

Working from the bottom up you can see that:

- line 17: an application main method was called from IntelliJ
  - `AppMain.java:120`
- lines 14-16: various reflection methods were called to start the code
  - `NativeMethodAccessorImpl.java:57`
- lines 10-13: JUnit was called
  - `JUnitStarter.java:63`
- lines 8 & 9: JUnit started a JUnit runner to run the `@Test` method
  - `JUnit4IdeaTestRunner.java:77`
- lines 5-9: then there were a bunch of lines all related to starting and executing the method
- lines 1-3: before our code failed on line 15
  - `ExceptionsExampleTest.java:15`

To be honest, I don't fully understand all the lines in that stack trace. But I can look at them and make a rough guess what is happening and I can see the most important parts.

The stack trace is useful because it shows the line numbers that were involved in calling the code, and for us, the most important is line 3 in the listing. Where the line (`15`) in `ExceptionsExampleTest.java` is described as the source of the exception. This helps us debug the code when an exception is thrown.

Exercise: Fix the `NullPointerException` in the code

Amend the code to assign `18` to the `age` and check the code runs successfully without throwing an exception.

Catching Exceptions

There are situations where we know in advance that an exception might happen, and we want to catch the exception and take action to handle the exception. e.g. we try to open a file, but it doesn't exist, so we catch the exception and then create the file.

This is where the `try` and `catch` keywords in Java help us.

```
Integer age=null;
String ageAsString;

try{
   ageAsString = age.toString();

}catch(NullPointerException e){
    age = 18;
    ageAsString = age.toString();
}
```

I made a few changes to the code to use the try catch:

- declare `String ageAsString;` before the `try`
- declare the type of exception to `catch`, in this case a `NullPointerException`.
- take action to handle the exception in the `catch` block. i.e. I assigned a value to the `Integer age`.

I have to declare `String ageAsString;` before the `try`. You can see that `try` has a code block delimited with `{` and `}`. If I declared `ageAsString` within that code block it would only be accessible for code within the try code block's { and }, and not available to code in the `catch` block or after the `try` and `catch` blocks.

In the `catch` I have to declare what type of exception I will catch. In this case I only want to catch `NullPointerExceptions`, so declare a variable `e` as a `NullPointerException`.

In the `catch` block, I assume that I have reached this code because `age` was `null`, so I assign it a value and repeat the `Integer` to `String` conversion. I use the `catch` block to fix the cause of the exception and take action to allow the rest of the code to run to completion.

try catch Notes

- Code in the `try` block will always run.
- The `catch` block will execute only if the declared exception is thrown.
- Exceptions that are thrown in the `catch` block will propagate up the stack i.e. to calling methods.

The code in the `try` block will always be run.

If an exception is thrown, and it is of the type declared by the `catch` block then the code in the `catch` block will be run.

If an exception is thrown within the catch block. Then it won't be re-caught because there is no `try catch` statement surrounding it.

If a different exception is thrown then it will not be caught because I have specified that only `NullPointerException` will be caught.

My full code looks like this:

```
@Test
public void catchANullPointerException(){
    Integer age=null;
    String ageAsString;

    try{
       ageAsString = age.toString();

    }catch(NullPointerException e){
        age = 18;
        ageAsString = age.toString();
    }
```

```
    String yourAge =
            "You are " + age.toString() + " years old";

    assertEquals("You are 18 years old", yourAge);
}
```

Exercise: Use a different exception instead of `NullPointerException`

Replace `NullPointerException` with `ArithmeticException`.

What happens?

Exercise: Don't fix the cause of the exception

Remove the `age = 18;` statement from within the catch block.

Run the `@Test` method and see what happens.

Exercise: Catch a Checked Exception

Use `NoSuchMethodException` instead of `NullPointerException`.

What happens?

An Exception is an object

```
}catch(NullPointerException e){
    age = 18;
    ageAsString = age.toString();
}
```

You can see in my catch block that I declared a parameter `e` as a `NullPointerException`.

This means that within the catch block I have access to a local variable `e`. You could name this variable whatever you want, a lot of people stick with `e` as a convention.

`e` is an object of type `NoSuchMethodException` so I have access to a variety of methods on this exception. A few useful methods are:

- `getMessage` - shows me the error message associated with the exception so I can log it
- `getStackTrace` - an Array of `StackTraceElement` object with method calls that reveal the lines of code which led up to the throwing of the exception, which can help with debugging
- `printStackTrace` - which prints the stack trace to the error output stream - typically your console or command line

Exercise: Use Exception as an object

Add the following code in your `catch` block, run the `@Test` method, and see what information you get from the exception itself.

The `getStackTrace` method returns an array of `StackTraceElement` objects, investigate what the methods on this object reveal.

```
System.out.println("getMessage - " +
        e.getMessage());
System.out.println("getStacktrace - " +
        e.getStackTrace());
System.out.println("printStackTrace");
e.printStackTrace();
```

Catch more than one exception

In the `try catch` code above, I only checked for a single type of exception.

The catch block can be repeated to write code that catches multiple exceptions.

```
Integer age=null;
String ageAsString;

try{
    ageAsString = age.toString();

}catch(NullPointerException e){

    age = 18;
    ageAsString = age.toString();
```

```
    }catch(IllegalArgumentException e){
        System.out.println("Illegal Argument: " +
                            e.getMessage());
    }
```

In the above code snippet, the catch blocks will handle either a `NullPointerException` or an `IllegalArgumentException`.

JUnit and Exceptions

JUnit has a handy feature to allow us to check for thrown exceptions.

```
@Test(expected = NullPointerException.class)
```

We can tell the `@Test` annotation to expect an exception of a particular class to be thrown.

The above code tells JUnit to expect to have an exception of type `NullPointerException` thrown during the execution.

If no `NullPointerException` is thrown then the method will fail.

If a `NullPointerException` is thrown then the method will pass.

For example, the following method passes because a `NullPointerException` is thrown:

```
@Test(expected = NullPointerException.class)
public void nullPointerExceptionExpected(){
    Integer age=null;
    age.toString();
}
```

Be careful with this parameter as the exception could be thrown anywhere in the method code and your method would still pass, so when you use this parameter make sure that your code is as small as possible to trigger the exception and you have other `@Test` methods which ensure that the setup code works. After all, if your setup code threw a `NullPointerException` then the method would pass, but would not have checked what you wanted.

Throwing an Exception

We are not limited to catching the exceptions from code that other people have written. We can also throw exceptions when we need to.

As an example of this I will revisit the abstraction layer we have for users, where we were able to construct a user by passing in the `username` and `password`.

I will amend this so that the password is checked and the constructor will throw an exception if the password is less than 7 characters in length.

I'll re-use the `setPassword` method in the constructor with parameters so that I only have to add the validation rule checking in the `setPassword` method.

```
public User(String username, String password) {
    this.username = username;
    setPassword(password);
}
```

Then finally I write code to implement the password validation length checking.

```
public void setPassword(String password) {

  if(password.length()<7){
     throw new IllegalArgumentException("Password must be > 6 chars");
  }

  this.password = password;
}
```

To explain this in more detail we will look at the password length check.

```
  if(password.length()<7){
     throw new IllegalArgumentException("Password must be > 6 chars");
  }
```

To validate the length of the password I check the `length` of the `String`. If the length is `< 7` (less than seven).

```
throw new IllegalArgumentException("Password must be > 6 chars");
```

Since an exception is an object, I have to create a `new` instance of an `IllegalArgumentException`. And the `throw` keyword is important because this is what causes the exception to interrupt the flow of execution.

Also note that when I create the new exception I add an explanatory message. This adds additional information to the stack trace to help anyone debug the code. The error output for this exception, if it was not caught and handled, looks as follows:

```
java.lang.IllegalArgumentException: Password must be > 6 chars
  at com.javafortesters.domainentities.interim.exceptions.User.setPassword
    (User.java:29)
  at com.javafortesters.domainentities.interim.exceptions.User.<init>
    (User.java:19)
  at com.javafortesters.exceptions.UserPasswordExceptionsTest.
    passwordMustBeGreaterThan6Chars(UserPasswordExceptionsTest.java:22)
  ...
```

You can see from the above error message output that the first thing in the stack trace is the explanatory text that I added when I threw the exception.

Throwing exceptions in your abstraction layers is a useful way to keep the code simple and clean, and help avoid making simple errors in your `@Test` methods.

finally

Sometimes we want to `try` and do something, `catch` and handle any exceptions, and then `finally`, always execute some code.

```
try{
    // try and do something

}catch(NullPointerException e){
    // handle the exception here

}finally{
    // perform the code here
    // regardless of whether an
    // exception was thrown or not
}
```

In the following code, the `finally` block is used to assign a value to the `yourAge` variable:

```
@Test
public void tryCatchFinallyANullPointerException(){
    Integer age=null;
    String ageAsString;
    String yourAge="";

    try{
        ageAsString = age.toString();

    }catch(NullPointerException e){

        age = 18;
        ageAsString = age.toString();

    }finally{

        yourAge = "You are " + age.toString() + " years old";
    }

    assertEquals("You are 18 years old", yourAge);
}
```

The `finally` block is mainly used when we want to re-throw an exception, but before we lose control over the code execution we want to tidy up resources.

In the following code, instead of fixing the age, I re-throw the `NullPointerException` as an `IllegalArgumentException`.

If I did not add the `finally` block, as soon as I throw the `IllegalArgumentException`, no more code in this method would be executed. Because I added the `finally` block, the `IllegalArgumentException` is thrown, but before control is passed down the call stack, the code in the `finally` block is executed:

```
@Test(expected = IllegalArgumentException.class)
public void exampleTryCatchFinally(){
    Integer age=null;

    try{
        System.out.println("1. generate a null pointer exception");
        System.out.println(age.toString());

    }catch(NullPointerException e){
        System.out.println("2. handle null pointer exception");
        throw new IllegalArgumentException
                    ("Null pointer became Illegal", e);
    }finally{
        System.out.println("3. run code in finally section");
    }
}
```

Which generates the following output:

```
1. generate a null pointer exception
2. handle null pointer exception
3. run code in finally section

java.lang.IllegalArgumentException: Null pointer became Illegal
  at com.javafortesters.exceptions.ExceptionsExampleTest.
    exampleTryCatchFinally(ExceptionsExampleTest.java:144)
  at sun.reflect.NativeMethodAccessorImpl.invoke0(Native Method)
  ... 26 more
```

You can see from the above that:

- the try block executes
- we catch the `NullPointerException`
- we throw an `IllegalArgumentException`
- since we are about to lose control of the execution due to the `IllegalArgumentException`, the finally block executes
- the `IllegalArgumentException` is triggered and the flow of execution is interrupted.

Summary

You will have to handle exceptions when you write automation code because many of the libraries you use will throw exceptions to alert you of unexpected events.

We will revisit exceptions in a future chapter so you learn how to create your own exceptions.

When writing abstraction layers for automation I try not to put asserts in my abstraction layers, rather I `throw` exceptions so that the `@Test` annotated method can either propagate them, or `catch` and handle them.

References and Recommended Reading

- Exceptions
  - docs.oracle.com/javase/tutorial/essential/exceptions[95]
- Official Definition of an Exception
  - docs.oracle.com/javase/tutorial/essential/exceptions/definition.html[96]
- StackTraceElement
  - docs.oracle.com/javase/7/docs/api/java/lang/StackTraceElement.html[97]

---

[95]http://docs.oracle.com/javase/tutorial/essential/exceptions/index.html

[96]http://docs.oracle.com/javase/tutorial/essential/exceptions/definition.html

[97]http://docs.oracle.com/javase/7/docs/api/java/lang/StackTraceElement.html

Chapter Twelve - Introducing Inheritance

Chapter Summary

In this chapter you will learn a brief overview of *Inheritance*:

- An Object can inherit from another Objects to reuse code
- An Object can re-implement inherited methods
- You can re-use code through composition, as well as inheritance
- use the keyword `extends` in Java to inherit from a Class

Before we provide more information about Exceptions we have to provide an overview of Inheritance and how you use Java to `extend` other classes.

Inheritance

Inheritance is an Object-oriented Design[98] concept. Java provides an implementation of some inheritance features. In this chapter you will receive a very brief overview of inheritance, mainly so that you understand some of the mechanisms that Java provides, and to help you understand some of the more advanced sections as we work through the book.

I have covered inheritance late in the book because you don't really need it for the early parts of this book. The book started by having you 'use' Java. You didn't really need to extend any classes.

When we start creating our own Exception classes, then we will need to extend other classes, so we need to understand the Java concept of Inheritance.

You have seen that Java Classes have methods and fields. And that those methods and fields could be made public or private.

[98]http://en.wikipedia.org/wiki/Object-oriented_design

Inheritance provides one way of allowing us to re-use those methods in other classes.

We make one object inherit from another by use of the `extends` keyword.

```
import com.javafortesters.domainentities.User;

public class EmptyUser extends User {
}
```

In the above example, the `EmptyUser` object inherits from the `User` object.

Any public methods on the `User` object, are 'inherited' by the `EmptyUser` object, so you, as a programmer, do not have to write those methods.

If you want the `EmptyUser` to have a different implementation of any of those methods then you can implement the method in `EmptyUser` and override the method inherited from `User`.

You can see from the previous code that `EmptyUser` has no code in the body of the class, but I can use it in an `@Test` method, because it 'inherits' the methods from the `User` object.

```
    @Test
    public void emptyUserExampleTest(){
        EmptyUser enu = new EmptyUser();
        assertEquals("username", enu.getUsername());
        assertEquals("password", enu.getPassword());
    }
```

At this point the `EmptyUser` offers the same functionality as the `User`.

Inheritance or Composition

Inheritance is an Object-oriented Design technique, and represents an 'is a' relationship. So when we extend an object we are really saying that the new object 'is a' type of object that we are extending.

Composition is an Object-oriented Design technique, and represents a 'has a' relationship, so one object 'has' some other object(s) e.g. a bottle has a top.

Object-oriented Design is beyond the scope of this book (see the references section for more detail). But it is important to understand that some of Java functionality, implements Object-oriented concepts.

Inheritance

Inheritance is an Object-oriented Design technique, and represents an 'is a' relationship. When we extend an object we are really saying that the new object 'is a' type of object that we are extending.

e.g. `SuperWidget` **'is a'** `Widget`, `EmptyUser` **'is a'** `User`

If we use inheritance only because we want to re-use code then we run the risk that we make our code harder to re-use, maintain and understand, because Java supports single inheritance i.e. you can only `extend` one object. If you later want to 'change' the superclass (the class we `extend`) then this can be hard to do without extensive changes in your code.

Note, the following example is a terrible example, never ever do something like the following in your code. While it is functionally possible to extend pretty much any other Class, that does not mean we should do so. See the later sections in this chapter for guidance. But just to reiterate - never do the following:

For example: I may decide that I want the `User` to be able to return the URL that they are using, currently I have this in the `TestAppEnv` object. I *could* re-use the code in `TestAppEnv` by having the `User` object extend the `TestAppEnv`. Then the `User` object inherits a `getUrl` method.

Unfortunately a `User` is not a `Test Application Environment`, so while this might seem like a useful shortcut to re-use some code, I do not consider it a good idea in practice.

Because a `User` is not a `TestAppEnv`, extending `TestAppEnv` to re-use code will lead to code which relies on unrelated Objects, and if you do this throughout your code base, it will eventually become unmaintainable, and unreadable, and changes in one area of the code will have unexpected consequences in other areas of the code.

Composition

Very often I don't use Inheritance in my code. I code using 'composition' and 'interfaces'. This basically means, implementing interfaces, and embedding other objects within my code and gaining re-use by using their methods.

For example, : If I did want a `getUrl` method in my `User` then I might find a way to re-use a `TestAppEnv` object in my `User` object. If the `TestAppEnv` object required instantiation then I would instantiate it in the `User` constructor. Then I would add a `getUrl` method to my `User`, but the method actually calls the `getUrl` on the `TestAppEnv`.

Exercise: Create a User that is composed of `TestAppEnv`

Try and implement the above **User** object, so that the **User** 'is a' `User` object, which also has a `getUrl` method, where the implementation of that method is achieved by delegating to a `TestAppEnv` object.

Using Inheritance

A better example for the use of inheritance, given our current small number of domain abstraction objects, might be to create an Admin User.

Assuming that the system under test has different types of users, and that Admin users have different permissions from a normal User. I could add a `getPermission` level to the `User`.

The following code would check for this:

```
@Test
public void aUserHasNormalPermissions(){
    User aUser = new User();
    assertEquals("Normal", aUser.getPermission());
}
```

Then I could implement the `getPermission` method on `User`.

```
public String getPermission() {
    return "Normal";
}
```

To create the `AdminUser` I would declare the `AdminUser` class as a class which `extends` User.

```
public class AdminUser extends User {
```

And re-implement the `getPermission` method in `AdminUser`, to return a different value.

```
public String getPermission(){
    return "Elevated";
}
```

I also have to create the constructors for my `AdminUser`:

```
public AdminUser(){
    this("adminuser", "password");
}

public AdminUser(String username, String password){
    super(username, password);
}
```

Note that I call the `super` constructor, which calls the constructor on `User` (the *superclass*)

I could check the `AdminUser` as follows:

```
@Test
public void anAdminUserDefaultConstructor(){
    AdminUser adminUser = new AdminUser();
    assertEquals("adminuser", adminUser.getUsername());
    assertEquals("password", adminUser.getPassword());
    assertEquals("Elevated", adminUser.getPermission());
}

@Test
public void anAdminUserHasElevatedPermissions(){
    AdminUser adminUser = new AdminUser("admin","Passw0rd");
    assertEquals("admin", adminUser.getUsername());
    assertEquals("Passw0rd", adminUser.getPassword());
    assertEquals("Elevated", adminUser.getPermission());
}
```

In all of the above note that, I didn't have to rewrite the `getUsername` or `getPassword` methods, since we inherited those from `User` when we **extended** it.

One last thing to note. I should really add the `@Override` annotation to the `getPermission` method. This tells the compiler to check that the `getPermission` method is really on the `User` object and is still the same declaration. This helps find any simple errors at compile time, rather than runtime.

So my final `AdminUser` class looks as follows:

```
public class AdminUser extends User {

    public AdminUser(){
        this("adminuser", "password");
    }

    public AdminUser(String username, String password){
        super(username, password);
    }

    @Override
    public String getPermission(){
        return "Elevated";
    }
}
```

Exercise: Create a `ReadOnlyUser`

Create a `ReadOnlyUser` which has the permission `ReadOnly`, with the same default "username" and "password" from `User`.

Inherit from Interfaces and Abstract Classes

In production Java code, a common recommendation is to *code to Interfaces*. Rather than Inheritance.

We haven't really covered Interfaces in detail in this book, because I'm trying to get you up and running fast.

But you saw this concept when using Collections.

Collections are based around interfaces.

The Collections themselves implement interfaces, and extend Abstract Classes.

Since you don't really need to worry about this until you have a larger code base, and have more familiarity with Java, I have delegated discussion of this into the "Advancing Concepts" chapter towards the end of the book.

Summary

Inheritance can be used as a 'code re-use' tool, but it is better used to construct objects which have an 'is a' relationship.

When we re-implement a method from the 'super' class that we `extend` then we annotate the method with `@Override` to make it clear to other people what we have done, and we gain some compile time checking of our actions.

We can add new methods into the class which is inheriting and these will not be added to the `super` class.

Any new methods in the `super` class will automatically be made available to the **extending** class.

Private methods and fields are not accessible through inheritance, only the super class's protected and public fields and methods are accessible through inheritance.

References and Recommended Reading

- Object Oriented Design Concepts
  - docs.oracle.com/javase/tutorial/java/concepts[99]
- Inheritance or Composition Discussion
  - en.wikipedia.org/wiki/Composition_over_inheritance[100]
- Object Oriented Programming Concepts
  - en.wikipedia.org/wiki/Object-oriented_programming[101]

---

[99]http://docs.oracle.com/javase/tutorial/java/concepts

[100]http://en.wikipedia.org/wiki/Composition_over_inheritance

[101]http://en.wikipedia.org/wiki/Object-oriented_programming

Chapter Thirteen - More About Exceptions

Chapter Summary

In this chapter you will learn more about exceptions:

- Unchecked Exception
- Checked Exception
- The Exception Inheritance hierarchy
- How to create your own Exception

After this chapter you will be able to use code that other people have written which throw exceptions and create your own exceptions to add into your own abstraction layers.

Unchecked and Checked Exceptions

All the examples you have seen so far in the book have been unchecked exceptions.

- An unchecked exception is one that can be thrown, by a method, without having to declare that the exception will be thrown.
- A checked exception, has to be declared, and generally represents a particular use case that, while 'exceptional' still has to be explicitly handled, or deliberately ignored by the calling code.

Unchecked Exceptions

Unchecked exceptions can bite without you knowing they will occur. You saw an example of this in the earlier chapters with the `NullPointerException`.

An unchecked Exception is also known as a Runtime Exception, as you are only made aware of them at run time.

If you want to create an unchecked exception you `extend` `RuntimeException` or any of the classes which already extend it.

e.g.

- `IllegalArgumentException`
- `ArithmeticException`
- `NoSuchElementException`
- etc.

I don't think I have ever created a custom exception that extended an unchecked exception. Generally when I create custom exceptions I want people to be aware of them and handle them in their code.

If I do want to throw an unchecked exception I will first of all try and use one of the standard `java.lang` unchecked exceptions.

For example you saw the use of a `java.lang` unchecked exception when we added the exception to the password validation in `User` I used the `IllegalArgumentException` because I was validating a parameter to a method.

It might be appropriate to create my own unchecked exceptions if I want to allow code to distinguish between exceptions that the abstraction layer has thrown at runtime, and those exceptions thrown by the Java runtime.

Checked Exceptions

You will be informed about the need to handle checked exceptions at compile time because a checked exception will be declared as being thrown by the method declaration.

For example, I could declare the `setPassword` method on `User` as throwing an `InvalidPassword` exception (assuming that `InvalidPassword` exception existed, which it doesn't, but it will when we come to the 'Create your own Exception class' section later in this chapter):

```
public void setPassword(String password) throws InvalidPassword {
```

Then, anywhere in the code that I use the `setPassword` method I either have to:

- handle the exception, as we saw before in a `try catch` block, or
- ignore the exception and allow it to propagate upwards

Ignoring Checked Exceptions

The way that we allow an exception to propagate upwards is to declare the method that we are 'ignoring' the method in, as throwing that particular exception.

For example, since the `User` constructor calls setPassword, I either have to handle the exception or, as shown below, allow it to propagate upwards:

```
public User(String username, String password) throws InvalidPassword{
    this.username = username;
    setPassword(password);
}
```

Handling checked exceptions in default constructor

If I call a constructor from another constructor e.g.

```
    this("username", "password");
```

Then the first statement in the constructor has to be the `this` call. Which means that I cannot wrap that call with a `try catch`.

I have to find a different way of delegating the construction call. In this code I chose to change the default constructor so that it calls a private constructor.

```
public User(){
        this("username", "password", false);
}

private User(String username, String password, boolean b) {
    // only call this because we don't want to throw the exception
    this.username = username;
    try{
        setPassword(password);
    }catch(InvalidPassword e){
        throw new IllegalArgumentException(
                        "Default password incorrect ", e);
    }
}
```

This way I ensure that anyone using the no-argument constructor doesn't have to handle an `InvalidPassword` exception for a hard coded password.

```
@Test
public void canCreateDefaultUserWithoutHandlingException(){
    User aUser = new User();
    assertEquals("username", aUser.getUsername());
    assertEquals("password", aUser.getPassword());
}
```

But they still have to handle the exception if they use the constructor where the `username` and `password` are passed in by the programmer.

```
@Test
public void haveToCatchIllegalPasswordForParamConstructor(){
    try {
        User aUser = new User("me","wrong");
        fail("An exception should have been thrown");
    } catch (InvalidPassword invalidPassword) {
        assertTrue("The exception was thrown", true);
    }
}
```

Note that in the above code I used `fail` from JUnit to cause the `@Test` method to fail if we did not throw an assertion after creating the user. Without the `fail` call, the method would have passed if an exception had not been thrown, even though the method had actually failed. Be very careful when working with exceptions as you need to make sure that you don't have 'false positives' i.e. an `@Test` method passing, when it should have failed.

Difference between `Exception`, `Error` and `Throwable`

Java has an Exception hierarchy:

- `Throwable`
  - `Error`
  - `Exception`
    * `RuntimeException`

The root object is `Throwable`, and both `Error` and `Exception` extend this.

`Error` is reserved for serious Java platform errors. The general guidance provided to Java programmers is "never catch a Java `Error`", which also means we should never catch a `Throwable`.

If we want to catch a generic runtime exception then we should catch `RuntimeException` because any runtime exceptions we raise will derive from `RuntimeException`.

Most of our Exceptions will derive from either `Exception` or a class that already extends `Exception`. We will rarely derive from `Throwable` and never derive from `Error`

Create your own Exception class

Throughout this chapter you have seen reference to a custom exception called `InvalidPassword`.

There is no magic around this class and it is a very small piece of code which implements a class that extends `Exception`.

```
public class InvalidPassword extends Exception {
    public InvalidPassword(String message) {
        super(message);
    }
}
```

Creating your own exception allows you to aggregate multiple Java exceptions into a single context specific exception.

For example, I could catch `IllegalArgumentException`, `NullPointerException`, etc. and throw an `IllegalPassword` exception so that code using my abstraction layer only has to handle a small set of exceptions.

Exercise: Create an `InvalidPassword` exception

To help people use the `User` domain object:

- create the `InvalidPassword` exception
- make the `InvalidPassword` exception describe the validation rules around password i.e. "Password must be > 6 chars"
- write `@Test` methods that check:
  - the `InvalidPassword` exception is thrown on `setPassword`
  - the `InvalidPassword` exception is thrown in the constructor
  - the `InvalidPassword` exception is not thrown in the default constructor
  - the error message thrown by the exception contains the text "Password must be > 6 chars"

Summary

In this chapter you saw how to create and throw a custom exception. Custom exceptions are useful when creating abstraction layers because we do not need to create a lot of return codes, we can throw the exceptions instead.

Custom exceptions 'help' people using our classes, to alert them to validation and exceptions that they might encounter using the class. We can do this through documentation, and we can do this through custom checked exceptions.

By creating a custom checked exception we alert people as they write the code, to the validation and usage rules of our class. If we create a custom `RuntimeException` then we need to rely on documentation to alert the user.

The `fail` method is very useful when writing checks for custom exceptions because we need to make sure that checks do not pass because the exception was not thrown in our `@Test` method.

References and Recommended Reading

- Java Exceptions
  - docs.oracle.com/javase/tutorial/essential/exceptions[102]

[102] http://docs.oracle.com/javase/tutorial/essential/exceptions

- A list of unchecked exceptions in Java
    - list4everything.com/list-of-unchecked-exceptions-in-java.html[103]

[103]http://www.list4everything.com/list-of-unchecked-exceptions-in-java.html

Chapter Fourteen - JUnit Explored

Chapter Summary

In this chapter you will learn more about JUnit features:

- `@Test` - annotate a method as a *JUnit Test*
- `assertEquals` - assert that two values are equal
- `@Test(expected=...)` - expect a specific exception class thrown
- `fail` - force a method to fail
- `@Rule` for `ExpectedException` to check for exceptions
- `@BeforeClass` - run once, before any `@Test` methods are run
- `@AfterClass` - run once, after all `@Test` methods have run
- `@Before` - run before each `@Test` method
- `@After` - run after each `@Test` method
- `@Ignore` - prevent an `@Test` method from running
- More JUnit assertions:
  - `assertEquals` - check expected and actual are equal
  - `assertFalse` - check actual is false
  - `assertTrue` - check actual is true
  - `assertArrayEquals` - check expected and actual arrays are equal
  - `assertNotNull` - check actual is not null
  - `assertNotSame` - check expected and actual are different
  - `assertNull` - check actual is null
  - `assertSame` - check expected and actual are the same
- Hamcrest matchers for literate assertions:
  - `assertThat` - literate assertion using Hamcrest Matcher
  - `is` - true when `assertThat(x, is(y))`
  - `equalTo` - true when `assertThat(x, equalTo(y))`
  - `not` - true when `assertThat(x, is(not(y)))`
  - `containsString` - true when `assertThat(x, containsString(y))`
  - `endsWith` - true when `assertThat(x, endsWith(y))`
  - `startsWith` - true when `assertThat(x, startsWith(y))`
  - `nullValue` - true when `assertThat(x, is(nullValue()))`

With the new JUnit features you will learn in this chapter you will gain the ability to refactor and remove code duplication, and use a greater range of assertion methods.

@Test

We have already seen that in order for a method to be recognized as a *JUnit test*, it has to be annotated with `@Test`.

```
@Test
public void thisTestWillNeverFail(){
}
```

A method will fail if an assertion fails, or an exception is thrown in the body of the method code.

You do not need to add '`test`' into the name of the method. Usually I don't, since '`Test`' is somewhere in the class name, and this gives me the ability to make my method names as expressive as possible.

Checking for Exceptions

Because a method will fail if an exception is thrown. JUnit gives us the ability to check for exceptions, and make an `@Test` method pass, only when the exception is thrown.

@Test(expected=...)

If I want to check that a particular exception is thrown then I can declare it in the `expected` parameter.

```
@Test(expected=InvalidPassword.class)
public void expectInvalidPasswordException() throws InvalidPassword {
    User user = new User("username", "<6");
}
```

Note that your `@Test` method will pass if an exception matching the expected class is thrown anywhere during the execution.

We can use the `ExpectedException` rule to be more specific about the exceptions we count as a pass.

`ExpectedException` rule

JUnit has the concept of 'rules' to extend and enhance JUnit. We won't cover many of the rules available in this book.

The `ExpectedException` rule allows you to be more specific about the exception and only count a particular exception as a pass when:

- a particular class of exception is thrown
- an exception has a particular message
- an exception has a particular cause
- any combination of the above

The following code would have the same effect as annotating with the parameter `expected`:

```
@Rule
public ExpectedException expected = ExpectedException.none();

@Test
public void invalidPasswordThrown()
                throws InvalidPassword {

    expected.expect(InvalidPassword.class);
    User user = new User("username", "<6");
}
```

You can see that I add an `@Rule` as a field in the `class`, instantiated with the static `none` method on `ExpectedException`.

```
@Rule
public ExpectedException expected = ExpectedException.none();
```

In the `@Test` method itself I configure the rule to expect an `InvalidPassword.class`, by calling the `expect` method on the `ExpectedException` object.

```
    expected.expect(InvalidPassword.class);
```

I can make the check more specific by specifying a substring of the expected message. By doing this, my method won't pass if an `InvalidPassword` exception is thrown , but with a different message.

```
expected.expect(InvalidPassword.class);
expected.expectMessage("> 6 chars");
User user = new User("username", "<6");
```

The substring, can also be a Hamcrest matcher:

```
expected.expectMessage(containsString("> 6 chars"));
```

Before & After

JUnit provides annotations for executing code before and after any tests are run, and before and after each test. This allows for setup and cleanup of data or environment conditions.

- `@BeforeClass` - run once, before any `@Test` methods
- `@AfterClass` - run once, after all `@Test` methods
- `@Before` - run before each `@Test` method
- `@After` - run after each `@Test` method

Any method annotated with `@BeforeClass` or `@AfterClass` has to be declared as a static method:

```
@BeforeClass
public static void runOncePerClassBeforeAnyTests(){
    System.out.println("@BeforeClass method");
}
```

Methods annotated with `@Before` and `@After` do not need to be static:

```
@Before
public void runBeforeEveryTestMethod(){
    System.out.println("@Before each method");
}
```

All methods need to be public.

`@After` and `@AfterClass` are run, regardless of whether the preceding method passed or failed.

@Ignore

We can annotate methods with `@Ignore` and the `@Test` annotated method will not be run.

```
@Ignore
@Test
public void thisTestIsIgnored(){
```

No `@Before` or `@After` method will be called for `@Ignore` annotated methods.

We can also add a text parameter to the `@Ignore` to provide a reason for its ignored state.

```
@Ignore("Because it is not finished yet")
```

When you `@Ignore` a method, I recommend you add a text parameter to describe why, otherwise people will forget, and the method is likely to be deleted.

JUnit Assertions

JUnit has its own assertions built in:

```
import static org.junit.Assert.*;
```

JUnit assertions mostly take the form of a method name, with a parameter for the expected result and then a parameter for the actual result, some only take an actual value as the expected is in the name of the assert e.g. `assertNull`:

```
    assertEquals(6, 3 + 3);
```

With JUnit asserts you can also add an optional message to describe the assertion:

```
    assertEquals("3 + 3 = 6", 6, 3 + 3);
```

If the assertion fails then the message is written as part of the message to make it easier to identify the problem e.g.

```
java.lang.AssertionError: 3 + 3 = 6 expected:<7> but was:<6>
```

JUnit provides the following assertions:

- `assertEquals` - check expected and actual are equal
- `assertFalse` - check actual is false
- `assertTrue` - check actual is true
- `assertArrayEquals` - check expected and actual arrays are equal
- `assertNotNull` - check actual is not null
- `assertNotSame` - check expected and actual are different
- `assertNull` - check actual is null
- `assertSame` - check expected and actual are the same

If I use JUnit asserts in my automation code, I mainly use `assertEquals`, `assertFalse` and `assertTrue`.

Exercise: Create an `@Test` method which uses all of the asserts

Experiment with the JUnit asserts by creating an `@Test` annotated method which passes, with all of the above asserts in it.

JUnit also provides an `assertThat` assertion for use with matchers.

Asserting with Hamcrest Matchers and `assertThat`

You can use the `assertThat` method in conjunction with matchers, e.g. from Hamcrest, to make your code more readable.

```
assertThat(3 + 3, is(6));
```

`assertThat`

When an `assertThat` without a reason fails, e.g.

```
assertThat(3 + 3, is(7));
```

Then the output looks like the following:

```
java.lang.AssertionError:
Expected: is <7>
     but: was <6>
```

`assertThat` can also be given a 'reason' message.

```
assertThat("3 + 3 = 6", 3 + 3, is(6));
```

If an assertThat with a reason fails, e.g.

```
assertThat("3 + 3 = 6", 3 + 3, is(7));
```

Then the output looks like the following:

```
java.lang.AssertionError: 3 + 3 = 6
Expected: is <7>
     but: was <6>
```

Since `assertThat` is so readable in the code, I tend not to add a reason, and just use the stacktrace to find the line with the error in it. You can choose your own style.

Hamcrest Core Matchers

JUnit has a dependency on Hamcrest core, so when you add JUnit as a dependency into your project you also get access to Hamcrest core.

Hamcrest core provides a set of 'matchers' which help us write literate asserts, so that our code becomes more readable.

Hamcrest core provides matchers such as:

- `is` - true when `assertThat(x, is(y))`
- `equalTo` - true when `assertThat(x, equalTo(y))`
- `not` - true when `assertThat(x, is(not(y)))`
- `containsString` - true when `assertThat(x, containsString(y))`
- `endsWith` - true when `assertThat(x, endsWith(y))`
- `startsWith` - true when `assertThat(x, startsWith(y))`
- `nullValue` - true when `assertThat(x, is(nullValue()))`

The matchers can be chained to make literate statements e.g.

```
assertThat("", is(not(nullValue())));
```

Exercise: Replicate all the JUnit Asserts using `assertThat`

Copy the `@Test` method you wrote for all the asserts. Then rewrite all the asserts to be `assertThat` with Hamcrest Matchers. e.g. `assertEquals(x,y)` becomes `assertThat(y, is(x))`

Do the above for all of the asserts below:

- `assertEquals` - check expected and actual are equal
- `assertFalse` - check actual is false
- `assertTrue` - check actual is true
- `assertArrayEquals` - check expected and actual arrays are equal
- `assertNotNull` - check actual is not null
- `assertNotSame` - check expected and actual are different
- `assertNull` - check actual is null
- `assertSame` - check expected and actual are the same

Exercise: Use all of the Hamcrest matchers listed

Create an `@Test` method which uses all of the Hamcrest matchers listed, try and use them in combination where you can to make the assertions literate.

- `is` - true when `assertThat(x, is(y))`
- `equalTo` - true when `assertThat(x, equalTo(y))`
- `not` - true when `assertThat(x, is(not(y)))`
- `containsString` - true when `assertThat(x, containsString(y))`
- `endsWith` - true when `assertThat(x, endsWith(y))`
- `startsWith` - true when `assertThat(x, startsWith(y))`
- `nullValue` - true when `assertThat(x, is(nullValue()))`

Hamcrest provides more matchers which you can access if you include the full Hamcrest as a dependency in your `pom.xml` file. e.g.

```
<dependency>
    <groupId>org.hamcrest</groupId>
    <artifactId>hamcrest-all</artifactId>
    <version>1.3</version>
</dependency>
```

For information on the full set of Hamcrest matchers see the Hamcrest Tutorial link in the references for this chapter.

`fail`

JUnit provides a `fail` method which can be used to deliberately cause a method to fail.

This can be called without a description:

```
fail();
```

Or with a description parameter:

```
fail("fail always fails");
```

When a `fail` is issued, then an `AssertionError` is thrown.

`static` importing

The main way you have seen JUnit assertions used so far is by statically importing the method from JUnit:

```
import static org.junit.Assert.assertEquals;
```

So that in the main `@Test` method code we can write the assertion directly:

```
@Test
public void canAddTwoPlusTwo(){
    int answer = 2+2;
    assertEquals("2+2=4", 4, answer );
}
```

Another style of writing JUnit assertions that you might see, or choose to adopt,

```
Assert.assertEquals("2+2=4", 4, answer);
```

In the above usage I have imported the `Assert` class rather than a single method.

```
import org.junit.Assert;
```

In the context of the `@Test` method it would look as follows:

```
@Test
public void canAddTwoPlusTwo(){

    int answer = 2+2;
    Assert.assertEquals("2+2=4", 4, answer);
}
```

Your preference may vary.

I think the first approach without the `Assert.` prefix is often more readable. But using the `Assert.` prefix often aids me when coding because I can see the full range of assertions available to me when I use IDE code completion.

Summary

JUnit offers multiple assertion methods. Try to use the range available to make your assertions expressive, although it is often possible to write all your assertions as `assertTrue` and `assertFalse`. But this means people reading your code have to parse the entire assertion condition, rather than use the assert method itself to help them understand your intent.

We can stick with those assertions offered by default JUnit, or we can choose to use those provided by the Hamcrest imports via the `assertThat` assertion.

Hamcrest offers more matchers than those listed in this chapter, so once you are familiar with the use of `assertThat` in your code, read through the Hamcrest web site and experiment with the additional features in Hamcrest.

Ideally we would write code which does more than simply *assert*. It should also make the intent behind those assertions easy to read and understand from the code. And we can do this by using a combination of assertion and matcher methods.

You will gain a lot of value from experimenting with the `Before` and `After` annotations to help you structure your code and move setup and tear down code to the correct level:

- class level (`@BeforeClass` and `@AfterClass`), or
- method level (`@Before` and `@After`).

References and Recommended Reading

- JUnit home page
  - junit.org[104]
- JUnit Exception Checking
  - github.com/junit-team/junit/wiki/Exception-testing[105]
- JUnit Assertions
  - github.com/junit-team/junit/wiki/Assertions[106]
- Java Hamcrest home page
  - ithub.com/hamcrest/JavaHamcrest[107]
- Hamcrest Tutorial
  - code.google.com/p/hamcrest/wiki/Tutorial[108]

---

[104]http://junit.org

[105]https://github.com/junit-team/junit/wiki/Exception-testing

[106]https://github.com/junit-team/junit/wiki/Assertions

[107]https://github.com/hamcrest/JavaHamcrest

[108]http://code.google.com/p/hamcrest/wiki/Tutorial

Chapter Fifteen - Strings Revisited

Chapter Summary

In this chapter you will revisit what you already know, and learn more about strings:

- `String` is an object with many useful method, not just a container for characters
- `System.out.println` - print a `String` to console
- Special characters encoded in string using \ e.g. `\t`, `\b`, `\n`, `\'`, `\"`, `\\`
- `String` concatenation using + and the `concat` method
- Convert to a `String` with the `toString` method of most objects
- Convert from a `String` to other objects using the `valueOf` method
- Construct `String` from `char[]`, `byte[]`, `StringBuffer`, `StringBuilder` and `String`
- `String` object has many comparison methods:
  - `.compareTo` - returns 0 if `Strings` are equal
  - `.compareToIgnoreCase` - same as `compareTo`, but ignoring case
  - `.contains` - returns `true` if parameter is in `String`
  - `.contentEquals` - returns `true` if `String` content equals to parameter
  - `.equals` - returns `true` if content is equal and the parameter is a `String`
  - `.equalsIgnoreCase` - same as `equals` but ignoring case
  - `.endsWith` - returns `true` if end of `String` equals parameter
  - `.startsWith` - returns `true` if start of `String` equals parameter
  - `.isEmpty` - returns `true` if length of `String` is 0
  - `.indexOf` - returns the index position of a substring
  - `.lastIndexOf` - returns the last index position of a substring
  - `.regionMatches` - compare a region of the substring to a region of the `String`
- `.matches` - easy to use regular expression `String` matching
- Replace sections of a `String` with `.replace`, `.replaceAll`, `.replaceFirst`
- Case conversion using `.toUppercase` and `.toLowercase`
- `.trim` - to remove white space from `String`
- `.substring` - to return a portion of a `String`
- `.format` - to use simple string templates
- `.split` - to parse a string
- `StringBuilder` - build strings: `append`, `delete`, `insert`, `replace`, `reverse`

You have already seen the use of `String` objects throughout the book.

This chapter will pull all that information together into a single chapter because the `String` is an essential object to use when building our `@Test` methods and abstraction layers.

A lot of fields on our objects will start as strings e.g. `username`, `password`. At some point we might choose to make them objects in their own right because then we can make them responsible for their own validation.

String Summary

Just a quick summary of what we have already learned.

A `String` is an object, in `java.lang` so we don't have to worry about importing it.

```
String aString = "abcdef";
```

A `String` literal is also an object, so we can call methods on a `String` literal.

```
assertThat("hello".length(), is(5));
```

We can concatenate strings with the + operator.

```
assertEquals("123456", "12" + "34" + "56");
```

A `String` is immutable. Once a `String` is created, we can't amend it, it might look like we are amending it, but really we are creating a new `String` object.

This means that Java can re-use the same `String` value throughout our code, so even if we type a `String` in multiple places, it doesn't take up any more memory. Of course, we should not use this as an excuse to duplicate `String` literals throughout our code as that can make our code harder to maintain.

System.out.println

You have seen `System.out.println` used in earlier code, this statement allows us to write `String` objects to the console.

It is very useful when trying to gain insight into a section of code and to generate adhoc files or strings to paste into applications.

It can be used as a simple logging tool e.g. for printing out progress of execution to the console, or printing the variables used as input data.

The following example shows this in action:

```
int i=4;
System.out.println("Print an int to the console " + i);
```

Note that in the example above, the `int` is automatically converted into a `String` and concatenated to the string literal:

```
Print an int to the console 4
```

Special character encoding

We encountered the escape sequences in an earlier chapter.

- `\t` - a tab character
- `\b` - backspace
- `\n` - a new line
- `\r` - a carriage return
- `\'` - a single quote
- `\"` - a double quote
- `\\` - a backslash

When building strings we have to make sure we escape the characters like `"`, and \ otherwise our strings will fail to build.

```
System.out.println("Bob said \"hello\" to his cat's friend");
System.out.println("This is a single backslash \\");
```

Will output:

```
Bob said "hello" to his cat's friend
This is a single backslash \
```

Exercise: Try using the other escape characters

Experiment with some `@Test` methods which use the other escape characters in a string e.g. `"\t"`, `"\b"`, `"\n"`, `"\r"` and see the effect when you use `System.out.println` to print to the console output.

`String` Concatenation

We have already seen + as a method of concatenating strings. The + is also useful as a way of adding primitives and other objects on to the `String`.

```
String ps1 = "This is " + "String2";
assertThat(ps1, is("This is String2"));
String ps2 = "This is " + 4;
assertThat(ps2, is("This is 4"));
```

The `String` class has a `concat` method which allows us to concatenate other strings. This does not allow us to concatenate other objects on to the `String`.

```
String thisIs = "This is ";
String s1 = thisIs.concat("String1");
assertThat(s1, is("This is String1"));
```

Converting to/from a `String`

Converting to a `String` with `toString`

Most classes override the `toString` method to provide a way of creating a `String` representation of the object.

This provides a useful way of converting to a `String`, and this is the method called when you concatenate a `String` with a different type using `+`.

For primitive types, the associated object version is used e.g. for `int` the `Integer.toString` is used.

```
String intConcatConvert = "" + 1;
assertThat(intConcatConvert, is("1"));

String integerIntConvert = Integer.toString(2);
assertThat(integerIntConvert, is("2"));
```

The `String` class itself has the `valueOf` method which takes objects and primitives and converts them to a `String`. For objects, the `toString` method on the object is used for the conversion.

```
String integerStringConvert = String.valueOf(3);
assertThat(integerStringConvert, is("3"));
```

In addition you can convert from `byte[]` and `char[]` (and other objects) to a `String` using the `String` constructor.

Converting from a `String`

Many objects have a `valueOf` method which can convert the value of the `String` to the associated object. e.g. `Integer`, `Float`, etc.

```
assertThat(Integer.valueOf("2"), is(2));
```

The `String` object also has a `toCharArray` to convert to a `Character` array.

```
char[] cArray = {'2','3'};
assertThat("23".toCharArray(), is(cArray));
```

We can convert a `String` to a `byte` array using the `getBytes` method.

```
byte[] bArray = "hello there".getBytes();
```

Converting to bytes from strings can be problematic if we want to move our code between different machines as they may have a different default character set or character encoding.

When we convert between `byte` and `String` we may need to control the encoding. If we use an incorrect encoding then an `UnsupportedEncodingException` will be thrown:

```
@Test
public void canConvertBytesUTF8() throws UnsupportedEncodingException {
    byte[] b8Array = "hello there".getBytes("UTF8");
}
```

Constructors

We can construct a new `String` with no arguments to create a `0` length `String`.

```
String empty = new String();
assertThat(empty.length(), is(0));
```

Or with arguments to construct from:

- `String`
- `char[]` - an array of `char`
- `byte[]` - an array of `byte`
- `StringBuffer` - a mutable `String`
- `StringBuilder` - a mutable `String`

e.g.

```
char[] cArray = {'2','3'};
assertThat(new String(cArray), is("23"));
```

Exercise: Construct a String

Construct a String from a `String`, `char[]`, and `byte[]`.

Experiment with the different combinations of parameters.

Comparing Strings

`String` provides many methods for comparison and searching:

- `.compareTo` - returns 0 if `Strings` are equal
- `.compareToIgnoreCase` - same as `compareTo`, but ignoring case
- `.contains` - returns `true` if parameter is in `String`
- `.contentEquals` - returns `true` if `String` content is equal to parameter
- `.equals` - returns `true` if content is equal and the parameter is a `String`
- `.equalsIgnoreCase` - same as `equals` but ignoring case
- `.endsWith` - returns `true` if end of `String` equals parameter
- `.startsWith` - returns `true` if start of `String` equals parameter

- `.isEmpty` - returns `true` if length of `String` is 0
- `.indexOf` - returns the index position of a substring in a `String`
- `.lastIndexOf` - returns the index position of a substring searching from the end of the `String` forwards
- `.regionMatches` - compare a region of the substring to a region of the `String`

`compareTo` & `compareToIgnoreCase`

`compareTo` compares the `String` you call the method on, with a `String` parameter:

If the two `Strings` are equal then `compareTo` returns `0`

```
String hello = "Hello";
assertThat(hello.compareTo("Hello"), is(0));
```

If the argument `String` is smaller than the `String` then `compareTo` returns a negative number

```
assertThat(hello.compareTo("hello") < 0, is(true));
assertThat(hello.compareTo("Helloo") < 0, is(true));
assertThat(hello.compareTo("Hemlo") < 0, is(true));
```

If the argument `String` is larger than the `String` then `compareTo` returns a positive number

```
assertThat(hello.compareTo("H") > 0, is(true));
assertThat(hello.compareTo("Helln") > 0, is(true));
assertThat(hello.compareTo("HeLlo") > 0, is(true));
```

Note that larger means both longer length or, a character difference. Similarly smaller means smaller length, or a character difference.

`compareToIgnoreCase` uses the same logic as `compareTo` but the case of the letters is ignored e.g

```
assertThat(hello.compareToIgnoreCase("hello"), is(0));
assertThat(hello.compareToIgnoreCase("Hello"), is(0));
assertThat(hello.compareToIgnoreCase("HeLlo"), is(0));
```

`contains`

The method `contains` returns `true` if the parameter `String` is contained within the `String`. The value `true` will also be returned if the parameter `String` equals the `String`.

```
String hello = "Hello";
assertThat(hello.contains("He"), is(true));
assertThat(hello.contains("Hello"), is(true));
```

Case is important when using contains:

```
assertThat(hello.contains("LL"), is(false));
```

The value `false` is returned if the parameter is not contained within the `String`

```
assertThat(hello.contains("z"), is(false));
```

`contentEquals` & `equals` & `equalsIgnoreCase`

The method `contentEquals` returns `true` if the `String` has the same content as the parameter and `false` if it does not.

```
String hello = "Hello";
assertThat(hello.contentEquals("Hello"), is(true));
assertThat(hello.contentEquals("hello"), is(false));
```

The `contentEquals` method will work with any object that implements the `CharSequence` interface, or against a `StringBuffer` (e.g. a `StringBuilder`).

The `equals` method enforces the additional rule that the parameter must be a `String`, as well as having equal content.

The `equalsIgnoreCase` method works the same as `equals` but ignores the case in the comparison.

```
assertThat(hello.equalsIgnoreCase("hello"), is(true));
```

`endsWith` & `startsWith`

The `endsWith` method compares the end of the `String` to the parameter.

```
String hello = "Hello";
assertThat(hello.endsWith("Hello"), is(true));
assertThat(hello.endsWith(""), is(true));
assertThat(hello.endsWith("lo"), is(true));
```

The `startsWith` method compares the start of `String` to the parameter.

```
assertThat(hello.startsWith("Hello"), is(true));
assertThat(hello.endsWith(""), is(true));
assertThat(hello.startsWith("He"), is(true));
```

Both `endsWith` and `startsWith` methods implement case sensitive searches.

```
assertThat(hello.startsWith("he"), is(false));
assertThat(hello.startsWith("Lo"), is(false));
```

isEmpty

The `isEmpty` method returns `true` if the length of the `String` is `0`, and `false` if the length is `> 0`.

```
String empty = "";
assertThat(empty.isEmpty(), is(true));
assertThat(empty.length(), is(0));
```

regionMatches

The `regionMatches` method allows you to compare part of one String, with part of another String. The 'part' being a 'region' which is specified by indexes.

The first `String` is the `String` which the `regionMatches` method has been called on. The other `String` is passed as an `other` argument to the `regionMatches` method.

The `regionMatches` method takes two forms:

```
regionMatches(boolean ignoreCase, int toffset,
              String other, int ooffset, int len)
```

- the `String` comparison can ignore case

- the region in the first `String` is defined as `toffset` index to the end of the first `String`
- `other` is the second `String`
- the region in the `other` `String` is defined from index `ooffset` (other offset) for length `len`

Or in a second case sensitive form:

```
regionMatches(int toffset,
              String other, int ooffset, int len)
```

Given a particular `String`:

```
"Hello fella"
 01234567890
```

I can search for a substring in the above `String` e.g.

```
String hello = "Hello fella";
assertThat(
        hello.regionMatches(true, 6, "fez", 0, 2),
        is(true));
```

In the above example I am specifying:

- perform a case insensitive comparison
- the region of the `hello` `String` to search as starting at position 6, until the end of the string
- the substring is `"fez"`, and
  - I want the region of this `"fez"` `String` to start at position `0`, and
  - only be 2 characters long

In effect I am looking for `"fe"` in the `hello` `String` starting at position 6.

This is a particularly complicated method to use, and I have rarely used it. I tend to use `contains` or `indexOf` instead.

Exercise: Use `regionMatches`

Write an `@Test` method which uses `regionMatches` to search in the `String` `"Hello fella"`. And match a region of the substring `"young lady"`. e.g. search for the `"la"` portion of `"young lady"` in `"Hello fella"`

`indexOf` & `lastIndexOf`

For the following examples I am using the `String`:

```
"Hello fella"
 01234567890
```

Declared, in the code, as follows:

```
String hello = "Hello fella";
```

Both the `indexOf` and `lastIndexOf` methods return the position in the `String` where the `Character` parameter or `String` parameter can be found.

The `indexOf` method returns the first place in the `String` where the parameter can be found.

```
assertThat(hello.indexOf("l"), is(2));
```

The `lastIndexOf` method returns the last place in the `String` where the parameter can be found. The search for the index begins from the end of the `String`, working towards the start of the `String`.

```
assertThat(hello.lastIndexOf("l"), is(9));
```

Both `indexOf` and `lastIndexOf` can be called with an additional parameter to specify the start position in the `String` to search from.

In the case of `indexOf` it searches from the given position, to the end of the `String`.

```
assertThat(hello.indexOf('l',3), is(3));
assertThat(hello.indexOf("l",4), is(8));
```

The `lastIndexOf` method searches from the given position towards the start of the `String`.

```
assertThat(hello.lastIndexOf('l',8), is(8));
assertThat(hello.lastIndexOf("l",7), is(3));
```

If `indexOf` or `lastIndexOf` cannot find an occurrence of the `Character` or substring in `String` then the method returns `-1` (negative one).

```
assertThat(hello.indexOf('z'), is(-1));
assertThat(hello.lastIndexOf("z"), is(-1));
```

Exercise: Find positions of all occurrences in a `String`

- Write a method, which takes a `String` and a substring as parameters and returns a `List<Integer>` where each Integer is the location of the substring in the `String`.
  - e.g. `findAllOccurrences("Hello fella", "l")` would return a `List<Integer>` with the values `2,3,8,9`
- For bonus points, write a `findAllOccurrences` method which returns the list in the reverse order i.e. `9,8,3,2`

Comparing With Regular Expressions

Regular Expressions are an incredibly powerful tool for working with strings.

Java has a whole package dedicated to regular expressions, '`java.util.regex`', but a detailed look at Regular Expression handling is beyond the scope of this book. I have listed the main on-line references I use in the References section of this chapter.

In this book I want to introduce you to regular expressions with the `.matches` method.

A regular expression is a `String` where some of the `Characters` have special meaning, e.g. wild cards, or grouping constructs. The phrase "Regular Expression" is often abbreviated to "Regex".

The `matches` method helps us to do the simplest regular expression task, which is answer the question "does this Regular Expression match this `String`?"

An example scenario for the use of Regular Expressions might be that we want to expand the `password` validation on our `User` class:

- password must contain a digit
- password must contain an uppercase letter

We could implement the above conditions using the `indexOf` operator and loop over digits or upper case letters and try and find them in the `String`. But that would be the hard way, it would require a complicated loop and could lead to buggy code.

Or, we could build a regular expression that only matches if each of those conditions is correct.

For example, I can write a regular expression of matching a `String` and check that it includes a digit `".*[0123456789]+.*"`.

At a high level the above regular expression means:

- `.*` - match 0 or more characters
- `[0123456789]+` - until we find 1 or more of the following characters "`0123456789`"
- `.*` - which can be followed by 0 or more characters

To detail it further:

- `.` - matches any single character
- `*` - means match 0 or more of the preceding element
- `[]` - matches any single character contained in the brackets
- `+` - means match 1 or more of the preceding element

I can use it in my Java code as follows:

```
String mustIncludeADigit = ".*[0123456789]+.*";
```

I assigned the regular expression into a `String` variable for re-use.

I call the `matches` method on a `String` and pass in the regular expression as a parameter, and if the regular expression matches the `String` then `matches` returns `true`.

```
assertThat("12345678".matches(mustIncludeADigit), is(true));
assertThat("1nvalid".matches(mustIncludeADigit), is(true));
```

If the match fails then `false` is returned.

```
assertThat("invalid".matches(mustIncludeADigit), is(false));
assertThat("Invalid".matches(mustIncludeADigit), is(false));
```

I can write a similar regular expression to match uppercase letters:

```
String mustIncludeUppercase = ".*[A-Z]+.*";
```

I used one additional construct in the above regular expression:

- `A-Z` in `[A-Z]` - means any character between `A-Z`, so I could do `a-z` or `0-9`

```
assertThat("Valid".matches(mustIncludeUppercase), is(true));
assertThat("val1D".matches(mustIncludeUppercase), is(true));
```

Exercise: Regular Expressions for `User` `setPassword`

Add the regular expression checks to the `setPassword` method on `User` so that an `IllegalPassword` exception is thrown if the password does not contain a digit, or does not contain an upper case letter.

Working with Regex

When you are new to Regular Expressions they can seem daunting.

Every time I return to them, they seem daunting, because I've forgotten a lot of the nuances and how to write them.

So I want to let you in on my secrets on how I get back up to speed.

1. I use regular-expressions.info[109] to help me remember the syntax
2. I use on-line tools like regexpal.com[110] to construct and check the regular expression against sample text

[109]http://www.regular-expressions.info
[110]http://www.regexpal.com

3. I use desktop tools like RegexBuddy (regexbuddy.com[111]) to help me construct and check the regular expression. RegexBuddy also builds code snippets to use.
4. I write *JUnit tests* to check my regular expression works
5. I write *JUnit tests* around the code using the regular expression e.g. to test the `setPassword` method

Regular expressions are a tremendous tool when you get used to them. As you grow more experienced with Java and start using the `java.util.regex` package you can use regular expressions to parse strings and pull out substrings using regular expressions.

But for the moment, start with the `.matches` method and get used to writing regular expressions for validation.

Manipulating Strings

Replacing Strings

Java provides three methods on `String` to help us generate a new `String` but with elements of the `String` replaced with other characters.

- `.replace` - replace all matching substrings with a new substring
- `.replaceAll` - replace all substrings that match a regular expression with a new substring
- `.replaceFirst` - replace the first substring matching the regular expression with a new substring

```
String hello = "Hello fella fella fella";

assertThat( hello.replace("fella", "World"),
            is("Hello World World World"));
```

You might wonder why there is no `replaceFirst` for normal `Strings`, rather than just using regular expressions. And the reason is that a 'normal' string, is a regular expression, but one which only matches that `String`.

This allows me to use `replaceFirst` to replace the first occurrence of `fella` with `World`:

[111]http://regexbuddy.com

```
assertThat( hello.replaceFirst("fella", "World"),
            is("Hello World fella fella"));
```

And, when the regular expression is a string literal with no regular expression special characters, I can use `replaceAll` instead of `replace`

```
assertThat( hello.replaceAll("fella", "World"),
            is("Hello World World World"));
```

`replaceFirst` and `replaceAll` offer us a very simple way of accessing additional power of regular expressions.

e.g. to replace numbers, with the `String` `"digit"`:

```
assertThat("1,2,3".replaceFirst("[0-9]","digit"),
            is("digit,2,3"));

assertThat("1,2,3".replaceAll("[0-9]", "digit"),
            is("digit,digit,digit"));
```

Uppercase and Lowercase

Java provides very self explanatory methods for converting an entire `String` to uppercase or lowercase

- `.toUppercase` - convert the `String` to uppercase
- `.toLowercase` - convert the `String` to lowercase

```
String text = "In the lower 3rd";

assertThat( text.toUpperCase(),
            is("IN THE LOWER 3RD"));

assertThat( text.toLowerCase(),
            is("in the lower 3rd"));
```

Removing Whitespace

The `String` `trim` method, removes leading and trailing white space from a `String`.

```
String padded = "    trim me    ";
assertThat(padded.length(), is(15));

String trimmed = padded.trim();

assertThat(trimmed.length(), is(7));
assertThat(trimmed, is("trim me"));
```

This is a very handy method to use when tidying up input data, or data read from files.

Substrings

`String` has two forms of `substring`:

- `substring(int beginIndex)` - from an index to the end of the `String`
- `substring(int beginIndex, int endIndex)` between a start index and an end index

Given a `String` of digits:

```
String digits = "0123456789";
```

We can get from (and including) the 5th digit, to the end of the `String`:

```
assertThat( digits.substring(5), is("56789"));
```

The `endIndex` is not included in the substring, so `(5,6)` means "from 5th to (but not including), the 6th":

```
assertThat(digits.substring(5, 6), is("5"));
```

`String.format`

Instead of concatenating strings all the time we can use the static `format` method on `String` to construct strings.

The `format` method allows us to create simple string templates, which we pass arguments into.

e.g. instead of having to concatenate `String` and other variables together:

```
int value = 4;
String output = "The value " + value + " was used";
assertThat(output, is("The value 4 was used"));
```

We could use `String.format` and a format string:

```
String template = "The value %d was used";
String formatted = String.format(template, value);
assertThat(formatted, is("The value 4 was used"));
```

A 'format' string is a `String` with embedded conversion placeholders for the arguments supplied to `String.format` . e.g.

- `%d` - means convert the argument to a decimal integer

Common placeholders are :

- %d - a decimal
- %s - a String

e.g.

```
String use = "%s %s towards %d large %s";
assertThat(
    String.format(use, "Bob", "ran", 6, "onions" ),
    is("Bob ran towards 6 large onions"));
```

The arguments are used in order to fill the placeholders in the format string.

The format string can specify exactly which argument it wants to use in each place holder by using `%<index>$` e.g. `%2$` would mean the 2nd argument:

```
String txt = "%2$s %4$s towards %3$d large %1$s";
assertThat(
        String.format(txt, "Bob", "ran", 6, "onions" ),
        is("ran onions towards 6 large Bob"));
```

This allows us to re-use arguments to fill the template in multiple places:

```
String txt2 = "%1$s %1$s towards %3$d large %1$s";
assertThat(
        String.format(txt2, "Bob", "ran", 6, "onions" ),
        is("Bob Bob towards 6 large Bob"));
```

The format string offers a lot of flexibility, and when you look at the official documentation for the String Formatting Syntax you will see this.

- docs.oracle.com/javase/7/docs/api/java/util/Formatter.html#syntax[112]

I tend to keep the format strings very simple, and mainly use them as place holders for `%s` and `%d`, but it is worth being aware of the possibilities open to you with the format place holders.

Basic String parsing with `split`

`split` allows us to convert a `String` into an array, where each array element is a portion of the `String` delimited by the `split` argument.

For example, I could 'parse' a comma separated value string with

```
String csv="1,2,3,4,5,6,7,8,9,10";
String[] results = csv.split(",");
```

The `results` array would have 10 elements, where each element was one of the numbers separated by "," in the original `String`:

[112]http://docs.oracle.com/javase/7/docs/api/java/util/Formatter.html#syntax

```
assertThat(results.length, is(10));
assertThat(results[0], is("1"));
assertThat(results[9], is("10"));
```

The `split`, argument is a regular expression, so can be used create sophisticated split functions with minimal code.

I frequently use `split` to parse simple CSV, or tab delimited files. I've also used it to parse HTML and XML, without bringing in other libraries.

Manipulating strings With `StringBuilder`

We have learned that `String` is immutable, but Java provides a Class for manipulating and creating strings called `StringBuilder`:

```
StringBuilder builder = new StringBuilder();
```

A `StringBuilder` allows us to:

- `append` values to the end of the string
- `delete` characters, or sub strings, from the string
- `insert` values into the string
- `replace` substrings with other strings
- `reverse` the string

It does this by holding an internal representation of the string which is only converted into a `String` when the `toString` method is called. e.g.

```
builder.append("Hello There").
        replace(7,11,"World").
        delete(5,7);
assertThat(builder.toString(), is("HelloWorld"));
```

A `StringBuilder` extends `StringBuffer`, and is slightly faster, but only for use with single threaded applications. If you advance your Java to the stage where you are using multiple threads, then you may need to use `StringBuffer` instead.

Construct a `StringBuilder`

We can construct an empty `StringBuilder`:

```
StringBuilder builder = new StringBuilder();
```

We can construct a `StringBuilder` with a starting `String` value from anything that implements the `CharSequence` interface e.g. `String`

```
StringBuilder sb = new StringBuilder("hello");
```

Capacity Management

Since `StringBuilder` maintains an internal representation of the `String` it allocates a particular `capacity` in memory for that internal representation. When items are appended to the `StringBuilder` the capacity is automatically increased.

By default, if you use the no-argument constructor, the capacity is 16.

```
StringBuilder builder = new StringBuilder();
assertThat(builder.capacity(), is(16));
```

You can find out the current capacity size using the `capacity` method.

You can construct a `StringBuilder` with a specific capacity if you want.

```
StringBuilder sblen = new StringBuilder(512);
assertThat(sblen.capacity(), is(512));
assertThat(sblen.toString().length(), is(0));
```

For automation code we typically don't worry about the capacity, but if you are writing code that needs to be fast then you might size the `StringBuilder` to avoid too much capacity re-allocation.

You can size the `StringBuilder` after construction using the `ensureCapacity` method:

```
builder.ensureCapacity(600);
```

If you have amended the capacity, or deleted a lot of the string then you can set the capacity to the minimum necessary to hold the string characters by issuing:

```
builder.trimToSize();
```

Appending to the `StringBuilder`

The `append` method works much like the + concatenation approach for `String`. We can append `Objects`, primitives, `Strings`, or `char[]` to the end of a `StringBuilder`.

```
StringBuilder builder = new StringBuilder();
builder.append("> ");
builder.append(1);
builder.append(" + ");
builder.append(2);
char[] ca = {' ', '=', ' ', '3'};
builder.append(ca);

assertThat(builder.toString(), is("> 1 + 2 = 3"));
```

If during the appending, we add more characters than the current capacity, then `StringBuilder` will automatically resize.

Exercise: Check `StringBuilder` resizes

Write an `@Test` annotated method which validates that a `StringBuilder` resizes when you append more characters than the current capacity.

Insert into the `StringBuilder`

The `insert` method supports the same objects and primitives as the `append` method.

When we `insert` into the `StringBuilder` we have to specify the position to `insert` into:

```
StringBuilder builder = new StringBuilder("123890");
builder.insert(3,"4567");
assertThat(builder.toString(), is("1234567890"));
```

In Java, indexes start at `0`, so the first space we can insert into in an Empty string is `0`.

If we use an `index` which is longer than the current internal representation of the String then a `StringIndexOutOfBoundsException` will be thrown.

When a `StringBuilder` has some values in the string we can insert at:

- index `0` to add it to the front,
- index `length` to append it
- anything in between to add it into the body

Exercise: Insert into a `StringBuilder`

Insert a `String` into an empty `StringBuilder`. Insert a `String` on the end. Insert a `String` in the middle.

When we insert a `char[]` we have additional options. In addition to the index, we can specify the offset in the `char` array, and the number of characters to copy from the `char` array.

Given the following `StringBuilder` which starts with the `String` `"abgh"`:

```
char[] ca = {'.', 'a', 'b', 'c', 'd', 'e', 'f'};
StringBuilder builder = new StringBuilder("abgh");
```

The code below will insert at position 2 in the string (i.e. after the 'b'). The characters from position 3 in the char array (`'c'`) to the next 4 characters e.g. (`cdef`);

```
// at position 2 in the string
// insert from the char[] ca
// starting at index 3 'c'
// inclusive the next 4 indexes
builder.insert(2, ca, 3, 4);
assertThat(builder.toString(), is("abcdefgh"));
```

Deleting from `StringBuilder`

We can `delete` substrings, based on indexes from the `StringBuilder`:

```
StringBuilder builder = new StringBuilder("abcdefg");
builder.delete(2,4);
assertThat(builder.toString(), is("abefg"));
```

Given the string `"abcdefg"` we:

- specify the start index to delete from, e.g. 2, which is "c", and
- specify the last index to delete up to, e.g. 4, which would span "cd"

```
abcdefg
0123456
```

Or we can delete a specific character at a specified index using `deleteCharAt`:

```
builder.deleteCharAt(2);
assertThat(builder.toString(), is("abdefg"));
```

Replace Sub Strings and Characters

We can replace sub strings with the `replace` method, which takes a *start index*, *end index*, and a *`String`* as parameters.

The characters from *start index*, to *end index* are replaced by the *`String`*:

```
StringBuilder builder = new StringBuilder("abcdefgh");
builder.replace(0,4,"12345678");
assertThat(builder.toString(), is("12345678efgh"));
```

In the example above, the string to replace was only 4 characters, but the 'gap' was lengthened to allow the replacement `String` to be inserted.

We can replace individual characters by using the `setCharAt` method:

```
StringBuilder builder = new StringBuilder("012345678");
builder.setCharAt(5,'f');
assertThat(builder.toString(), is("01234f678"));
```

Reverse

The ability to reverse strings comes in surprisingly useful.

Having this method built into `StringBuilder` means that I often simply construct a `StringBuilder` with a `String` and call `.reverse().toString()`.

```
StringBuilder builder = new StringBuilder("0123456789");
assertThat(builder.reverse().toString(), is("9876543210"));
```

Sub Strings

The `substring` method returns a `String` from a start index to an end index:

```
StringBuilder builder = new StringBuilder("0123456789");
assertThat(builder.substring(3,7), is("3456"));
```

Or from a start index to the end of the string:

```
assertThat(builder.substring(3), is("3456789"));
```

StringBuilder Summary

StringBuilder is a very powerful class that prevents needing to use a lot of Strings and constantly concatenating them together. The use of StringBuilder is also very efficient since it uses an internal representation rather than constructing new String objects on each method call.

For efficiency we could maintain the capacity ourself, and size the StringBuilder appropriately for the task at hand, rather than have the StringBuilder resize on the fly with each method.

StringBuilder has other methods that we haven't covered here, this has been an overview of the main StringBuilder functionality that you will use most often.

I find that I use StringBuilder most for String construction, so mainly the append and insert methods. I rarely use the replace, and sub string methods, preferring to replace and work with substrings directly with the String class.

You will develop your own style, and work with the classes that make most logical sense to you.

For full documentation, of all the methods, see the link in the References or use code completion in your IDE. Remember in IntelliJ pressing ctrl + q (on Windows) or ctrl + j (on Mac) in the code completion pop-up shows the JavaDoc documentation for the method.

Concatenation, .format, or StringBuilder

How do you choose the right way to build Strings?

We have seen many different ways to construct strings:

- simple concatenation either with + or concat
- simple templates using String.format

- `StringBuilder` flexibility with inserts, appends and deletes

So which is best?

Well, I use them all.

For simple string building I use concatenation.

I use formats when I have too many concatenations and the code becomes hard to read and maintain, or when I want to reuse the format string in multiple places. I try to remember to use `String.format` more, even when I have a small set of concatenations, but sometimes I get lazy and concatenate `Strings` together.

I tend to use `StringBuilder` if I'm building a `String` over a long period of time, or need to build the `String` over a number of method calls.

I don't think there is a right answer. But do be aware that you have options.

Try to make your code as readable and maintainable as possible. Choose the method that helps you build code that lasts.

Summary

When automating I work with strings all the time: representing data, parsing files, processing JSON, creating HTTP requests, etc.

So I use a lot of basic `String` processing methods and `StringBuilder` generation methods.

This chapter has covered a lot of the basics, even though we haven't gone into depth in many of the areas. Refer back to this chapter when working with automation and data and you'll find many of the basic functions that you are using, or could use, listed here.

I've tried to cover the methods and classes behind the bulk of my string processing needs, hopefully that will match your initial future needs.

References and Recommended Reading

- Java Escape Sequences
  - docs.oracle.com/javase/tutorial/java/data/characters.html[113]
- Java Strings tutorial

[113]http://docs.oracle.com/javase/tutorial/java/data/characters.html

  - docs.oracle.com/javase/tutorial/java/data/strings.html[114]
- Java Byte Encoding and Strings
  - docs.oracle.com/javase/tutorial/i18n/text/string.html[115]
- String Formatting syntax
  - docs.oracle.com/javase/7/docs/api/java/util/Formatter.html#syntax[116]
- StringBuilder Tutorial
  - docs.oracle.com/javase/tutorial/java/data/buffers.html[117]
- StringBuilder Documentation
  - docs.oracle.com/javase/7/docs/api/java/lang/StringBuilder.html[118]
- Java Regular Expressions
  - docs.oracle.com/javase/tutorial/essential/regex[119]
- Regular Expressions Information and Tutorials
  - regular-expressions.info/[120]
- Wikipedia Regular Expressions
  - en.wikipedia.org/wiki/Regular_expression[121]
- On-line Regular expression tester
  - regexpal.com[122]
- RegexBuddy Desktop Tool
  - regexbuddy.com[123]

---

[114] http://docs.oracle.com/javase/tutorial/java/data/strings.html
[115] http://docs.oracle.com/javase/tutorial/i18n/text/string.html
[116] http://docs.oracle.com/javase/7/docs/api/java/util/Formatter.html#syntax
[117] http://docs.oracle.com/javase/tutorial/java/data/buffers.html
[118] http://docs.oracle.com/javase/7/docs/api/java/lang/StringBuilder.html
[119] http://docs.oracle.com/javase/tutorial/essential/regex
[120] http://www.regular-expressions.info
[121] http://en.wikipedia.org/wiki/Regular_expression
[122] http://regexpal.com
[123] http://www.regexbuddy.com

Chapter Sixteen - Random Data

Chapter Summary

In this chapter you will learn how to use Java's Random functionality to create Random Data:

- `Math.random` - easy to use `static` wrapper to generate a random double between 0.0 and 1.0
- `java.util.random` - the main Java random package:
  - `nextBoolean` - return either `true` or `false`
  - `nextLong` - return a random `long` value
  - `nextInt` - random `int` over the range of all `Integer` values
  - `nextInt(int below)` - random `int` greater than or equal to `0` and less than `below`
  - `nextDouble` - flat distribution where each value between 0.0 and 1.0 has equal chance of being returned
  - `nextGaussian` - a Gaussian distribution with a mean of 0.0 and a standard deviation of 1.0, meaning about 70% values hovering around the 0.0 mark (+ or - 1.0)
  - `nextFloat` - random `float` greater than or equal to 0.0 and less than 1.0
  - `nextBytes` - fill a given `byte[]` with random bytes
- *seeding* random number generation with `new Random(seed)`
- Generating random strings

Random data in automation is a contentious subject. Some people argue that automation should be completely deterministic and always run the same way - implying that we always use the same data. I prefer to vary data that is not important to the conditions checked, i.e. data that should be part of an equivalence class. By doing this we increase the data coverage of the automation, and increase the possibility that the automated check will reveal a bug.

Java has a very simple set of random methods and classes.

- `java.util.random`
- `Math.random()`

Java, as part of the Security packages has a `SecureRandom` class, which exposes the same methods as we discuss in this chapter. I do not cover `SecureRandom` in this book because:

- I have never used it in production automation code,
- It is slightly slower to instantiate,
- It is slightly harder to use well.

Most of the randomness you need in your automation code you can achieve with:

- `java.util.random`

`Math.random`

The static `random` method on `Math` provides a 'pseudo random' number.

It is actually a wrapper for the `java.util.random` `nextDouble` method. But makes it simpler to use.

When `Math.random()` is first called, a new random number generator is created which is used for each call to `Math.random()`

`Math.random()` returns a double, greater than or equal to `0.0` and less than `1.0`

```
double rnd = Math.random();

System.out.println(
    String.format(
            "generated %f as random number", rnd));

assertThat(rnd < 1.0d, is(true));
assertThat(rnd >= 0.0d, is(true));
```

`java.util.random`

The `java.util.random` package provides methods to generate random values as follows:

- `boolean`
    - `nextBoolean` - return either `true` or `false`

- `long`
  - `nextLong` - return a random `long` value
- `int`
  - `nextInt` - random `int` over the range of all `Integer` values
  - `nextInt(int below)` - random `int` greater than or equal to `0` and less than `below`
- `double`
  - `nextDouble` - flat distribution where each value between 0.0 and 1.0 has equal chance of being returned
  - `nextGaussian` - a Gaussian distribution with a mean of 0.0 and a standard deviation of 1.0, meaning about 70% values hovering around the 0.0 mark (+ or - 1.0)
- `float`
  - `nextFloat` - random `float` greater than or equal to 0.0 and less than 1.0
- `byte[]`
  - `nextBytes` - fill a given `byte[]` with random bytes.

To use the methods we first have to instantiate a `Random` Object:

```
Random generate = new Random();
```

Then call the appropriate method to generate the random value that we require:

```
boolean randomBoolean = generate.nextBoolean();
int randomInt = generate.nextInt();
int randomIntRange = generate.nextInt(12);
long randomLong = generate.nextLong();
double randomDouble = generate.nextDouble();
double randomGaussian = generate.nextGaussian();
byte[] bytes = new byte[generate.nextInt(100)];
generate.nextBytes(bytes);  // fill bytes with random data
```

Most of the above methods are pretty self explanatory and I encourage you to experiment with them by doing the exercises listed in this chapter.

I will go into two of the methods in more detail, after the exercise:

- `nextInt(int below)`
- `nextGaussian`

Exercise: Create `@Test` Methods Which Confirm Random Limits

- Create `@Test` methods for each of the random methods. i.e. `nextInt`, `nextLong`, etc.
- For each random method, generate 1000 random values and assert that the returned values meet the description:
  - `nextInt` generates from `Integer.MIN_VALUE` and `Integer.MAX_VALUE`
  - `nextBoolean` generates either `true` or `false`
  - `nextLong` generates a `long` between `Long.MIN_VALUE` and `Long.MAX_VALUE`
  - `nextFloat` generates a `float` between `0.0f` and `1.0f`
  - `nextDouble` generates a `double` between `0.0d` and `1.0d`
  - `nextBytes` fills a `byte[]` with random data
  - `nextInt(x)` generates an `int` from `0` to `x-1`

`nextInt(int below)`

When generating a random `int` we can specify the upper range for the generation.

- `nextInt(int below)`

For a given value `below`, the `nextInt` method will generate a value between 0 (inclusive) and the value of the `below` parameter (exclusive) e.g:

- `nextInt(5)` generate a random between 0 and 4 inclusive
  - a number greater than or equal to 0 (inclusive) but less than 5 (exclusive)
- `nextInt(200)` generate a random number between 0 and 199 inclusive
  - a number greater than or equal to 0 (inclusive) but less than 200 (exclusive)

If we want to use `nextInt` to generate an integer from a specific number, e.g. 1 instead of 0 then we have to use an algorithm:

- calculate the range of numbers
- add 1 to this, since the `nextInt` maximum is one less than desired
- and add the start number.

e.g.

```
int minValue = 1;
int maxValue = 5;
int randomIntRange = generate.nextInt(
        maxValue - minValue + 1) + minValue;
```

Exercise: Create an `@Test` method which generates 1000 numbers inclusively between 15 and 20

Use the algorithm above to generate 1000 numbers between 15 and 20 and assert that all numbers 15,16,17,18,19,20 were generated.

`nextGaussian`

A `double` drawn from a Gaussian distribution with a mean of 0.0 and a standard deviation of 1.0, meaning:

- about 70% values hovering around the 0.0 mark (+ or - 1.0),
- about 95% values between -2.0 and 2.0
- about 99% values between -3.0 and 3.0
- about 99.9% values between -4.0 and 4.0

Theoretically there is no limit to the value of the `double` that could be returned by `nextGaussian` because it is not a limited range, it is a probability distribution around a given mean.

You can find references to 'Standard Deviation' at the end of the chapter.

Exercise: Write an `@Test` method that shows the distributions

- Write an `@Test` method that generates 1000 `double` values using `nextGaussian`.
- Count those that are within 1 standard deviation, within 2 standard deviations etc.
- Calculate the percentages of numbers within each standard deviation range and see if they align roughly with the values above.

e.g. the output after running the method could be:

```
about 70% one standard deviation = 67.299995
about 95% two standard deviation = 95.3
about 99% three standard deviation = 99.8
about 99.9% four standard deviation = 100.0
```

Use `nextGaussian` to generate a range of integers

The `nextGaussian` method is typically used in combination with other methods to distribute the range of random values over a probability curve.

e.g. if 'most' of our users are aged 30 - 40, then we have a mean of 35 with a standard distribution of 5, then we could use Gaussian distribution to generate the age:

```
int age = (int)(generate.nextGaussian() * 5) + 35;
```

- about 70% values hovering around the 35 +/- 5 mark (30 - 40),
- about 95% values between 35 +/- 10 mark (25 - 45)
- about 99% values between 35 +/- 15 mark (20 - 50)
- about 99.9% values between 35 +/- 20 mark (15 - 55)

When dealing with ages you might need to add additional code to ensure a minimum and maximum value, even though the probability of getting an extreme value is low, it might happen.

Exercise: Write an `@Test` method which generates 1000 ages using `nextGaussian`

Write an `@Test` method which generates 1000 ages using `nextGaussian` with a mean of 35 and a standard deviation of 5. Count each age generated and output the sorted list of ages and counts to the console.

e.g.

```
...
34 : 70
35 : 167
36 : 83
37 : 80
38 : 66
39 : 51
...
```

Seeding random numbers

The random numbers are 'pseudo random' because they are based on a 'seed', and each call to 'random' is deterministic if the 'seed' is controlled.

For example:

```
Random generate = new Random(1234567L);
```

Would generate a random number generator where the `nextInt` returns `1042961893`

Exercise: Create an `@Test` method for Random with Seed

Create an `@Test` method for the seed `1234567L` and assert that:

- `nextInt` == `1042961893` then
- `nextLong` == `-6749250865724111202L`
- continue the assertions and add:
  - `nextDouble`,
  - `nextGaussian`,
  - `nextFloat`,
  - `nextBoolean`

Make sure you can re-run the method and you get the same 'random' numbers.

This is useful when you want to make method execution repeatable. e.g. if at the start of a run you seed the `Random` with the current date time, then if you log the date and time, you could repeat the run exactly, even if random data was used.

For Example:

```
long currentSeed = System.currentTimeMillis();
System.out.println("seed used: " + currentSeed);
Random generate = new Random(currentSeed);
```

If the `System.out.println` was a logging call, then I could recreate the run by seeding random with the seed value logged in the output.

Using Random Numbers to generate Random Strings

A crude way to generate random strings is to build a `String` by randomly adding a valid character to the String.

For Example if I want to build a `String` from the uppercase letters and space:

```
String validValues = "ABCDEFGHIJKLMNOPQRSTUVWXYZ ";
```

Then I can randomly select a character from that String:

```
int rndIndex = random.nextInt(validValues.length());
char rChar = validValues.charAt(rndIndex);
```

If I loop around this generation process and concatenate the results then I can generate a random `String`.

Exercise: Generate a Random String 100 chars long

Generate a random string, 100 characters long, containing the characters `' '` (space) and `'A'` to `'Z'`.

Discussion random data in automation

Many people do not like to add random data to their automation.

I do.

I view automated checks as exercising a particular path through the system, with variable data.

Some data, is needed in order to control the path, and if I vary that data then I run a different path.

For Example: If I am only asked for my passport number when I am 65, then if I create a user who is not 65, I can't cover that path. So I would not vary the age. But if I am asked for a passport number when I am 65 or over, then I have an equivalence class. And if I randomly generate an age which is 65 or older then I can cover that path. It should make no difference to the `@Test` methods, so I can vary the data. If I vary the data and the `@Test` method does not run as expected then I may have found a bug with our understanding of the equivalence class, but I might also have found a bug related to the way the application processes a particular age.

I use randomness to generate data for equivalence classes, and control the data which needs to be static for the execution path preconditions to be met.

Importance of Logging when using Random data

When I use random data, I need to log it.

The simplest logging mechanism to start with is `System.out.println` so if my `@Test` methods write to the console an output of what data they have used, then I can recreate the run later by using the output logs. Because the methods may have failed due to the specific combination of random values, and I need to recreate any failing assertion with that particular data.

I may need to create a mechanism to rerun methods with particular data values, in which case seeding the random mechanism, and logging the seed value, might be an appropriate solution.

I have managed to get by in most of my production use of randomization by logging the output of the random data generation to `System.out.println`. The log appears in System.out when the code ran as part of continuous integration and if an assertion fails due to data then we can look at the log and use the seed, or data, to recreate the execution, or re-running the failing `@Test` method manually with the generated data.

Start simple with your automation.

Don't think that because you've started using random data you need the ability to recreate all the runs exactly and seed your data in the continuous integration environment. You probably don't. You probably need to start with the ability to see what data you have used so that you can re-run any failing methods manually and determine if the random data combination you used, triggered a bug.

Summary

You have seen with the later examples using `nextGaussian` and the random `String` generation that even with a small set of random number generation functions we can fairly easily use them to generate complicated data sets.

I frequently use random data to help me build Domain objects e.g. random Users. And then I set the specific values I need for my `@Test` method. i.e. instead of a default `username` and `password` in the constructor, I might assign a randomly generated `username` and `password`.

References and Recommended Reading

- Standard Deviation
  - en.wikipedia.org/wiki/Standard_deviation[124]
- `Math.random`
  - docs.oracle.com/javase/7/docs/api/java/lang/Math.html#random()[125]
- `java.util.random`
  - docs.oracle.com/javase/7/docs/api/java/util/Random.html[126]
- Hints on generating values in a range
  - http://stackoverflow.com/questions/363681[127]

---

[124]http://en.wikipedia.org/wiki/Standard_deviation

[125]http://docs.oracle.com/javase/7/docs/api/java/lang/Math.html#random()

[126]http://docs.oracle.com/javase/7/docs/api/java/util/Random.html

[127]http://stackoverflow.com/questions/363681/generating-random-number-in-a-range-with-java

Chapter Seventeen - Dates and Times

Chapter Summary

In this chapter you will learn how to use Java's native Date functionality

- `System.currentTimeMillis` - current system time in milliseconds since midnight January 1st, 1970
- `System.nanoTime` - current JVM time source in nanoseconds
- The native classes associated with dates:
  - `Date` - simple to use class for comparison and working from milliseconds
  - `SimpleDateFormat` - create a `String` from a `Date` using a format pattern
  - `Calendar` - a wrapper for `Date` to allow working with days, months, etc.

Dates in Java are handled a little rough and ready, as a result, many Java developers use external libraries like 'Joda-Time'. External libraries are beyond the scope of this book, and while the internal Java classes may not offer the flexibility of 'Joda Time', they are still very powerful.

In addition to working with dates, I also use the Date/Time functionality to:

- seed random numbers
- generate unique data e.g. filenames, and user ids

`currentTimeMillis` and `nanoTime`

- `System.currentTimeMillis` - returns current system time in milliseconds since midnight January 1st, 1970
- `System.nanoTime` - returns current JVM time source in nanoseconds

`System.currentTimeMillis` returns a `long` which represents the current time on your local machine. The time is represented as the number of milliseconds since midnight of the January 1st, 1970.

```
long startTime = System.currentTimeMillis();
```

`System.nanoTime` returns a long which represents the current nanoseconds as calculated by the current JVM. This doesn't necessarily map on to the current system time, but the difference between two calls to `nanoTime` represents the passage of time (in nanoseconds) between the two calls.

```
long startTime = System.nanoTime();
```

A nanosecond is one thousand-millionth of a second.

I typically use these methods to:

- calculate the time that a task takes to execute
- create unique ids and filenames

Calculate the time that a task takes to execute

To calculate the length of time that a task takes, I would :

- instantiate a `startTime`
- perform the task
- instantiate an `endTime`
- calculate the `totalTime` as `endTime - startTime`

For example to calculate how long it takes to output the currentTimeMillis to the console ten times, I can write code like the following:

```
@Test
public void currentTimeMillis(){
    long startTime = System.currentTimeMillis();

    for(int x=0; x < 10; x++){
        System.out.println("Current Time " +
                           System.currentTimeMillis());
    }

    long endTime = System.currentTimeMillis();
    System.out.println("Total Time " + (endTime - startTime));
}
```

When I run this I normally get a totalTime value of around `1`, but sometimes I will get a total value of `0` because the entire task takes place within the same 'millisecond' as calculated by `currentTimeMillis`.

The resolution of values represented by `currentTimeMillis` can vary between operating systems, it is not guaranteed to be a 'millisecond', it might be more e.g. tens of milliseconds. As such this isn't a great method for exact time, but it very often good enough for automation timings, particularly if you are rounding up to the nearest second anyway.

What it is very good for, are unique numbers or values, assuming that you don't reset your computer clock into the past.

Exercise: Re-write the timing `@Test` method using nanoTime

Re-write the millisecond `@Test` method shown above using `nanoTime` and see the difference in output.

When using `nanoTime`, again the resolution is determined by the underlying operating system, but is reported in nanoseconds.

- `nanoTime` is much better for calculating the time duration of an activity which runs quickly, and for which you want a more accurate measurement.
- `nanoTime` is not useful for creating unique numbers because you don't really know the basis for the JVM time.

Create unique values with `currentTimeMillis`

To create unique identifiers or names I often prefix a `String` to the `currrentTimeMillis` value:

```
String userID = "user" + System.currentTimeMillis();
```

This is crude and simple, but fast and obvious.

e.g.

```
user1424101386462
```

Exercise: Use currentTimeMillis to create a unique name with no numbers

We need to create a unique name, that has all alphabetic characters i.e. no numbers in it.

- Create a test which generates a unique string from `currentTimeMillis` but has no numbers in the final string.

Date

The `Date` class exposes a small set of methods.

```
Date date = new Date();
```

Methods that `Date` provides:

- `after` - return true if the parameter date is after the `Date` object
- `before` - return true if the parameter date is before the `Date` object
- `compareTo` - returns 0 if the `Date` objects are equal, negative if the `Date` object is less than parameter and positive if the `Date` object is greater than the parameter

- `equals` - return true if the parameter and `Date` object represent the same time and date
- `setTime`- set the time represented by the `Date` object to a specific millisecond value
- `getTime` - return the number of milliseconds after midnight, January 1 1970 that this `Date` represents
- `toString` - return a `String` representation of the date

Instantiating `Date` without a parameter will default the time represented by the `Date` to the same value as `System.currentTimeMillis`.

The following two statements are essentially equivalent:

```
Date equivDate1 = new Date();
Date equivDate2 = new Date(System.currentTimeMillis());
```

The `toString` method provides a simple method of outputting a `String` representation of the date.

```
System.out.println(date.toString());
```

On my machine `toString` outputs the following string format:

- `Thu Jun 20 12:18:04 BST 2013`

We will learn how to control the output of a `Date` in the next section.

We can also instantiate a `Date` with a `long`, in order to set the `Date` to a specific time.

For example, I could create a `Date` 7 days in the future from one `Date` by manipulating the `long` that I instantiate the `Date` with:

```
long oneWeekFromNowTime = date.getTime();
oneWeekFromNowTime = oneWeekFromNowTime +
                     (1000 * 60 * 60 * 24 * 7);
Date oneWeekFromNow = new Date(oneWeekFromNowTime);
System.out.println(oneWeekFromNow.toString());
```

In the above code I take the time from one `Date` then I add 7 days worth of milliseconds to the `long` value, and instantiate a new `Date` from that milliseconds value. Resulting in the following output:

- `Thu Jun 27 12:18:04 BST 2013`

We can use the `setTime` to set the milliseconds time value of a date after constructing it, so I can create a `Date` with a duplicate time using the constructor or the `setTime` method:

```
Date sameDate = new Date();
sameDate.setTime(date.getTime());
assertThat(date.equals(sameDate), is(true));
assertThat(date.compareTo(sameDate), is(0));
```

SimpleDateFormat

`SimpleDateFormat` allows us to output the value of a `Date` object as a String, in a format that we choose.

```
SimpleDateFormat sdf = new SimpleDateFormat();
```

So if I instantiate a `Date` to the 1st of January 1970:

```
Date date = new Date(0L);
```

Then the following table shows example patterns and the associated generated output, when I apply the pattern:

Pattern	Output
`"MM/dd/yyyy"`	`"01/01/1970"`
`"MMM/dd/yyy"`	`"Jan/01/1970"`
`"MMMM/d/yy"`	`"January/1/70"`

I can use the `applyPattern` method to set the pattern for a `SimpleDateFormat` and use the pattern on a date with the `format` method.

```
sdf.applyPattern("MM/dd/yyyy");
assertThat(sdf.format(date), is("01/01/1970"));
```

- `applyPattern` - set the pattern that the next `format` will use

- `format` - format the given `Date` with the defined pattern

I can also instantiate `SimpleDateFormat` with the pattern that I want to use e.g. "year month day 24hour:minutes:seconds.milliseconds" shown below

```
SimpleDateFormat sdf = new SimpleDateFormat("y M d HH:mm:ss.SSS");
```

You can use `SimpleDateFormat` to generate a `Date` for a given date string e.g. the date of "15th December 2013" and a time of "11:39 pm" and "54 seconds and 123 milliseconds":

```
Date date = sdf.parse("2013 12 15 23:39:54.123");
```

Important elements for use in the pattern format are listed below, using

Element	Description	Output
`"y"`	year	`"2013"`
`"yy"`	year	`"13"`
`"yyy"`	year	`"2013"`
`"yyyy"`	year	`"2013"`
`"yyyyy"`	year	`"02013"`
`"M"`	Month	`"12"`
`"MM"`	Month	`"12"`
`"MMM"`	Month	`"Dec"`
`"MMMM"`	Month	`"December"`
`"d"`	Day in Month	`"15"`
`"dd"`	Day in Month	`"15"`
`"ddd"`	Day in Month	`"015"`
`"h"`	Hour in AM/PM Time	`"11"`
`"hh"`	Hour in AM/PM Time	`"11"`
`"hhh"`	Hour in AM/PM Time	`"011"`
`"H"`	Hour in 24 Hr Time	`"23"`
`"HHH"`	Hour in 24 Hr Time	`"023"`
`"m"`	Minute in Time	`"39"`
`"mm"`	Minute in Time	`"39"`
`"mmm"`	Minute in Time	`"039"`
`"s"`	Second in Minute	`"54"`
`"ss"`	Second in Minute	`"54"`
`"sss"`	Second in Minute	`"054"`
`"S"`	Milllisecond	`"123"`
`"E"`	Week Day Name	`"Sun"`
`"EEEE"`	Week Day Name	`"Sunday"`
`"a"`	AM/PM	`"PM"`

More unusual date format patterns are listed below. These, I haven't tended to use much:

Element	Description	Output
`"w"`	Week in the year	`"50"`
`"www"`	Week in the year	`"050"`
`"W"`	Week in the month	`"2"`
`"WW"`	Week in the month	`"02"`
`"WWW"`	Week in the month	`"002"`
`"D"`	Day in the year	`"349"`
`"F"`	Day of week in the month	`"3"`
`"FF"`	Day of week in the month	`"03"`
`"FFF"`	Day of week in the month	`"003"`
`"u"`	Day number in the week	`"7"`
`"uu"`	Day number in the week	`"07"`
`"k"`	Hour in the day (1-24)	`"23"`
`"kkk"`	Hour in the day (1-24)	`"023"`
`"H"`	Hour in the am/pm (0-11)	`"23"`
`"HHH"`	Hour in the am/pm (0-11)	`"023"`
`"z"`	General Time Zone	`"GMT"`
`"Z"`	RTC 822 Time Zone	`"+0000"`
`"X"`	ISO 8601 Time Zone	`"Z"`

The reason for showing so many different combinations e.g. `"y"`, `"yy"`, `"yyyyy"` was to demonstrate that some patterns will truncate, or pad, or expand depending on the value in the `Date`.

`SimpleDateFormat` has other methods available, I suggest you read the on-line documentation for `SimpleDateFormat` if you want to learn more. Typically I create a `SimpleDateFormat` with the pattern I want to use, and then `format` a `Date` with that pattern. You'll get a lot of mileage out of that simple approach.

Calendar

`Calendar` provides a wrapper for the `Date` class which allows us to edit it in terms of its individual components, e.g. change the date, or the month, or the year, rather than working directly with the millisecond time.

Instantiate a new `Calendar` using the static `getInstance` method on the `Calendar` class.

```
Calendar cal = Calendar.getInstance();
```

Initially I will compare `Calendar` with `Date` so you gain basic familiarity with it, then we will explore the methods and capabilities in more detail.

We have many of the methods that you already encountered with `Date`, but the methods work with `Calendar` parameters:

- `after` - returns `true` if the parameter is after the `Calendar`
- `before` - returns `true` if the parameter is before the `Calendar`
- `equals` - returns true if the parameter represents the same date and time as the `Calendar`
- `compareTo` - returns `0`, `-ve` or `+ve`; if the parameter is equal, after, or before the `Calendar`

We have a method `getTime` on `Calendar` just as we did with `Date` but the `getTime` method on `Calendar` returns a `Date` so the following lines are equivalent when working with `Calendar`:

```
System.out.println(cal.getTime().getTime());
System.out.println(System.currentTimeMillis());
```

The `Calendar` method `toString` does not print a nicely formatted version of the date and time, instead it shows all the attributes of the `Calendar` Object.

Exercise: Write the `toString` to console

Write an `@Test` method which instantiates a `Calendar` object and writes the output of `toString` to the console.

I can control the `Date` details of a `Calendar` with the `setTime` method:

```
Calendar sameDate = Calendar.getInstance();
sameDate.setTime(cal.getTime());
assertThat(cal.equals(sameDate), is(true));
assertThat(cal.compareTo(sameDate), is(0));
```

Since I'm using the `Date` from another `Calendar` I can compare the two `Calendars` with `equals` and `compareTo` and expect them to have the same date and time details.

To advance the date and time details for a `Calendar` I can use the `add` method. e.g. to add on 7 days, as I did previously with the `Date`:

```
Calendar oneWeekFromNow = Calendar.getInstance();
oneWeekFromNow.setTime(cal.getTime());
oneWeekFromNow.add(Calendar.DATE,7);
```

I can then compare the `Calendar` objects as we saw before with `after`, `before`, `compareTo`.

```
assertThat(oneWeekFromNow.after(cal), is(true));
assertThat(cal.before(oneWeekFromNow), is(true));
assertThat(cal.compareTo(oneWeekFromNow), is(-1));
assertThat(oneWeekFromNow.compareTo(cal), is(1));
```

Setting Calendar Values

Calendar Constants

Calendar provides some constants for working with fields in a literal way:

- `DATE`
- `YEAR`
- `MONTH`
- `DAY_OF_MONTH`
- `HOUR`
- `MINUTE`
- `SECOND`
- etc.

You can find a full list of these constants in the on-line reference[128] or through code completion on the `Calendar` object.

We use these constants when we `add`, `set` or `get` the fields on the `Calendar`.

`set` individual `Calendar` fields

We can `set` individual `Calendar` fields using the Calendar constants:

[128] http://docs.oracle.com/javase/7/docs/api/java/util/Calendar.html

```
cal.set(Calendar.YEAR, 2013);
cal.set(Calendar.MONTH, 11);  // starts at 0
cal.set(Calendar.DAY_OF_MONTH, 15);
cal.set(Calendar.HOUR_OF_DAY, 23);
cal.set(Calendar.MINUTE, 39);
cal.set(Calendar.SECOND, 54);
cal.set(Calendar.MILLISECOND, 123);
```

Since it can be confusing to see Months as zero based in the code there are also constants for the Month names themselves.

```
cal.set(Calendar.MONTH, Calendar.DECEMBER);
```

`set` the `Calendar`

You can also call the `set` method with multiple fields. These are then in a fixed order:

- Year
- Month
- Day of Month
- Hour of day
- Minute
- Second

```
cal.set(2013, 11, 15);
cal.set(2013, Calendar.DECEMBER, 15);
cal.set(2013, 11, 15, 23, 39);
cal.set(2013, Calendar.DECEMBER, 15, 23,39, 54);
```

Note that the combinations do not let you set the hour without also setting the minute.

We can use `Date` to set the time on a Calendar with the `setTime` method:

```
cal.setTime(new Date(0L));
```

We can also set the `Calendar` from a millisecond value in the same way we did for `Date`:

```
cal.setTimeInMillis(0L);
```

We can also set the `Calendar` from a relative perspective of weeks e.g. Thursday in the 3rd Week of January 2013:

```
cal.setWeekDate(2013, 3, Calendar.THURSDAY);
```

The above sets the date to 17th January 2013. Feel free to double check this on an actual calendar.

`get` details from the `Calendar`

Just as we use the `Calendar` constants to `set` values in a `Calendar` we can use the same constants to `get` information from the `Calendar`.

Given a `Calendar` set to 15th December 2013, at 23:49 and 54 seconds:

```
cal.set(2013, Calendar.DECEMBER, 15, 23,39, 54);
```

We can use the constants to assert that the `Calendar` has been created as we expected:

```
assertThat(cal.get(Calendar.MONTH), is(Calendar.DECEMBER));
```

Exercise: Use the other Calendar constants

Write an `@Test` method which instantiates a `Calendar`, and assert on the values you expect for the following constants:

Use a `Calendar` set to 15th December 2013, at 23:49 and 54 seconds.

Assert on the values you expect for:

- `MONTH`
- `YEAR`
- `DAY_OF_MONTH`
- `HOUR_OF_DAY`
- `MINUTE`
- `HOUR` - AM/PM hour
- `AM_PM` - Calendar.AM or Calendar.PM

Exercise: Experiment with other constants

Experiment with the other constants so that you are sure you understand them. e.g. confirm the following for the 15th December 2013:

- it is a Sunday
- it is the 1st day in the week
- it is the 349th day in the year

`get` more information from `Calendar`

- `getTime` - returns the `Calendar` as a `Date` object
- `getTimeInMillis` - returns the `Calendar` as a `long`

There are other methods on `Calendar` to retrieve more information about the calendar, but I suggest you read the on-line documentation or code completion to help you understand the scope of all the information you can retrieve from this object.

In practice. I tend to setup dates as I need them, retrieve dates, and then move dates forward or backwards in time. Which we will cover next.

`add` and subtract to `roll` dates through time

There are two main mechanisms with the `Calendar` object for moving the time in a relative fashion:

- `add` - add or subtract an amount from a field
- `roll` - change a single field without affecting others

We can use `add` to increment or decrement field values. For example I could take a Calendar date of 23:39 and decrement the hour of the time:

```
cal.add(Calendar.HOUR_OF_DAY, -1);
assertThat(cal.get(Calendar.HOUR_OF_DAY), is(22));
```

Similarly I could increment the minutes on the time:

```
cal.add(Calendar.MINUTE, 10);
assertThat(cal.get(Calendar.MINUTE), is(49));
```

Exercise: Increment and Decrement other Fields

Experiment with the add method and change the fields in different ways to move the date from 23rd December 2013 to 3rd June 2011.

With the `roll` method I can change a single field, without affecting any of the larger units e.g. given the date 15th December 2013, I can roll forward 17 Days of the month to roll over to the 1st, and it will still be December 2013. If I were to do this with an add the date would become 1st January 2014 because the other fields would advance as well to keep the date valid.

```
cal.roll(Calendar.DAY_OF_MONTH,17);

assertThat(cal.get(Calendar.YEAR), is(2013));
assertThat(cal.get(Calendar.MONTH), is(Calendar.DECEMBER));
assertThat(cal.get(Calendar.DAY_OF_MONTH), is(1));
```

Exercise: Confirm add Moves the Year

Write an `@Test` method that demonstrates that adding 17, to 23rd of December 2013, instead of rolling 17 moves the date to 1st January 2014.

Summary

In the production environment, in the main application, we very often use the Joda-Time library. But I'm trying to keep coverage of 'libraries' out of scope for this book, to make it easier for you to get started, and to help you build knowledge and experience with the in-built features.

Relying too much on external libraries often means adding another library into the code-base when all that is really required is a quick wrapper around existing core Java.

The chapter covered basic examples of:

- timing how long a set of code takes to execute
- creating unique ids and names for files
- formatting dates
- date arithmetic and manipulation

I frequently have to format dates in different ways, when I'm generating input data for application automation.

I time the how long code runs, when I'm writing simple performance automation. I often use `nanoTime` to do this.

I very often create unique file-names using the value returned by `currentTimeMillis`. You saw examples of simple ways to convert the numeric file names into alphabetic characters. I sometimes generate unique `usernames` for input data in this way, with `currentTimeMillis`.

We also covered basic date time arithmetic in the chapter. A very useful thing to be able to do, when generating random data.

I think I've covered the basics of Date and Time for the core Java classes well enough for you to start using them in your `@Test` methods.

I have only ever had to drop down to Joda-Time once or twice in my career. I encourage you to experiment with the in-built Date Time functionality, before bringing in an external library. You might be surprised how much you can do.

References and Recommended Reading

- Joda-Time
  - joda-time.sourceforge.net[129]
- `currentTimeMillis`
  - docs.oracle.com/javase/7/docs/api/java/lang/System.html#currentTimeMillis%28%29[130]
- `nanoTime`
  - docs.oracle.com/javase/7/docs/api/java/lang/System.html#nanoTime%28%29[131]
- `nanosecond`
  - en.wikipedia.org/wiki/Nanosecond[132]
- `Date`
  - docs.oracle.com/javase/7/docs/api/java/util/Date.html[133]

---

[129] http://joda-time.sourceforge.net

[130] http://docs.oracle.com/javase/7/docs/api/java/lang/System.html#currentTimeMillis%28%29

[131] http://docs.oracle.com/javase/7/docs/api/java/lang/System.html#nanoTime%28%29

[132] http://en.wikipedia.org/wiki/Nanosecond

[133] http://docs.oracle.com/javase/7/docs/api/java/util/Date.html

- `SimpleDateFormat`
  - docs.oracle.com/javase/7/docs/api/java/text/SimpleDateFormat.html[134]
- `Calendar`
  - docs.oracle.com/javase/7/docs/api/java/util/Calendar.html[135]

[134]http://docs.oracle.com/javase/7/docs/api/java/text/SimpleDateFormat.html
[135]http://docs.oracle.com/javase/7/docs/api/java/util/Calendar.html

Chapter Eighteen - Properties and Property Files

Chapter Summary

In this chapter you will learn how to use the `Properties` class

- A property file has "key, value" pairs on each line
- `Properties` class makes it easy to load and save "key, value" pair data
- `setProperty` method to add a property key and value
- `getProperty` method to get the value for a property key
- `size` method to return the number of property keys
- Iterate through properties by key using `stringPropertyNames`
- `list` to display properties to output
- `containsKey` check if a property key exists
- An introduction to Java System properties
  - `user.dir` - current working directory for the code
  - `user.home` - home directory of current user
  - `line.separator` - end of new line string
  - `file.separator` - character separator for directory paths
  - `java.io.tmpdir` - location of the current temporary directory
- Loading and Saving Property files
  - `store` to save property files
  - `load` property files in combination with a `FileReader`

One of the early problems I had when working with Java, was working with files for my data. Files aren't really that hard, and we'll cover them in a later chapter, but my initial workaround was to use property files, via the `Properties` class.

Property files are those very simple files you see many tools use for configuration, with a `key=value` pair e.g.

```
# Define the browsers to use
browser=chrome
port=8080
```

- A property file treats lines starting with `# as comments.`
- Blank lines are ignored.
- Lines with content are treated as "key, value" pairs separated by an = sign.
- If a property file has multiple entries with the same key, then only the last one will be used
- trailing and leading spaces before and after either the key or the value are ignored, e.g. the following entries are all equivalent

```
browser     =     chrome
browser=chrome
browser     =     chrome
```

In the early days I would very often use Property files as input files which I didn't have to struggle to parse e.g.

```
step1 = OPEN_APP
step2 = TYPE 12345
step3 = CLICK_ENTER
step4 = CLOSE_APP
```

You can probably guess that the above example is a simple keyword driven script. I don't recommend this approach, I'm just pointing out that when I was learning Java, I used the basic knowledge that I had to get things done, without worrying too much about the 'best' way of doing it. And Properties, with associated property files, made certain things easy.

Properties Basics

The Java `Properties` object in `java.util.Properties` is the main class we will use for working with Properties.

It works much like a hash map, with a "key, value" pair, where both key and value are `String` objects.

`Properties` also has additional methods for loading and saving the properties to files.

Warning: Don't go crazy

When I first learned about `Properties` I think I went a bit crazy and used it everywhere. I used it instead of using a Map. Instead of defining all parameters in methods, I just stuck everything in a `Properties` object and passed that in to the method. I don't do this anymore. And neither should you since you already know how to use the collection classes.

Creating new `Properties`

We create new `Properties` objects using the `Properties` class from `java.util.Properties`

```
Properties properties = new Properties();
```

The above will give us a `Properties` object with no properties. i.e. `size` of `0`

```
assertThat(properties.size(), is(0));
```

Setting and Getting Property values

Use the `setProperty` and `getProperty` methods to *set* and *get* property values:

```
properties.setProperty("browser", "firefox");
properties.setProperty("port", "80");
```

`setProperty` will create the property if it does not exist, or overwrite the value of the property if it already exists.

`getProperty` returns the value for the property:

```
assertThat( properties.getProperty("browser"),
            is("firefox"));
assertThat( properties.getProperty("port"),
            is("80"));
```

If the property key we provide to `getProperty` does not exist then `null` will be returned.

```
assertThat( properties.getProperty("missing"),
            is(nullValue()));
```

When we call `getProperty` we can specify a default value, so that we don't receive 'null', instead we receive the default value if the property key has not been set.

```
assertThat( properties.getProperty("missing", "default"),
            is("default"));
```

Working with Properties

Generally, if we have setup the properties then we will work with the `getProperty` method.

But, sometimes you want to work with the `Properties` using the set of keys. We use the `stringPropertyNames` method for this:

If I want to iterate over the property keys and output all the values, then I can iterate over the `Set` of `String` property keys:

```
for( String key : properties.stringPropertyNames()){
    System.out.println("Key: " + key + " " +
                       "Value: " + properties.getProperty(key));
}
```

The above would output:

```
Key: port Value: 80
Key: browser Value: firefox
```

The `Properties` class has a method called `list` which outputs the property name and value pair to the given print stream:

```
properties.list(System.out);
```

Calling the `list` method would output:

```
-- listing properties --
port=80
browser=firefox
```

I can also check for property existence with the `containsKey` method:

```
assertThat( properties.containsKey("browser"), is(true));
```

Exercise: Create and List a `Properties` object

Write an `@Test` annotated method which:

- Creates a `Properties` object
- Add the following "key, value" pairs: `name=bob`, `gender=male`, `password=paSSw0rd`
- Assert that the size of the `Properties` object is 3
- Output the "key, value" pairs to the console by iterating over the keys
- Use the `list` method to output the properties
- Assert that the `Properties` object contains the key `gender`
- Assert that the value of the property `name` is `bob`
- Use `getProperty` with a default value and assert that the value of key `"permission"` is `"Admin"`

Java's `System` Properties

Reading System Properties

Java's `System` object has a set of properties that come in very hand when writing automation code.

e.g. `"user.dir"` returns the working directory for the running application

```
String workingDirectory = System.getProperty("user.dir");
```

I can use this for accessing data files that I want to use in my automation e.g. if I create a directory in my project called `property_files` under `/src/test/resources/` then I could build the full path to a file by prefixing the current working directory:

```
String resourceFilePath = workingDirectory +
                          "/src/test/resources/" +
                          "property_files/" +
                          "static_example.properties";
```

Note that in the above code, I use `/` as the directory separator. Even if working in Windows, this should work for most file operations. Although building paths by hand can be problematic, so it is recommended to use `File` or `Paths` to do that. We cover these classes in the next chapter, and you'll see use of `File` a few pages hence.

You can work directly with the `Properties` object on System, by using the `getProperties` method.

For example if I wanted to list the System properties then I can use the following code:

```
Properties sys = System.getProperties();
sys.list(System.out);
```

A partial output of the above command is shown below:

```
-- listing properties --
java.runtime.name=Java(TM) SE Runtime Environment
sun.boot.library.path=C:\Program Files\Java\jdk1.7.0_10\jre...
java.vm.version=23.6-b04
java.vm.vendor=Oracle Corporation
java.vendor.url=http://java.oracle.com/
path.separator=;
java.vm.name=Java HotSpot(TM) 64-Bit Server VM
```

Exercise: Output the `System` `Properties` object

Write an `@Test` annotated method which will `list` the contents of the `System Properties`

Read the System Properties documentation so you understand the range of properties available for you to use by default.

- docs.oracle.com/javase/tutorial/essential/environment/sysprop.html[136]

System properties I use most often are:

- `user.dir` - current working directory for the code
- `user.home` - home directory of current user
- `line.separator` - end of new line string
- `file.separator` - character separator for directory paths e.g. \ on windows, / on linux
- `java.io.tmpdir` - location of the current temporary directory

Setting System Properties

You can set `System` properties, the same as you can with a normal `Properties` object using the `setProperty` command.

I frequently do this if I want to control some environmental configuration from within my running code.

As an example, when using WebDriver and working with Chrome, I have to set a `System` property, so that the Chrome driver knows where to find the `ChromeDriver.exe` that it uses to control the Chrome browser.

- `webdriver.chrome.driver`

I generally don't add the `ChromeDriver.exe` into version control and have a convention that it is located in a directory relative to my working directory. So I set the property relative to my working directory.

Since this is a property that might have been set already, I tend to check if it has been set outside the running application before I overwrite it. Leading to code like the following:

[136]http://docs.oracle.com/javase/tutorial/essential/environment/sysprop.html

```
if(!System.getProperties().containsKey("webdriver.chrome.driver")){
    String currentDir = System.getProperty("user.dir");
    String chromeDriverLocation
                = currentDir +
                "/../tools/chromedriver/chromedriver.exe";
    System.setProperty("webdriver.chrome.driver", chromeDriverLocation);
}
```

In the above code I first check if the property is set, if it is then I don't overwrite it. If the property is not set then I use the current `"user.dir"` and set the path relative to that working directory.

Working with Property files

In this section we are going to look at the methods on the `Properties` Object associated loading and saving files.

Save

`Properties` does have a `save` method, but this is deprecated because it does not throw an `IOException`.

Deprecated

Deprecated means that the method should not be used, and that the method may be removed in future versions of Java. The method will work, but your code may fail in the future when you update the Java library or SDK you are using.

Instead we use the `store` method, which writes the file to a `Writer` or an `OutputStream`.

Because I will create a file that I'm only using as part of the `@Test` method execution, I'm going to create it as a temporary file.

Java 7 provides a way of creating temporary files, which we will cover in the Files Chapter.

Since this is the `Properties` chapter, we will use the System property `"java.io.tmpdir"` which returns the path of the system temp directory.

```
String tempDirectory = System.getProperty("java.io.tmpdir");
String tempResourceFilePath =
            new File(tempDirectory,
                "tempFileForPropertiesStoreTest.properties")
                    .getAbsolutePath();
```

Use `File` to create a simple path

You can see that I have cheated and used a `File` object that I haven't explained yet (although I will do in the next chapter). I'm using `File` to build up the path in a cross platform manner. On some platforms the temp directory property has a `/` on the end and on some it does not. If I use the `File` to build up the path and then retrieve the path as a `String` using the `getAbsolutePath` method then my code should work cross platform. Building paths by hand using string concatenation can make your code platform dependent.

We then need to create the properties that we will `store` to the file:

```
Properties saved = new Properties();
saved.setProperty("prop1", "Hello");
saved.setProperty("prop2", "World");
```

We need to create a `FileOutputStream` to store the properties into, and write them with the `store` method. The `store` method leaves the `OutputStream` open so we have to `close` it when we are finished with it.

```
FileOutputStream outputFile =
                    new FileOutputStream(tempResourceFilePath);
saved.store(outputFile, "Hello There World");
outputFile.close();
```

Note that the `store` method takes two parameters:

- the `OutputStream` that we write the details to
- a comment `String`

The String comment is written to the `OutputStream` prior to the properties, and in addition a TimeStamp for when the properties are written is added to the file.

So the final file output from the above method execution looks as follows:

```
#Hello There World
#Mon Aug 05 15:12:24 BST 2013
prop2=World
prop1=Hello
```

Note that the property ordering is not retained when writing to the file.

Load

Since I have already created a file in my project (using the `store` method), all I have to do is load it from the directory I saved it to.

I can use either an `InputStream` or a `FileReader` for this. We will cover these in more detail in the Files Chapter. But for now, we will use a `FileReader`.

```
FileReader propertyFileReader =
                    new FileReader(tempResourceFilePath);
Properties loaded = new Properties();

try{
    loaded.load(propertyFileReader);
}finally{
    propertyFileReader.close();
}
```

I have wrapped the `load` method in a `try/finally` block, because the `load` method leaves the `InputStream` or `FileReader` open when it finishes, so we have to close it. And I want it to close even if the `load` method throws an `IOException`.

Once the property file has loaded into the `Properties` object, I can access the property with the `getProperty` method as we did before:

```
assertThat(loaded.getProperty("prop1"), is("Hello"));
assertThat(loaded.getProperty("prop2"), is("World"));
```

Delete Files

We will cover files in more detail in a later chapter. But for now, since we have created a file. We should learn how to delete it:

```
new File(tempResourceFilePath).delete();
```

Exercise: Store and Load a Saved Properties File

Using the code presented above:

- Create a `Properties` object
- Add some "key, value" pairs to the `Properties`
- Store the `Properties` file in the `"java.io.tmpdir"`
- Read the `Properties` file and assert on the values
- Delete the `Properties` file when you are finished

Summary

I still find property files very useful and before writing complicated file parsing and storing routines. I first see if I can prototype any file storage functionality with property files.

Property files have the advantage that they are easy to edit by humans, since they are a simple format of text file.

They are also easy to parse for the application code.

References and Recommended Reading

- `Properties` official documentation -
  - docs.oracle.com/javase/7/docs/api/java/util/Properties.html[137]
- `Properties` Java Tutorial
  - docs.oracle.com/javase/tutorial/essential/environment/properties.html[138]
- System Properties official documentation
  - docs.oracle.com/javase/tutorial/essential/environment/sysprop.html[139]
- Create a Temporary directory in Java
  - stackoverflow.com/questions/617414/create-a-temporary-directory-in-java[140]

---

[137]http://docs.oracle.com/javase/7/docs/api/java/util/Properties.html

[138]http://docs.oracle.com/javase/tutorial/essential/environment/properties.html

[139]http://docs.oracle.com/javase/tutorial/essential/environment/sysprop.html

[140]http://stackoverflow.com/questions/617414/create-a-temporary-directory-in-java

Chapter Nineteen - Files

Chapter Summary

In this chapter you will learn how to use the basic Java file handling classes

- `File` the general wrapper for a file
  - `createTempFile` - create a temporary file
  - `createNewFile` - create the file
  - `delete` - delete the file now
  - `deleteOnExit` - delete the file when the application closes
  - `getName` - return the filename or directory name
  - `getParent` - return the path of the parent directory
  - `getAbsolutePath` - return the full filename and path
  - `getCanonicalPath` - return the unique full representation of the `File`
  - `mkdir` - creates a single directory
  - `mkdirs` - creates a directory and all necessary directories in the path
  - `isDirectory`, `isFile` - determing type of physical `File`
  - `separator`, `pathSeparator` - for files e.g. '\' and Path e.g. ';'
  - `listRoots` an array of the root paths in the file system
  - `length` - the length of the `File` in bytes
  - `getFreeSpace`, `getTotalSpace`, `getUsableSpace` - disk space
  - `renameTo` - rename a file
  - Directory methods
    * `list` - a list of the filenames as String
    * `listFiles` - a list of `File` objects for each file and directory
  - Attribute methods
    * `canRead`, `canWrite`, `canExecute`, `lastModified`
    * `setExecutable`, `setReadable`, `setWritable`,
    * `setReadOnly`, `setLastModified`
- `Files` class with static methods to `copy` and `move` a file or directory
- `PrintWriter` - has methods to make writing easier e.g. `print`, `println`
- `FileWriter` - write to character based files
- `BufferedWriter`, `BufferedReader` - buffer output and input for efficiency
- `FileReader` - read from an input stream
- `Paths.get` - to 'make' a `Path` rather than concatenate strings

I tend to keep my file code as simple as possible, because my use cases are usually fairly simple:

- reading files that other people have written - sometimes to check validity of the data
- reading simple CSV or tab delimited files - often as input to data driven test code
- copying files - to keep a folder of data used during automation, or for setup data
- creating directories - to make my work-flow simpler
- moving files - screen shot images, log files
- deleting files
- writing report - simple log files or HTML report output

In this chapter I'll cover the basic classes and approaches for implementing the above use cases.

Example of reading and writing a file

I will quickly show you some code that writes a file, and reads the same file.

If you want to immediately experiment then feel free. The rest of the chapter will work through the various methods and classes used, explaining them in more detail.

Write a Temp File

```
private File writeTheTestDataFile() throws IOException {
    File outputFile = File.createTempFile("forReading", null);
    PrintWriter print = new PrintWriter(
                            new BufferedWriter(
                                new FileWriter(outputFile)));

    for(int lineNumber = 1; lineNumber < 6; lineNumber++){
        print.println("line " + lineNumber);
    }

    print.close();
    return outputFile;
}
```

The above code, creates a temporary file, in the system 'Temp' directory.

e.g. `forReading2536453396676632859.tmp` in

- `%TEMP%` on Windows
- `$TMPDIR` on Mac

It uses 3 classes to wrap around the file: `FileWriter`, `BufferedWriter` and `PrintWriter`. Then prints 5 lines of text to the file, closes the file, and returns the `File` to the calling method.

Read the temp file

```
@Test
public void outputFileToSystemOutWithBufferedReader() throws IOException {

    File inputFile = writeTheTestDataFile();
    BufferedReader reader = new BufferedReader(new FileReader(inputFile));

    try{
        String line;
        while((line = reader.readLine())!=null){
            System.out.println(line);
        }
    }finally{
        reader.close();
    }
}
```

The code above, calls the `writeTheTestDataFile` method to create a temporary file. Then it uses the returned `File`, and wraps it with a `FileReader` and a `BufferedReader`, then reads each line and prints it out.

It wraps the reading code in a `try/finally` block when reading to make sure that the file actually closes if an exception is thrown.

Basic Notes

It seems like a lot of classes are involved there. But as you will see later, they build on each other to make the reading and writing of files easy for you.

If you start by copying the code above, and amending it slightly, you can probably meet at least 3 of the use cases I mentioned at the top of this chapter as my common use cases.

And you could probably figure out the other use cases by reading the context sensitive code completion on the classes.

The remainder of this chapter will cover each of the classes involved in more detail.

File

The `File` class provides the main class to represent a 'file' or 'directory' and methods for creating directories and other local file actions.

The `File` class also provides a set of static methods that can help us.

`File` is in the `java.io` package.

Static Methods

- `createTempFile`
  - create a temporary file in the system's temporary directory (on Windows this is '`%TEMP%`' and on Mac this is `$TMPDIR`)
- `separator`
  - the separator for file values e.g. '\' or '/'
- `pathSeparator`
  - the system separator in the Path e.g. '`;`'
- `listRoots`
  - an array of the root paths in the file system

I only really use the `createTempFile` and `separator` but will cover all the above methods.

createTempFile

```
File outputFile = File.createTempFile("forReading", null);
```

This method creates an empty physical file in the system temporary directory (`%TEMP%` or `$TMPDIR`).

In the above example I assign the `File` into a variable called `outputFile` so that I can use it.

The mandatory parameters to this method are:

- `prefix`
  - e.g. `forReading`.
  - The prefix needs to be 3 chars or longer otherwise and exception is thrown:
    * `java.lang.IllegalArgumentException`
- `suffix`

  - The value to add at the end of the temp file name.
  - If you leave this as `null` then the file will be given the suffix `.tmp` but you can add your own suffix if you want to.

In the above example I pass in a prefix of `forReading`, and `null` for the suffix, so the end result is an empty file with a name like:

- `forReading1653577725464964274 1.tmp`

The number is added by the Java method to try and make the filename unique in the temp folder.

The optional final parameter to this method is:

- `directory`
  - A `File` object for the directory to create the temp file in.

```
aTempFile = File.createTempFile("pre", null,
                      new File(System.getProperty("user.dir")));
```

In the above code, I left the suffix as `null` so it will use '`.tmp`' as the suffix, and will create the file in the User Directory where I am running the code. On my system this created a file named and located as follows:

`D:\Users\Alan\Documents\javaForTesters\pre4051399336820173102.tmp`

Exercise: Create a Temp File and Vary the Parameters

Write an `@Test` method which creates a temp file.

Find the file in your System's temporary directory and make sure it was written.

Vary the prefix, and the suffix to see the impact of the output file.

`separator` and `pathSeparator`

The `separator` method is the main one I use, since it provides the separator between values in file paths, i.e. the directory separator '\' on Windows and '/' on Linux.

I use this if I manually build up `String` values to act as paths for files.

```
        assertTrue("Unrecognised OS file separator",
                File.separator.equals("\\") ||
                File.separator.equals("/"));
        assertTrue("Unrecognised OS path separator",
                File.pathSeparator.equals(";") ||
                File.pathSeparator.equals(":"));
```

The `pathSeparator` is the value you use in the `PATH` variables.

The `separator` and `pathSeparator` return system dependent values so help you make your code platform agnostic i.e. run on Linux or Windows.

listRoots

`listRoots` returns an array of `File` objects which represent the 'root' file paths in the system.

```
        File[] roots = File.listRoots();
```

On my windows system this returns a list of the 'drives' on my system, e.g.:

```
C:\
D:\
E:\
F:\
G:\
```

Have I ever used this method? No. But it might come in handy for someone.

Exercise: Write out the roots

Write an `@Test` method which prints to `System.out` the result of calling the `getAbsolutePath` method on each of the `File` objects returned by `listRoots`.

Constructor And Basic Operations

```
File aTempFile = new File("d:/tempJavaForTesters.txt");
```

The above code shows the simplest constructor for the `File` object. Simply create a `new File` with the full path you want to use. The above example shows an example for Windows.

File will convert '/' to '\'

Note that, I have used the Linux format for the file path, even though I primarily wrote the book on a Windows machine.

The `File` will convert from `/` to `\` if you are working on a different platform.

If you wrote an `@Test` method with the above code, then upon running it, you will note that instantiating a `File` object, does not create a physical file on the disk.

```
@Test
public void aNewFileDoesNotCreateAFile() throws IOException {
    File aTempFile = new File("d:/tempJavaForTesters.txt");
    assertThat(aTempFile.exists(), is(false));
}
```

I used the `exists` method on the `File` object to check existence. Since the code does not create a file, it will also work on Mac.

The `File` object creates a representation of the 'file' or 'directory', and allows us to interact with the file.

We use 'streams', 'readers' or 'writers' to interact with the actual file content.

The `File` object has methods for file creation and deletion:

- `createNewFile` will create the file
- `delete` will delete the file

e.g.

```
@Test
public void createAFileAndDeleteIt() throws IOException {
    File aTempFile = new File("d:/tempJavaForTesters.txt");
    assertThat(aTempFile.exists(), is(false));

    aTempFile.createNewFile();
    assertThat(aTempFile.exists(), is(true));

    aTempFile.delete();
    assertThat(aTempFile.exists(), is(false));
}
```

When you type the above code, ensure that you change the `d:/` part of the path to a filepath that exists on your machine.

Another form of the constructor allows us to pass in the file path and the file as separate arguments.

```
    File aTempFile = Paths.get("d:", "tempJavaForTesters.txt").toFile();
```

In this example, the '`d:`" is the *parent* part of the path.

Note that I don't have to worry about trailing directory separators when I use both parameters in the `File` constructor. This makes it a very useful constructor when creating simple paths, rather than concatenating strings together.

`File` operations can throw a variety of exceptions but the `java.io.IOException` is a catch all for the exceptions that are likely to be thrown.

In this short section we covered:

- Two `File` Constructors
- `exists` method to check if a file or directory exists
- `delete` to delete a file or directory
- `createNewFile` to create an empty file

Exercise: Create a Temporary File With Custom Code

Simulate the `createTempFile` method using the normal `File` object and the `createNewFile` method.

Hints: The system temporary directory is accessible from the `"java.io.tmpdir"` `System` property.

Use `System.currentTimeMillis` to create a 'unique' number as part of the file name.

`Paths.get` and `Path` to create `File`

You may not have to make your code cross platform. In which case concatenating strings will work fine for your initial code.

However, manually creating paths can make your code vulnerable.

The `File` constructor which takes two parameters will concatenate the two paths to create a well formed path, compensating for any trailing '/' or '\' in the *parent* and any prefixing the *child*.

For example, the `"java.io.tmpdir"` `System` property does not have a trailing '/' on Linux, but does on Windows, so I would have to add extra code to compensate for that if I was building the path manually. But I don't have to worry about it if I use the `File` constructor.

```
String tempDir = System.getProperty("java.io.tmpdir");
File aTempFile = new File(tempDir, "tempJavaForTesters.txt");
```

I can also chain `File` constructors if I want to make a more complicated path, since the `File` constructor will accept a `File` as the *parent*. So to construct the folders `1/2/3/4` under `"java.io.tmpdir"` I could use the `File` constructor:

```
String tempDirectory = System.getProperty("java.io.tmpdir");
File aFile = new File(tempDirectory);
aFile = new File(aFile, "1");
aFile = new File(aFile, "2");
aFile = new File(aFile, "3");
aFile = new File(aFile, "4");
```

The above is slightly unwieldy. But we have an alternative.

Using the `Paths` object, from `java.nio.file`, we can create a `Path` object with a single call to the static method `get`.

```
Path aPath = Paths.get(tempDirectory, "1", "2", "3", "4");
```

The `Paths.get` method returns a `Path` object, and we can covert this into a `File` using the `toFile` method to achieve the same result as chaining all those `File` calls.

```
assertEquals(aFile.getAbsolutePath(),
             aPath.toFile().getAbsolutePath());
```

`Paths.get` can also be used to replicate the functionality of the `File` constructor:

```
String tempDir = System.getProperty("java.io.tmpdir");
File aTempFile = Paths.get(tempDir, "tempJavaForTesters.txt").toFile();
```

`Path` has other methods which you can see in the JavaDoc[141]. The main purpose for introducing it here is to help you avoid concatenating strings to make paths.

`Paths` and `Path` were added in Java 1.7.

Other Basic `File` Methods

The basic methods on `File` we need to learn initially are:

- `deleteOnExit` - delete the file when the application closes
- `getName` - the filename or directory name

[141]https://docs.oracle.com/javase/8/docs/api/java/nio/file/Path.html

- `getParent` - the path of the parent directory
- `getAbsolutePath` - the full filename including root, folder hierarchy and filename used to create the `File`
- `getCanonicalPath` - the unique full representation of the `File`
- `mkdir` - creates a single directory
- `mkdirs` - creates a directory and all necessary directories in the path

deleteOnExit

As soon as you have a `File` you can add it to the 'delete on exit' queue.

```
File aTempFile = File.createTempFile("prefix", "suffix");
aTempFile.deleteOnExit();
```

When the application finishes. When all the `@Test` methods have run. All files in the 'delete on exit' queue will be deleted.

This is a useful method to combine with the `createTempFile` method because it means your temporary files are deleted after the run of the `@Test` method. Rather than relying on your operating system temporary directory clean up routines.

getName, getParent, getAbsolutePath, getCanonicalPath

If I create a temp file:

```
File aTempFile = File.createTempFile("prefix", "suffix");
```

I don't know exactly what the name of that file is.

When working with the `File` object `aTempFile`. I don't need to know the actual name because I operate with the `File` object directly.

If I do want to work with the name or path, then I can use the methods:

- `getName`,
- `getParent`,
- `getAbsolutePath` and
- `getCanonicalPath`.

`getName` returns the filename, without the path. So for the example above I would have a filename like `prefix12345678901234567890suffix` created.

```
assertThat( aTempFile.getName().startsWith("prefix"), is(true));
assertThat( aTempFile.getName().endsWith("suffix"), is(true));
```

`getParent` returns the path structure for the parent directory.

```
assertTrue(System.getProperty("java.io.tmpdir").
        startsWith(aTempFile.getParent()));
```

`getAbsolutePath` and `getCanonicalPath` both return the full path, including the filename of the `File`:

```
assertThat(aTempFile.getAbsolutePath().endsWith("suffix"),
            is(true));
assertThat(aTempFile.getAbsolutePath().startsWith(
               System.getProperty("java.io.tmpdir")), is(true));
```

```
assertThat(aTempFile.getCanonicalPath().endsWith("suffix"),
            is(true));
assertThat(aTempFile.getCanonicalPath().contains(
        System.getProperty("java.io.tmpdir")), is(true));
```

An 'absolute' path would display any relative file operators in the name, e.g. '../..' but 'canonical' would not.

Canonical is the unique path, so any relative elements are made absolute.

e.g. the following absolute paths:

- `C:/1/2/3/4/../../..`
- `C:/1/2/../../1`

would be represented as the following canonical path

- `C:/1`

Exercise: Write an `@Test` method To Check Canonical Conversion

Write an `@Test` method which checks the assertion that the absolute paths below are represented by the canonical path `C:/1`:

- `C:/1/2/3/4/../../..`
- `C:/1/2/../../1`

Do this by creating a `File` for each path. Then comparing the values from `getAbsolutePath` with `getCanonicalPath`.

If you write this on a Mac or Linux then you may need to exclude the operating system extras before `C:/` or use `"java.io.tmpdir"` as the *parent*

`mkdir` and `mkdirs`

Both `mkdir` and `mkdirs` are used for creating directories.

Both `mkdir` and `mkdirs` return either `true` or `false` to let you know if they managed to create the directory.

The difference between them is that `mkdir` will create a single directory, but only if the parent path already exists.

`mkdirs` will create the necessary parent directories to allow the operation to succeed.

An example

If I want to create a directory structure in the temp directory like the following:

```
- %TEMP% (or $TMPDIR)
  - 1234567890
    - 0987654321
```

The existing `%TEMP%` (or `$TMPDIR`) directory, with a subdirectory '`1234567890`', and another subdirectory '`0987654321`'. Where each of these numbers is supposed to represent a call to `System.currentTimeMillis()`

```
String tempDirectory = System.getProperty("java.io.tmpdir");

File aDirectory = Paths.get(tempDirectory,
                        Long.toString(System.currentTimeMillis()),
                        Long.toString(System.currentTimeMillis()))
                    .toFile();
```

A call to `mkdir` will fail, because the middle directory '`1234567890`' does not exist, and `mkdir` is only supposed to create the final directory, in our example '`0987654321`'. `mkdir` needs the rest of the directory structure to exist.

```
assertThat(aDirectory.mkdir(), is(false));
```

A call to `mkdirs` will pass, because it will create any necessary directories in the directory structure.

```
assertThat(aDirectory.mkdirs(), is(true));
```

Useful Checks

For a particular `File` object, you can check if it is a file or directory using the following methods:

- `isDirectory` returns `true` if the `File` object is a directory
- `isFile` returns `true` if the `File` object is a file

Exercise: Check that the Temp Directory is a Directory

Create a `File` object that represents the temporary directory.

`System.getProperty("java.io.tmpdir")`

Assert that `isDirectory` returns `true` and `isFile` returns `false`.

Writing And Reading Files

Writing Text Files

Java provides some wrapper classes which hide lower level input and output classes to make reading and writing files easier.

You saw the use of those in the initial examples in the chapter.

- `FileWriter` is a wrapper around `FileOutputStream` for character based files. e.g. text files.
- `BufferedWriter` makes writing more efficient by waiting until the buffer is full and then flushing the buffer to the writer. For file writing this queues up the writing of bytes to the file.
- `PrintWriter` provides convenience methods for writing lines to files for human readable output. e.g. `println`, `print`

For example:

```
File outputFile = File.createTempFile("printWriter", null);
FileWriter writer = new FileWriter(outputFile);
BufferedWriter buffer = new BufferedWriter(writer);
PrintWriter print = new PrintWriter(buffer);
```

You can append to existing files by creating the `FileWriter` with an append parameter set to true.

```
writer = new FileWriter(outputFile, true);
```

Writing with a `PrintWriter`

Using a `PrintWriter` is the same as using the `System.out.println` that you have seen throughout the book.

We can write a line to the file by using `println`

```
print.println("Simple Print to Buffered Writer");
print.println("===============================");
```

By using the `PrintWriter` and `println` to write text files, we don't have to worry about end of line characters as it will use the appropriate end of line for the system.

You can also add to the file without a new line using `print`.

Just remember to `close` the file when you have finished writing to it.

Exercise: Write to a PrintWriter then Append

Create a temp file. Then use `PrintWriter` to `println` text to the file. Remember to `close` the file.

After you have closed it, re-open the file, by creating a new `FileWriter`. This time setting the append parameter to `true`. Then:

- `println` some new lines to the file.
- `close` the file.
- manually open the file in a text editor to check that your line was appended to the file.

Writing with a `FileWriter`

You can write files directly with a `FileWriter`.

```
File outputFile = File.createTempFile("fileWriter", null);

FileWriter fileWriter = new FileWriter(outputFile);
fileWriter.write("Simple Report With OutputWriter");
fileWriter.write("===============================");
fileWriter.close();
```

Since this is a raw text writer, there are no line endings after each line, as there were with the `PrintWriter`'s `println` so the output file would look as follows:

```
Simple Report With OutputWriter===============================
```

Reading Text Files

- `FileReader` is a wrapper around `InputStreamReader` and `FileInputStream` which uses the default character encoding stream.
- `BufferedReader` makes the reading more efficient.

Use the `readLine` method to read the next line from the file into a string. `readLine` will strip the end of line characters from the line it reads.

If we have reached the end of the file then `readLine` will return `null`.

e.g. the following code will read a `File inputFile` and display the contents to the console.

```
BufferedReader reader = new BufferedReader(new FileReader(inputFile));

try{
    String line;
    while((line = reader.readLine())!=null){
        System.out.println(line);
    }
}finally{
    reader.close();
}
```

Additional File Methods

The `File` object has a lot of very useful methods for accessing the various properties of the file.

Space

The following methods on files can be used to find information about the size of the file, or the disk the file is located on.

Remember the length contains the end of line characters as well.

- `length` - the length of the `File` in bytes
- `getFreeSpace` - number of bytes of free space
- `getTotalSpace` - number of bytes of total space

- `getUsableSpace` - number of bytes of usable space

Exercise: Create a File and Calculate the length

Create a file, write data to it, calculate, and then check, the expected file length.

Hint: Use `System.lineSeparator()` to get the line end character(s).

Directory Methods

For a particular `File` that represents a directory. You can get a list of the files contained in the directory.

- `list` will return a list of the filenames as `String`
- `listFiles` will return a list of `File` objects representing every contained file and directory

e.g. to get a list of the filenames for the items in the temp directory I could use the `list` method:

```
@Test
public void listTempDirectory(){
    File tempDir = new File(System.getProperty("java.io.tmpdir"));

    String[] fileList = tempDir.list();

    for(String fileInList : fileList){
        System.out.println(fileInList);
    }
}
```

Exercise: Use `listFiles` to show the Temp Directory contents

Use the `listFiles` method on `File` to output the name of each file in the temp directory.

For each file, also write beside it "DIR:" if it is a directory and "FIL:" if it is a file.

Attributes

You can check and amend the file Attributes with the following methods.

- `canRead` - `true` if the file is readable
- `canWrite` - `true` if the file is writable
- `canExecute` `true` if the file is executable
- `lastModified` - the last modified date as a `long`

You can set the above attributes using the methods below:

- `setExecutable`
- `setReadable`
- `setWritable`
- `setReadOnly`
- `setLastModified`

Exercise: Output Attributes of Files In Temp Directory

Extend the `@Test` method you wrote for `listFiles` to also output the read, write, execute attributes, and the last modified date.

Files

`Files` is part of the `java.nio` package. `nio` being the "New IO" classes, introduced in Java 1.4; so not really that new any more, but they add some useful functionality that we often look for other libraries to manage.

The `nio` package offers a lot of methods, but we will primarily look at the `Files` `move` and `copy` methods.

- `copy` - will create a copy of a file or directory
- `move` - will move a file or directory, creating a new one and deleting the old

Rename vs Move

`File` has a 'renameTo' method, but I tend to use the `move` method on `Files`, even when I want to rename a file.

`move` and `copy` can be used to move and copy entire directory trees.

Both `move` and `copy` operate on `Path` objects rather than `File` objects. Fortunately the `File` object has a `toPath` method we can use to return a `Path` object.

```
Files.copy(copyThis.toPath(), toThis.toPath());
```

Both `move` and `copy` can take an optional parameter list which specifies the 'copy options'.

The copy options are contained in `java.nio.file.StandardCopyOption.` so you have to add an additional import to your class.

```
import static java.nio.file.StandardCopyOption.*;
```

When you import the copy options you can use:

- `REPLACE_EXISTING` - will allow the operation to complete even if destination exists
- `COPY_ATTRIBUTES` - preserve the file attributes during the copy
- `ATOMIC_MOVE` - any operating system follow on file actions wait till the move is complete

The `move` below uses copy options:

```
Files.move(moveThis.toPath(), toThis.toPath(),
          REPLACE_EXISTING, ATOMIC_MOVE);
```

Exercise: `copy` And `move` a `File`

- Write a file to the temporary directory and `copy` it to a new file with a ".copy" suffix.
- Write a file to the temporary directory and `move` it to a new file with a ".moved" suffix.

Summary

We haven't covered all the methods available for working with files.

I recommend you use code completion and the official help documentation to explore the classes available to you on the Java input output packages. Do read the 'Java IO Official Documentation' linked to in the References section.

The methods and classes we covered in this chapter should give you enough information for tackling the initial problems you will need for automation to support your testing.

Certainly you should be armed with enough information to read and write text files: either for input data or for writing ad-hoc reports.

Read the pages linked to below. There is a rich set of libraries in Java core for working with files.

Also in this chapter we concentrated on working with text files since I suspect that most of the files you will have to parse and write while automating will be text files.

References and Recommended Reading

- Java IO Official Documentation
  - docs.oracle.com/javase/tutorial/essential/io/index.html[142]
- Java File Official Documentation
  - docs.oracle.com/javase/7/docs/api/java/io/File.html[143]
- Java Files Official Documentation
  - docs.oracle.com/javase/7/docs/api/java/nio/file/Files.html[144]
- Java Nio vs Java IO
  - blogs.oracle.com/slc/entry/javanio_vs_javaio[145]
- Buffered Writer
  - docs.oracle.com/javase/7/docs/api/java/io/BufferedWriter.html[146]
- PrintWriter
  - docs.oracle.com/javase/7/docs/api/java/io/PrintWriter.html[147]

---

[142] http://docs.oracle.com/javase/tutorial/essential/io/index.html

[143] http://docs.oracle.com/javase/7/docs/api/java/io/File.html

[144] http://docs.oracle.com/javase/7/docs/api/java/nio/file/Files.html

[145] https://blogs.oracle.com/slc/entry/javanio_vs_javaio

[146] http://docs.oracle.com/javase/7/docs/api/java/io/BufferedWriter.html

[147] http://docs.oracle.com/javase/7/docs/api/java/io/PrintWriter.html

- Reading and writing file practices
  - www.javapractices.com/topic/TopicAction.do?Id=42[148]
- Different ways of reading files
  - stackoverflow.com/questions/4716503/best-way-to-read-a-text-file[149]
- Copy
  - docs.oracle.com/javase/tutorial/essential/io/copy.html[150]
- Move
  - docs.oracle.com/javase/tutorial/essential/io/move.html[151]
- Paths
  - docs.oracle.com/javase/7/docs/api/java/nio/file/Paths.html[152]
- Path
  - docs.oracle.com/javase/8/docs/api/java/nio/file/Path.html[153]

---

[148]http://www.javapractices.com/topic/TopicAction.do?Id=42

[149]http://stackoverflow.com/questions/4716503/best-way-to-read-a-text-file

[150]http://docs.oracle.com/javase/tutorial/essential/io/copy.html

[151]http://docs.oracle.com/javase/tutorial/essential/io/move.html

[152]http://docs.oracle.com/javase/7/docs/api/java/nio/file/Paths.html

[153]https://docs.oracle.com/javase/8/docs/api/java/nio/file/Path.html

Chapter Twenty - Math and BigDecimal

Chapter Summary

In this chapter you will learn how to use additional ‘number’ classes:

- `BigDecimal` - a class that offers accurate math operations without rounding, important for financial applications
  - `subtract` - a method to subtract a value from the `BigDecimal`
  - `add` - a method to add a value to the `BigDecimal`
  - `multiply` - a method to multiply the `BigDecimal` by the value
  - `divide` - a method to divide the `BigDecimal` by the value
  - `valueOf` - a static method to return a `BigDecimal` representing the supplied `double` or `long`
  - `BigDecimal` does not support ==, `!=`, `<`, `>` etc. instead use the methods `equals` and `compareTo`
- `Math` - a class that has additional methods for working with `float` and `double`
  - `max` - compare two values and return the larger
  - `min` - compare two values and return the smaller
  - `abs` - return the absolute value
  - `random` - return a random number `>= 0.0` and `< 1.0`
  - trigonometric functions: `sin`, `cos`, `tan`, `asin`, `acos`, `atan`, `toDegrees`, `toRadians`

The `Math` class can help you with a set of methods to help you work with `double` and `float`, so we will look at that class in this chapter.

For most of your automation you’ll probably get away with `float` and `double`. But you have to be careful as these types use rounding and approximation in their calculations. They do not represent 0.1 in a form that you can use for exact calculations, for exact operations and values you use `BigDecimal`.

e.g.

```
0.10 + 0.73 = 0.83
```

but…

```
float total = 0.1f + 0.73f;
assertThat(total, is(0.83f));
```

The above code fails when part of an `@Test` method because:

```
java.lang.AssertionError:
Expected: is <0.83F>
     but: was <0.83000004F>
```

With `double` and `float` you have to be careful and handle rounding yourself throughout the calculation process.

Or you can use the `BigDecimal` class.

You could also use `int` or `long`

If you use an `int` then you don't worry about rounding, particularly when doing a calculation like the example which actually represents 10 pence, plus 73 pence. i.e 0.1 pounds + 0.73 pounds.

I could have done the calculation in pennies and been fine.

BigDecimal

`BigDecimal` is imported using the `java.math` package.

```
import java.math.BigDecimal;
```

`BigDecimal` is not a primitive, so is a little clumsier to work with, and will perform more slowly than the primitives.

```
BigDecimal bdtotal = new BigDecimal("0.1").add(new BigDecimal("0.73"));
assertThat(bdtotal, is(new BigDecimal("0.83")));
```

`BigDecimal` maintains the decimal point precision. Particularly useful for financial calculations

So if, as a tester working in finance, you need to read values from a file and compare the calculations produced from some other system. You are likely to use `BigDecimal` to ensure that your calculations are as accurate as you can make them.

You could use `int` or `long` and manage the rounding yourself. Or take the easy route and use `BigDecimal` when you want to maintain the precision.

Joshua Bloch, the author of "Effective Java", summarizes the situation as "If the quantities don't exceed nine decimal digits, you can use `int`; if they don't exceed eighteen digits, you can use `long`. If the quantities might exceed eighteen digits, you must use `BigDecimal`".

Be aware of the choices now, so you don't raise defects against systems when the bugs are actually in your math calculation code.

Exercise: Convince Yourself of `BigDecimal` or `int`

Create an `@Test` method which calculates the result of the following situation.

(There are 100 pence to the pound, or 100 cents to the dollar) In this example I use pounds and pence. Feel free to mentally translate this into any currency you want, just be aware that there are 100 pence to the pound when you translate.

- I start with 5 pounds.
- I spend 43 pence,
- then I spend 73 pence,
- then I spend 1 pound and 73 pence.

i.e. 5 - 0.3 - 0.47 - 1.73

In my hand I have 2 pounds 50 pence (or 2.5 pounds).

- How much does your `double` have?
- Recreate the code with `int`.
- Recreate the code with `BigDecimal` using the `subtract` method.

`BigDecimal` Methods

Constructor

You can construct a `BigDecimal` from:

- `int`
- `long`
- `String`
- `double`
- `BigInteger` - an unbounded integer e.g. larger than a 64 bit long.

```
BigDecimal fromInt = new BigDecimal(5);
BigDecimal fromLong = new BigDecimal(5L);
BigDecimal fromString = new BigDecimal("5");
BigDecimal fromDouble = new BigDecimal(5.0);
BigDecimal fromBigInteger = new BigDecimal(BigInteger.valueOf(5L));
```

Static Methods

`BigDecimal` provides some factory methods for creating a `BigDecimal` object.

- `ONE`
- `TEN`
- `ZERO`
- `valueOf` - convert a `double` or a `long` to a `BigDecimal`

```
BigDecimal bd0 = BigDecimal.ZERO;
BigDecimal bd1 = BigDecimal.ONE;
BigDecimal bd10 = BigDecimal.TEN;
BigDecimal bdVal = BigDecimal.valueOf(5.0);
```

Basic Arithmetic Methods

The basic arithmetic operator methods on `BigDecimal` are:

- `add`
- `subtract`
- `multiply`
- `divide`

Each of these takes a `BigDecimal` as argument and returns a new `BigDecimal` representing the result of the associated operator `+`, `-`, `*`, or `/`

Exercise: Basic Arithmetic with `BigDecimal`

Create an `@Test` annotated method which implements the following calculation using `BigDecimal` methods:

- `aBigDecimal = 0`
- `(((aBigDecimal + 10) * 2) - 10) / 2) = 5`

Comparison Operators

You can't use the normal comparison operators on `BigDecimal` i.e. `>`, `<`, `==`, `!=`, `>=`, or `<=`

You can use `equals` to compare `BigDecimal` objects.

```
assertThat( BigDecimal.ONE.equals(
                new BigDecimal(1.0)), is(true));
assertThat( BigDecimal.ONE.equals(
                new BigDecimal("1")), is(true));
```

You can also use the `compareTo` method:

- `compareTo(value)` returns:
  - -1 if the `BigDecimal` is less than `value`,

- 0 if the `BigDecimal` is equal to `value`,
- 1 if the `BigDecimal` is greater than `value`

The official documentation suggests the following usage

```
BigDecimal.TEN.compareTo(BigDecimal.ONE) > 0
```

Which would be equivalent to:

```
BigDecimal.TEN > BigDecimal.ONE
```

Exercise: Compare TEN and ONE

Write an `@Test` annotated method to compare TEN and ONE.

Simulating each of the comparison operators:

`>, <, ==, !=, >=,` or `<=`

Follow the suggested usage pattern above e.g. `> 0`

Using `BigDecimal`

If you start working with `BigDecimal` then read the official documentation or using code completion in your IDE to see the additional range of methods offered. In this chapter we covered a small subset of `BigDecimal` methods to help you get started, and to help you understand the difference between `BigDecimal` and the earlier primitives `double` and `float`.

`BigDecimal` supports different rounding methods which you can use in conjunction with the arithmetic operations. You can also provide a 'scale' to work at different powers of ten.

Java also offers a `BigInteger` object in the `java.math` package which works with greater than 64 bit integers. The normal operators and functions associated with an `int` or `long`, are accessible via methods on `BigInteger`.

You can also convert from `BigDecimal` using `floatValue`, `doubleValue`, `intValue`, `longValue` etc. This is useful when you want to use some of the methods in the Math class after a series of calculations.

Math

The `java.lang.Math` class provides a range of mathematical methods for working with `float` or `double`, and sometimes with an `int` or `long`.

The official documentation lists the set of methods available so you can find the range easily enough on-line or in your IDE.

The methods on the class are all static, so are used without instantiating a `Math` object, and you will not need to import the `java.lang.Math` package.

e.g. to find the maximum of two values:

```
assertThat( Math.max(23.0, 42.0), is(42.0));
```

I've described a small set of `Math` methods I have found useful in the past below.

The following methods operate on `int`, `long`, `double` or `float`:

- `max` - compare two values and return the larger
- `min` - compare two values and return the smaller
- `abs` - return the absolute value
- `random` - return a random number `>= 0.0` and `< 1.0`

You also have trigonometric functions: `sin`, `cos`, `tan`, `asin`, `acos`, `atan`, `toDegrees`, `toRadians`.

I do not intend to cover all the methods in this book. I simply want to make you aware of the built in `Math` class. And now, when you start working with mathematical functionality in your tests, going beyond the typical arithmetic operations, you can examine the `Math` class in more detail to see if it has existing methods that meet your needs.

Summary

This was a chapter introducing two important classes at a very high level:

- `BigDecimal`
- `Math`

Use `BigDecimal` when working with currency values or when you need accuracy in the calculations, and avoiding rounding.

Use `Math` when you need to go beyond the simple mathematical operators `+-*/`.

Remember also the `BigInteger` class when you need to work with larger than 64 bit `integer` values.

References and Recommended Reading

- Java BigDecimal
  - docs.oracle.com/javase/7/docs/api/java/math/BigDecimal.html[154]
- BigInteger official documentation
  - docs.oracle.com/javase/7/docs/api/java/math/BigInteger.html[155]
- Java Math class official documentation
  - docs.oracle.com/javase/7/docs/api/java/lang/Math.html[156]

[154]http://docs.oracle.com/javase/7/docs/api/java/math/BigDecimal.html

[155]http://docs.oracle.com/javase/7/docs/api/java/math/BigInteger.html

[156]http://docs.oracle.com/javase/7/docs/api/java/lang/Math.html

Chapter Twenty One - Collections Revisited

Chapter Summary

In this chapter you will revisit the collection classes.

- *Core Collections* - Core collection interfaces:
  - `SortedSet` - like a `Set` but maintains an order
    - * `first` - return the first item
    - * `last` - return the last item
    - * `headSet(e)` - return the elements, before element `e`
    - * `tailSet(e)` - return the elements after and including element `e`
    - * `subSet(e1,e2)` - the elements from (and including) element e1, to (but excluding) e2
    - * `comparator` - return the `Comparator` object used for comparison for sort order
  - `SortedMap` - like a `Map` but maintains an order
    - * `firstKey` - the first key based on the sort order
    - * `lastKey` - the last key based on the sort order
    - * `headMap(k)` - every "key, value" pair before key `k`
    - * `tailMap(k)` - every "key, value" pair after and including the key `k`
    - * `subMap(k1,k2)` - every "key, value" pair between k1 and k2 (including k1, excluding k2)
    - * `comparator` - the `comparator` used to determine the sort order of the keys
  - `Queue` - a first in first out collection
  - `Deque` - add elements either at front or end but not middle
- *Core Implementations* - Core collection implementations:
  - `TreeSet` - implements a `SortedSet`
  - `TreeMap` - implements a `SortedMap`

Core Collection Interfaces Revisited

The official documentation lists the following as the Core Collection interfaces:

- `Collection`
  - `List`
  - `Set`
    - `SortedSet`
  - `Queue`
  - `Deque`
- `Map`
  - `SortedMap`

The following table provides a summary of the key methods on the Interfaces. I have removed `List` and added the `SortedSet` and `SortedMap` so you can see the additional nuances.:

Collection	Set	SortedSet	Map	SortedMap
`add(e)`	*All in Collection*	`first`	`put(k,v)`	`firstKey`
`remove(e)`		`last`	`remove(k)`	`lastKey`
`removeAll(c)`		`headSet(e)`	`entrySet`	`headMap(k)`
`retainAll(c)`		`tailSet(e)`	`get(k)`	`tailMap(k)`
`clear`		`subSet(i1,i2)`	`clear`	`subMap(k,k)`
`contains(e)`			`containsKey(k)`	
`containsAll(c)`			`containsValue(v)`	
`size`		`comparator`	`size`	`comparator`
`isEmpty`		*All in Collection*	`isEmpty`	*All in Map*
`toArray`			`values`	
`toArray(a)`			`keySet`	
`addAll(c)`			`putAll(m)`	

where: e == element, c == collection, a == array, i == index, k == key, v == value, m == map

Set

We described `Set` in the earlier collection chapter.

In this chapter we will build on `Set` and consider the `SortedSet`.

`SortedSet`

The `SortedSet`, like the `Set` strips out duplicates if you try to add them.

The `SortedSet` also:

- guarantees the order of the elements based on a `Comparator` or the `compareTo` method of the elements

The sorting relies on the elements in the set to implement a `Comparable` interface which mandates the implementation of a `compareTo` method. Or you can provide a `Comparator` to the `SortedSet` implementation at instantiation, and the `Comparator` knows how to compare the objects.

For the examples I will mainly use `String` but will also provide a short overview of the `Comparator`.

- `first` - return the first item
- `last` - return the last item
- `headSet(e)` - return the `SortedSet` of elements, before element `e`
- `tailSet(e)` - return the `SortedSet` of elements after and including element `e`
- `subSet(e1,e2)` - the `SortedSet` from (and including) element e1, to (but excluding) e2
- `comparator` - return the `Comparator` object used for comparison for sort order

With a `SortedSet` you also have access to all methods in the `Collection` interface.

With a `SortedSet` I use the `TreeSet` from `java.util` as my default implementation.

The following example shows:

- the `SortedSet` maintaining the order of the elements, even though I added them out of order
- the `SortedSet` does not add the duplicated `"a"` element

```
@Test
public void sortedSetCanMaintainSortOrder(){

    SortedSet<String> alphaset = new <String>TreeSet();

    alphaset.add("c");
    alphaset.add("d");
    alphaset.add("a");
    alphaset.add("b");
    alphaset.add("a");

    assertEquals(4, alphaset.size());

    String[] alphas = new String[alphaset.size()];
    alphaset.toArray(alphas);

    assertEquals("a", alphas[0]);
    assertEquals("b", alphas[1]);
    assertEquals("c", alphas[2]);
    assertEquals("d", alphas[3]);
}
```

In the above listing, I `add` the `String` values to the `alphaset` in a random order, but when I convert the `alphaset` to an array, the array has the `String` values in order.

Also, although I added the `String` `"a"` twice, it is only added to the `alphaset` once: as evidenced by the `size()` method returning `4`, and the conversion to array only containing the `String` `"a"` once.

`first` retrieves first element in sort

When new elements are added to the `SortedSet`, the sort order of elements is maintained so that `first` always returns the first element in the set based on the sort order.

```
@Test
public void canRetrieveFirstFromSortedSet(){
    SortedSet<String> alphaset = new <String>TreeSet();

    alphaset.add("c");
    assertEquals("c", alphaset.first());

    alphaset.add("d");
    assertEquals("c", alphaset.first());

    alphaset.add("b");
    assertEquals("b", alphaset.first());

    alphaset.add("a");
    assertEquals("a", alphaset.first());
}
```

`last` retrieves last element in sort

When new elements are added to the `SortedSet`, the sort order of elements is maintained so that `last` always returns the last element in the set based on the sort order.

```
@Test
public void canRetrieveLastFromSortedSet(){
    SortedSet<String> alphaset = new <String>TreeSet();

    alphaset.add("c");
    assertEquals("c", alphaset.last());

    alphaset.add("b");
    assertEquals("c", alphaset.last());

    alphaset.add("d");
    assertEquals("d", alphaset.last());

    alphaset.add("a");
    assertEquals("d", alphaset.last());
}
```

`headSet` subset before an element

You can create a sorted sub set of all elements in the set *before* a specific element.

```
SortedSet<String> subset = alphaset.headSet("c");
```

The above statement would return every element before "c" i.e "a" and "b", as the full example below illustrates.

```
@Test
public void sortedSetcanReturnHeadSet(){

    SortedSet<String> alphaset = new <String>TreeSet();

    alphaset.add("c");
    alphaset.add("d");
    alphaset.add("b");
    alphaset.add("a");

    SortedSet<String> subset = alphaset.headSet("c");

    assertEquals(2, subset.size());

    String[] alphas = new String[subset.size()];
    subset.toArray(alphas);

    assertEquals("a", alphas[0]);
    assertEquals("b", alphas[1]);
}
```

`tailSet` subset after, and including, an element

```
SortedSet<String> subset = alphaset.tailSet("c");
```

The `tailSet` creates a subset, but this time the set of all elements in the set which are greater than or equal to the element, so the subset also includes the element itself.

This is illustrated by the example below:

```
@Test
public void sortedSetcanReturnTailSet(){

    SortedSet<String> alphaset = new <String>TreeSet();

    alphaset.add("c");
    alphaset.add("d");
    alphaset.add("b");
    alphaset.add("a");

    SortedSet<String> subset = alphaset.tailSet("c");

    assertEquals(2, subset.size());

    String[] alphas = new String[subset.size()];
    subset.toArray(alphas);

    assertEquals("c", alphas[0]);
    assertEquals("d", alphas[1]);
}
```

`subSet` between two elements

```
SortedSet<String> subset = alphaset.subSet("b", "d");
```

The `subSet` contains a subset from, and including, the first element argument, to, but excluding the second element argument. e.g. given `"a", "b", "c", "d"` then a `subSet("b", "d")` would be from and including "b", to (but excluding) `"d"`, giving `"b", "c"`.

This is illustrated by the example below:

```
@Test
public void sortedSetcanReturnSubSet(){

    SortedSet<String> alphaset = new <String>TreeSet();

    alphaset.add("c");
    alphaset.add("d");
    alphaset.add("b");
    alphaset.add("a");

    SortedSet<String> subset = alphaset.subSet("b", "d");
```

```
        assertEquals(2, subset.size());

        String[] alphas = new String[subset.size()];
        subset.toArray(alphas);

        assertEquals("b", alphas[0]);
        assertEquals("c", alphas[1]);
    }
```

`comparator` used for sorting

`comparator` returns the `Comparator` object which the `SortedSet` is using for comparisons.

Therefore we should learn how to create a `Comparator`.

I have chosen to expand on `Comparator` but not `hashSet` and `equals` because I think the `Comparator` offers more re-use potential and likelihood of you implementing it.

To illustrate this functionality we are going to create a `SortedSet` of the `User` domain object that we created earlier.

We didn't add a `compareTo` method to that object, nor did we create `equals` or `hashCode`.

In the example below, our first attempt at creating a `SortedSet` of `User` objects would fail with a `ClassCastException`. The `ClassCastException` would be thrown as soon as we try to add the `User` named `"Bob"` to the `SortedSet`. Because our `User` object does not implement the `Comparable` interface.

```
        User bob = new User("Bob", "pA55Word");    // 11
        User tiny = new User("TinyTim", "hello"); //12
        User rich = new User("Richie", "RichieRichieRich"); // 22
        User sun = new User("sun", "tzu"); // 6
        User mrBeer = new User("Stafford", "sys"); // 11

        SortedSet<User> userSortedList = new TreeSet<User>();

        userSortedList.add(bob);
```

Our immediate thought might be to implement the `Comparable` interface on the `User` class. But sometimes we don't have control over all the classes we use, and sometimes we don't want to implement that interface for all our domain objects. We might only want to sort them once or twice.

Creating a custom `Comparator` can be very useful. Also we might want to sort them in different ways, at different times, and embedding the comparison code in the object itself might not give us that flexibility.

In this book I will take the approach of creating a `UserComparator`. The `UserComparator` is a class which will compare `User` objects.

In the `@Test` method where I want to create the `SortedSet` I instantiate the `TreeSet` as follows:

```
SortedSet<User> userSortedList = new TreeSet<User>(new UserComparator());
```

Here I create a `new UserComparator` and pass it as an argument to the `TreeSet` constructor. This provides flexibility because if I want to sort or compare the objects in different ways then I could construct the `TreeSet` with a different `Comparator` object.

To help you understand the comparison that I want to use, I will show you the full method code:

```
@Test
public void sortedSetWithComparatorForUser(){
    User bob = new User("Bob", "pA55Word");   // 11
    User tiny = new User("TinyTim", "hello"); //12
    User rich = new User("Richie", "RichieRichieRich"); // 22
    User sun = new User("sun", "tzu"); // 6
    User mrBeer = new User("Stafford", "sys"); // 11

    SortedSet<User> userSortedList =
                        new TreeSet<User>(new UserComparator());

    userSortedList.add(bob);
    userSortedList.add(tiny);
    userSortedList.add(rich);
    userSortedList.add(sun);
    userSortedList.add(mrBeer);

    User[] users = new User[userSortedList.size()];
    userSortedList.toArray(users);

    assertEquals(sun.getUsername(), users[0].getUsername());
    assertEquals(bob.getUsername(), users[1].getUsername());
    assertEquals(mrBeer.getUsername(), users[2].getUsername());
```

```
        assertEquals(tiny.getUsername(), users[3].getUsername());
        assertEquals(rich.getUsername(), users[4].getUsername());
    }
```

I want the sort order to be based on the length of the `username` + the length of the `password`. This is the algorithm that the `UserComparator` will implement.

You can see that I have added the lengths as comments after each of the `User` instantiations so that I know what to assert on.

The rest of the code is pretty simple:

- create the `User` objects
- instantiate a `SortedSet` with the `UserComparator`
- convert the set to an array so that we can assert on the expected order

The next step is to create the `Comparator`.

I will create it in the `src\main\java` branch as I'll probably reuse it in more places. And I'll add it to the `com.javafortesters.domainentities` package.

This is the first class you are seeing us create which implements an interface. In this example we will implement the `Comparator` interface:

```
public class UserComparator implements Comparator {
```

In order to satisfy this interface, I have to implement a `compare` method which takes two `Object` as arguments, and returns an `int`:

```
    public int compare(Object oUser1, Object oUser2) {
```

The `int` has to correspond to:

- `0` if the two objects are `equal` in the terms of the sorting algorithm
- negative `-ve` if `object1` is less than `object2`
- positive `+ve` if `object1` is greater than `object2`

Since the arguments have to be of type `Object` we need to cast them in the code to the correct type, which for us is `User`:

```
User user1 = (User)oUser1;
User user2 = (User)oUser2;
```

Implement the algorithm decided upon to compare the two values:

```
int user1Comparator = user1.getPassword().length() +
                      user1.getUsername().length();

int user2Comparator = user2.getPassword().length() +
                      user2.getUsername().length();
```

Then calculate the return `int`

```
int val =  user1Comparator - user2Comparator;
```

Great. And all of that implements the sorting algorithm. The problem is that `SortedSet` also uses the `Comparator` to decide if the values in the `SortedSet` are unique. And the implementation above would not let me add any `User` into the `SortedSet` where the `username + password` length is the same.

In the code above I would fail to add `mrBeer` because he has the same length as `bob`. And I want `mrBeer` in the `SortedSet`.

Beer

I don't actually like to drink beer. In fact I can't stand the stuff. I much prefer to drink wine. But I do love the books of **Mr Stafford Beer**. A particularly splendid Systems Thinker and Cybernetician. If you get the chance, read his work.

I have to add one little adjustment to the `Comparator` to allow for duplicate lengths, but I will exclude duplicate lengths with a duplicate `username` from the SortedSet. This would still allow in Users with duplicate names (provided they have different length passwords) but that is fine for this comparison algorithm.

```
if(val==0){
    val = user1.getUsername().compareTo(user2.getUsername());
}
```

And with that we can `return val;`

The full code for the `UserComparator` which allows the `@Test` method to complete is below:

```
public class UserComparator implements Comparator {

    public int compare(Object oUser1, Object oUser2) {

        User user1 = (User)oUser1;
        User user2 = (User)oUser2;

        int user1Comparator = user1.getPassword().length() +
                              user1.getUsername().length();

        int user2Comparator = user2.getPassword().length() +
                              user2.getUsername().length();

        int val =  user1Comparator - user2Comparator;

        if(val==0){
            val = user1.getUsername().compareTo(user2.getUsername());
        }

        return val;
    }
}
```

Exercise: Remove `if(val==0)`

Remove the `if(val==0)` block of code and run the `@Test` method. Ensure that you understand why we added that line of code.

Exercise: Disallow Duplicate UserNames

Create a `DupeUserComparator` which implements the length check as above, but also does not allow `User` with a duplicate `username` to be added to the `SortedSet`.

Use it in an `@Test` annotated method to demonstrate it works.

Exercise: `User` class `implements Comparable`

Add code to the `User` class such that it implements `Comparable` with the algorithm for disallowing a `User` with duplicate `username` as well as the length check in the `compareTo` method.

Use it in an `@Test` annotated method to demonstrate it works.

Exercise: See the sort in action

Add the line of code below, to your `Comparator`. Just before the `return val` line and see the `Comparator` in action in your console.

```
System.out.println("Compare " + user1.getUsername() +
        " with " + user2.getUsername() + " = " + val);
```

Set & SortedSet Documentation

You can find the details of Set and SortedSet on the official documentation site.

Interface:

- docs.oracle.com/javase/tutorial/collections/interfaces/set.html[157]
- docs.oracle.com/javase/tutorial/collections/interfaces/sorted-set.html[158]

Implementation:

- docs.oracle.com/javase/tutorial/collections/implementations/set.html[159]

Map

We described `Map` in the earlier collection chapter.

In this chapter we will build on `Map` and consider the `SortedMap`.

SortedMap

`SortedMap` is to `Map`, as `SortedSet` is to `Set`. The interface and function of the methods of `SortedMap` are almost the same as `SortedSet`, so it won't take long for you to figure out how `SortedMap` works.

- A `SortedMap` is ordered on its keys, not its values.

[157]http://docs.oracle.com/javase/tutorial/collections/interfaces/set.html
[158]http://docs.oracle.com/javase/tutorial/collections/interfaces/sorted-set.html
[159]http://docs.oracle.com/javase/tutorial/collections/implementations/set.html

- The `comparator` is used to determine the ordering, or the `compareTo` method on the *key*

The methods should be familiar as they are almost the same as `SortedSet`

- `firstKey` - the first key based on the sort order
- `lastKey` - the last key based on the sort order
- `headMap(k)` - the `SortedMap` containing every "key, value" pair before key `k`
- `tailMap(k)` - the `SortedMap` containing every "key, value" pair after and including the key `k`
- `subMap(k1,k2)` - the `SortedMap` containing every "key, value" pair between `k1` and `k2` (including `k1`, excluding `k2`)
- `comparator` - the `comparator` used to determine the sort order of the keys

For the sake of brevity, since we covered the `SortedSet` in detail, and `SortedMap` is much the same, I will use examples to explain `SortedMap` rather than a lot of descriptive text. All the examples for the `SortedMap` methods use the following `Map` declaration and instantiation:

```
SortedMap<String, String> map = new TreeMap<>();

map.put("key1", "value1");
map.put("key3", "value3");
map.put("key2", "value2");
map.put("key5", "value5");
map.put("key4", "value4");
```

`firstKey` & `lastKey` to retrieve key limits

`firstKey` and `lastKey` respectively return the first and last keys in the map:

```
assertEquals("key1", map.firstKey());
assertEquals("key5", map.lastKey());
```

Create sorted extracts with `headMap`, `tailMap` and `subMap`

`headMap(k)` returns a `SortedMap` containing every key, value pair before the key passed as argument. e.g.

```
SortedMap<String, String> headMap;
headMap = map.headMap("key3");

assertEquals(2, headMap.size());
assertTrue(headMap.containsKey("key1"));
assertTrue(headMap.containsKey("key2"));
```

`tailMap(k)` returns a `SortedMap` containing every key, value pair after and including the key passed as argument. e.g.

```
SortedMap<String, String> tailMap;
tailMap = map.tailMap("key3");

assertEquals(3, tailMap.size());
assertTrue(tailMap.containsKey("key3"));
assertTrue(tailMap.containsKey("key4"));
assertTrue(tailMap.containsKey("key5"));
```

`subMap(k,k)` returns a `SortedMap` containing every key, value pair after and including the key passed as first argument and before, but excluding, the key passed as second argument. e.g.

```
SortedMap<String, String> subMap;
subMap = map.subMap("key2", "key4");

assertEquals(2, subMap.size());
assertTrue(subMap.containsKey("key2"));
assertTrue(subMap.containsKey("key3"));
```

`comparator` for sorting

The `comparator` usage for `SortedMap`, differs from `SortedSet` only because the key is sorted and not the value (or element).

Whenever I have used a `SortedMap`, my keys typically are `Strings` and so natural sort order is normally adequate.

A `Map` can use any object as the key, so I have used the same example from `SortedSet` to illustrate the comparator on `SortedMap`. Even though this represents a fairly obtuse use of the `Map`.

In this example you should imagine that the `User` is the key and the value is a description of the `User`

I instantiate the `SortedMap` with the `UserComparator` as I did with `SortedSet`:

```
SortedMap<User,String> userSortedMap =
        new TreeMap<User,String>(new UserComparator());
```

Then the rest of the code is the same as `SortedSet`

- create a bunch of `User` objects
- instantiate the `SortedMap`
- put all the `User` objects into the `Map` as the key, and add a description as the value
- extract the keys to an array - they will be in the sort order specified by the `comparator`
- assert on the sort order

```
@Test
public void sortedMapWithComparatorForUser(){
    User bob = new User("Bob", "pA55Word");   // 11
    User tiny = new User("TinyTim", "hello"); //12
    User rich = new User("Richie", "RichieRichieRich"); // 22
    User sun = new User("sun", "tzu"); // 6
    User mrBeer = new User("Stafford", "sys"); // 11

    SortedMap<User,String> userSortedMap =
            new TreeMap<User,String>(new UserComparator());

    userSortedMap.put(bob, "Bob rules");
    userSortedMap.put(tiny, "Tiny Time");
    userSortedMap.put(rich, "Rich Richie");
    userSortedMap.put(sun, "Warfare Art");
    userSortedMap.put(mrBeer, "Cybernetician");

    User[] users = new User[userSortedMap.size()];
    userSortedMap.keySet().toArray(users);

    assertEquals(sun.getUsername(), users[0].getUsername());
    assertEquals(bob.getUsername(), users[1].getUsername());
    assertEquals(mrBeer.getUsername(), users[2].getUsername());
    assertEquals(tiny.getUsername(), users[3].getUsername());
    assertEquals(rich.getUsername(), users[4].getUsername());
}
```

Map KeySet Explored

`keySet` returns a `Set` where each element is a key from the `Map`:

```
Set<String> keys = map.keySet();
```

I could use this to create a SortedSet of keys:

```
SortedSet<String> keys = new TreeSet<String>(map.keySet());
```

Exercise: Access Values in a Map in Key order

- Create a Map
- Use a `SortedSet` for the keys to iterate through the `Map` in key order.

Map & SortedMap Documentation

You can find the details of Map and SortedMap on the official documentation site.

Interface:

- docs.oracle.com/javase/tutorial/collections/interfaces/map.html[160]
- docs.oracle.com/javase/tutorial/collections/interfaces/sorted-map.html[161]

Implementation:

- docs.oracle.com/javase/tutorial/collections/implementations/map.html[162]

[160]http://docs.oracle.com/javase/tutorial/collections/interfaces/map.html
[161]http://docs.oracle.com/javase/tutorial/collections/interfaces/sorted-map.html
[162]http://docs.oracle.com/javase/tutorial/collections/implementations/map.html

Queue & Deque

I'm not going to go into detail on the Queue and Deque (*deck*). Simply because I've never had to use them in the real world.

A `Queue` provides a first in, first out collection. Where you add elements at the back of the queue and remove them from the front.

A `Deque` allows you to add elements at the front or back of the queue, but not the middle.

It is worth knowing that these collection types exist, but if you need to use them, I'm sure you'll now be able to understand the documentation on the official site.

Queue & Deque Documentation

You can find the details of `Queue` and `Deque` on the official documentation site.

Interface:

- docs.oracle.com/javase/tutorial/collections/interfaces/queue.html[163]
- docs.oracle.com/javase/tutorial/collections/interfaces/deque.html[164]

Implementation:

- docs.oracle.com/javase/tutorial/collections/implementations/queue.html[165]
- docs.oracle.com/javase/tutorial/collections/implementations/deque.html[166]

Implementations

You have seen in the listings above the Implementations I used.

For completeness I've listed below the implementations for the various Collection interfaces that we covered in both chapters.

- **`Collection` & `List`**:

[163]http://docs.oracle.com/javase/tutorial/collections/interfaces/queue.html
[164]http://docs.oracle.com/javase/tutorial/collections/interfaces/deque.html
[165]http://docs.oracle.com/javase/tutorial/collections/implementations/queue.html
[166]http://docs.oracle.com/javase/tutorial/collections/implementations/deque.html

    - `ArrayList`
- **Set**:
    - `HashSet`
    - `TreeSet` - for sorted
- **Map**:
    - `HashMap`
    - `TreeMap` - for sorted on keys

Periodically I have had to call upon the `ConcurrentHashMap` in `java.util.concurrent` when I was writing code to share objects in memory across `@Test` methods running in parallel. I didn't know about the `ConcurrentHashMap` before I started. But I knew about collections, and I knew I needed something to work concurrently so I did a few Internet searches and found the collection I needed.

What I'm really suggesting in the above paragraph is that you learn a few classes to start with. Then, if you have time, look around at others, or wait until you need one. You'll know you need a new implementation because you are having to code workarounds with your existing implementation, and chances are someone else has already experienced your problem, and written a class so solve it. You just need to hunt it out.

Summary

The `SortedMap` and `SortedSet` require a little extra work - specifically the implementation of a `Comparator` or an Object to implement `Comparable`.

In practice, I default to implementing `Comparator` objects as this gives me more flexibility and I don't have to clutter my domain objects with the `Comparable` interface.

References and Recommended Reading

- Sorted Set Interface
    - docs.oracle.com/javase/tutorial/collections/interfaces/set.html[167]
    - docs.oracle.com/javase/tutorial/collections/interfaces/sorted-set.html[168]
- Sorted Set Implementation

[167]http://docs.oracle.com/javase/tutorial/collections/interfaces/set.html

[168]http://docs.oracle.com/javase/tutorial/collections/interfaces/sorted-set.html

    - docs.oracle.com/javase/tutorial/collections/implementations/set.html[169]
- Sorted Map Interface
    - docs.oracle.com/javase/tutorial/collections/interfaces/map.html[170]
    - docs.oracle.com/javase/tutorial/collections/interfaces/sorted-map.html[171]
- Sorted Map Implementation
    - docs.oracle.com/javase/tutorial/collections/implementations/map.html[172]
- Queue and Deque Interface
    - docs.oracle.com/javase/tutorial/collections/interfaces/queue.html[173]
    - docs.oracle.com/javase/tutorial/collections/interfaces/deque.html[174]
- Queue and Deque Implementation
    - docs.oracle.com/javase/tutorial/collections/implementations/queue.html[175]
    - docs.oracle.com/javase/tutorial/collections/implementations/deque.html[176]

---

[169]http://docs.oracle.com/javase/tutorial/collections/implementations/set.html
[170]http://docs.oracle.com/javase/tutorial/collections/interfaces/map.html
[171]http://docs.oracle.com/javase/tutorial/collections/interfaces/sorted-map.html
[172]http://docs.oracle.com/javase/tutorial/collections/implementations/map.html
[173]http://docs.oracle.com/javase/tutorial/collections/interfaces/queue.html
[174]http://docs.oracle.com/javase/tutorial/collections/interfaces/deque.html
[175]http://docs.oracle.com/javase/tutorial/collections/implementations/queue.html
[176]http://docs.oracle.com/javase/tutorial/collections/implementations/deque.html

Chapter Twenty Two - Advancing Concepts

Chapter Summary

This chapter provides a brief overview of each of the following areas, with links for you to start conducting your own research on the topic.

- Interfaces
- Abstract Classes
- Generics
- Logging
- Enum
- Regular Expressions
- Reflection
- Annotations
- Design Patterns
- Concurrency
- Additional File considerations

And we are almost finished now.

The original intent behind this book was to cover the basics of Java that you need to understand, in an order that allowed you to use the concepts quickly, without being distracted by too much additional overhead.

This chapter provides an overview of 'advancing' concepts which are not necessarily required to be functional in Java, but it is important to know they exist, and give you something to research in your next steps.

You probably won't need these concepts for writing simple *JUnit tests.*

You may need these when you start building a lot of code that has to hang together well, and when the Java code itself needs to embody good design principles.

For the first 3 or 4 years of my writing automation code, I probably didn't use any of these concepts very much at all.

- I used composition to re-use code, without using Interfaces.
- I rarely used Inheritance.
- I never used Abstract Classes.
- I didn't really know what an `enum` was
- etc.

My code was simple, but didn't have design principles holding it together. Which is why I think of these as "Advancing Concepts".

They are not 'advanced' since they are fundamental to the way that Java and good programming works. But in terms of your usage of them, they only need to become relevant when you are "Advancing" your understanding of Java and the robustness of your abstraction layers.

Interfaces

In earlier sections of the book we used Interfaces without actually explaining much about them.

An Interface declares a set of methods that a Class must implement. Anywhere in our code that we only want to use the set of interface methods, we can cast objects to the interface, or declare objects *as*, that interface, rather than working with concrete classes.

e.g use a `List` rather than an `ArrayList`

Each object that implements an interface then has freedom to decide how to implement the methods on that interface, such that they are appropriate to that particular object.

I tend to introduce interfaces into my code when I start to see similar usage patterns of the objects.

As an example. When automating a web site I might create objects to represent each Page on the site. Pages on the site tend to have similar components e.g. header or footer. Early in my code I might have a `getHeader` method on some pages, but not others and I might have repeated code as a result.

When I spot this, I can create an interface called `HasHeader` and this might force the page to implement the `getHeader` method. And I can write methods that operate on a `Header` of a page which take a `HasHeader` interface as a parameter instead of individual page objects, or an generic `Object`.

Research `Interfaces` so you understand their capabilities. And use them to help you organize your abstraction layers.

Research Links:

- Interface Definition
  - docs.oracle.com/javase/tutorial/java/concepts/interface.html[177]
- How to create an Interface
  - docs.oracle.com/javase/tutorial/java/IandI/createinterface.html[178]

Abstract Classes

Abstract classes are classes which you can extend, but can't instantiate directly since not all the methods in the Abstract class will have been implemented in the Abstract class.

I rarely use Abstract classes. I tend to use interfaces and delegate out to other concrete classes. I do this because I know that my automation abstractions are likely to change frequently and I need a lot of flexibility in my code.

Research Links:

- Abstract Classes Offical Documentation
  - docs.oracle.com/javase/tutorial/java/IandI/abstract.html[179]
- Abstract Classes vs. Interfaces
  - javaworld.com/javaqa/2001-04/03-qa-0420-abstract.html[180]

Generics

In the main body of this book you saw Generics used when instantiating Collections and we declared the type of objects that the collection would hold.

---

[177]http://docs.oracle.com/javase/tutorial/java/concepts/interface.html

[178]http://docs.oracle.com/javase/tutorial/java/IandI/createinterface.html

[179]http://docs.oracle.com/javase/tutorial/java/IandI/abstract.html

[180]http://www.javaworld.com/javaqa/2001-04/03-qa-0420-abstract.html

You can use Generics when creating your own objects and methods, such that you don't know exactly what object they will use.

This is a very powerful coding style, to make your automation abstractions flexible, but one that I tend not to have to use very often.

Research Links:

- Official Java Tutorial on Generics
  - docs.oracle.com/javase/tutorial/java/generics[181]

Logging

We didn't cover logging in this book. The closest we came was writing information out to a `File`, and using `System.out.println` to output to the console.

For most of my automation code I can get away with writing log messages to `System.out` since they will be displayed in continuous integration systems, and we rarely have to configure the level of logging when running automation.

Java logging allows you to write code that outputs log messages e.g. warnings, errors, etc. The level of logging output when running the code can be configured externally to the application by the user running the application.

When you need this level of flexibility, it is time to learn about logging frameworks.

Java has a built in logging framework. And a lot of external frameworks which increase the ease of use, or flexibility of configuration.

Research Links:

- Official Java Logging Overview
  - docs.oracle.com/javase/7/docs/technotes/guides/logging/overview.html[182]
- Tutorial by Lars Vogel
  - vogella.com/articles/Logging/article.html[183]

[181]http://docs.oracle.com/javase/tutorial/java/generics

[182]http://docs.oracle.com/javase/7/docs/technotes/guides/logging/overview.html

[183]http://www.vogella.com/articles/Logging/article.html

Enum

An `enum` can be thought of as a set of predefined constants. Useful when organizing constants in your abstraction layers.

An `enum` can be used as the argument in a switch statement. This can lead to readable and simple code.

These constants can also have methods making them very flexible, and might even remove the need to put them in a `switch` statement, and instead use the `enum`'s method itself.

Research Links:

- Official Enum documentation
  - docs.oracle.com/javase/tutorial/java/javaOO/enum.html[184]

Regular Expressions

We briefly touched upon regular expressions in the main text.

Regular Expressions provide a massive amount of power and flexibility for parsing and processing input.

When your code starts to look complicated, and you have a series of nested `if` statements, or complicated transformations. Then it might be time to graduate to the use of Regular Expressions.

Research Links:

- docs.oracle.com/javase/tutorial/essential/regex/[185]

Reflection

Most of our programming work uses specific objects, and we know the methods and interfaces available at the time of coding.

[184]http://docs.oracle.com/javase/tutorial/java/javaOO/enum.html

[185]http://docs.oracle.com/javase/tutorial/essential/regex

Reflection means querying the class at runtime to find out information about the object, e.g. finding out which methods are on the object, what are their parameters, what annotations exist etc.

You can also amend the method signatures to allow you to call private methods, or access private variables etc.

Most programmers I know spurn reflection. And indeed most of the time in an application it isn't used, it can be slow, and it can be dangerous to perform these actions at Runtime.

Some of the problems I've faced in the past however, could only be solved using reflection:

- Trying to use libraries without documentation
- Using pieces of functionality out of sequence
- Working around limitations in abstraction layers

Some of the tools we use e.g. JUnit, can only work because of reflection, and all the annotations you added to your code are accessed via reflection.

Learn about reflection so that you know what it is capable of. Then you can try and use it when you encounter a problem that you see no other way to solve.

Research Links:

- docs.oracle.com/javase/tutorial/reflect[186]

Annotations

You used annotations when you put `@Test` atop your method code.

Annotations are meta-data. Meaning they are used by the compiler and when your code is accessed at runtime using Reflection.

I have in the past used annotations when trying to find ways of reporting on execution coverage and creating custom JUnit runners.

Important to know about, but I imagine you will not use them very often.

Research Links:

- docs.oracle.com/javase/tutorial/java/annotations[187]

[186]http://docs.oracle.com/javase/tutorial/reflect

[187]http://docs.oracle.com/javase/tutorial/java/annotations

Design Patterns

Design Patterns are those statements that you hear on the project that everyone assumes that everyone else understands and never explains, e.g.

- Singleton
- Observer
- Visitor
- Factory
- Proxy
- etc.

These are common approaches to solving common problems. The famous book "Design Patterns" by Gamma, Helm, Johnson and Vlissides lists 23 common patterns and some solutions.

Some familiarity with them is important because they offer approaches to problems that other people have solved. They will also help you understand what developers are talking about when they explain their code to you.

Research Links:

- c2.com/cgi/wiki?DesignPatternsBook[188]
- oodesign.com/[189]

Concurrency

Concurrency is important in Java. It allows you to run code in multiple threads and potentially achieve some results faster, or run more than one `@Test` method at the same time.

You will often read that certain classes are not "Thread Safe" which means they should not be used when you try and use concurrency.

There are different approaches to concurrency, ranging from simple use of `synchronized` which means that a method can only be called by a single thread at a time. To full non-blocking concurrency.

[188]http://c2.com/cgi/wiki?DesignPatternsBook

[189]http://www.oodesign.com

This topic is far too advanced for this book. Unfortunately many testers try and tackle this subject early because they want to run their `@Test` methods in parallel. Often before there is even a compelling need to run the automation checks in parallel.

Concurrency is a very interesting part of Java to study, and I have had to create automation abstractions that were usable in a multi-threaded manner. But not early when I was learning Java. I recommend you read about it, but don't try and do any concurrent programming until you are very comfortable understanding how your application works. Otherwise you may create code that fails intermittently that is hard to debug and fix.

I primarily added Concurrency in this section to warn you off trying to use it too quickly.

Research Links:

- docs.oracle.com/javase/tutorial/essential/concurrency[190]

Additional File considerations

In the file chapter I skipped over a lot of information, to try and create example code and basic information that will cover many of your initial file processing needs.

I also covered most of the things that I use files for. I rarely have to work with the basic file building blocks: streams and channels.

I rarely worry about File encoding, because most of my files are created and read from within the same *JUnit test* `class`, and because they are temporary, they get deleted after the `@Test` methods finish.

I include the links below as research items in case you need them in your environment.

Research Links:

- Streams
  - docs.oracle.com/javase/tutorial/i18n/text/stream.html[191]
- File IO
  - docs.oracle.com/javase/tutorial/essential/io/file.html[192]

[190]http://docs.oracle.com/javase/tutorial/essential/concurrency

[191]http://docs.oracle.com/javase/tutorial/i18n/text/stream.html

[192]http://docs.oracle.com/javase/tutorial/essential/io/file.html

Summary

I know this chapter has very few examples. The main purpose was to make you aware of additional areas of functionality available in Java.

I did not explain any in detail because each are areas that could have entire books dedicated to them, and in some cases books do exist dedicated to them, and I mention some of those books in the next chapter.

I've tried to make you aware of the circumstances that will lead you to using the concepts. But I hope you follow and read the provided research links so you have a basic memory of the capability, even if you haven't used it, or don't yet understand it.

Chapter Twenty Three - Next Steps

Chapter Summary

This chapter will provide you with a recommended set of next steps:

- Recommended Reading List
- Recommended Videos
- Recommended Web Sites
- Recommended Next Steps

I hope that if you made it this far into the book, that you attempted the exercises. If you did, and you followed the suggestions peppered throughout the book, then you now have a grasp of the fundamentals of writing Java code. This chapter suggests books and websites to visit to help you continue to learn.

Certainly you've seen a lot of code snippets. Most of the code you have seen has been written in the form of `@Test` annotated methods with assertions. Pretty much what you will be expected to write in the real world.

Recommended Reading

I don't recommend a lot of Java books because they are a very personal thing. There are books that people rave about that I couldn't get my head around. And there are those that I love that other people hate.

But since I haven't provided *massive* coverage of the Java language. I've pretty much given you "just enough" to get going and understand the code you read. I'm going to list the Java books that I gained most from, and still refer to:

- "Effective Java"
  - by Joshua Bloch
- "Implementation Patterns"

    - by Kent Beck
- "Growing Object-Oriented Software, Guided by Tests"
    - by Steve Freeman and Nat Pryce
- "Core Java: Volume 1 - Fundamentals"
    - by Cay S. Horstmann and Garry Cornell
- "Covert Java : Techniques for Decompiling, Patching and Reverse Engineering"
    - by Alex Kalinovsky
- "Java Concurrency in Practice"
    - by Brian Goetz
- "Mastering Regular Expressions"
    - by Jeffrey Friedl

Now, to justify my selections...

Effective Java

"Effective Java" by Joshua Bloch, at the time of writing in its 2nd Edition. This book works for beginners and advanced programmers.

Java developers build up a lot of knowledge about their language from other developers. "Effective Java" helps short cut that process.

It has 78 chapters. Each, fairly short, but dense in their coverage and presentation.

When I first read it, I found it heavy going, because I didn't have enough experience or knowledge to understand it all. But I re-read it, and have continued to re-read it over the time I have developed my Java experience. And each time I read it, I find a new nuance, or a deeper understanding of the concepts.

Because each chapter is short, I return to this book to refresh my memory of certain topics.

This was also the book that helped me understand `enum` well enough to use them and helped me understand concurrency well enough to then read, and understand, "Java Concurrency in Practice".

I recommend that you buy and read this book early in your learning. Even if you don't understand it all, read it all. Then come back to it again and again. It concentrates on very practical aspects of the Java language and can boost your real-world effectiveness tremendously.

You can find a very good overview of the book, in the form of a recording of a Joshua Bloch talk at "Google I/O 2008 - Effective Java Reloaded" on YouTube:

- youtu.be/pi_I7oD_uGI[193]

Implementation Patterns

Another book that benefits from repeated reading. You will take different information from it with each reading, depending on your experience level at the time.

"Implementation Patterns" by Kent Beck explains some of the thought processes involved in writing professional code.

This book was one of the books that helped me:

- concentrate on keeping my code simple,
- decide to learn the basics of Java (and know how to find information when I needed it),
- try to use in built features of the language, before bringing in a new library to my code.

The book is thin and, again dense. Most complaints I see on-line seem to stem from the length of the book and the terseness of the coverage. I found that beneficial, it meant very little padding and waste. I have learned, or re-learned, something from this book every time I read it.

Other books that cover similar topics include "Clean Code" by Robert C. Martin, and "The Pragmatic Programmer" by Andrew Hunt and David Thomas. But I found "Implementation Patterns" far more useful and applicable to my work.

For more information on Kent Beck's writing and work, visit his web site:

- threeriversinstitute.org[194]

Growing Object-Oriented Software

Another book I benefited from reading when I wasn't ready for it. I was able to re-read it and learn more. I still gain value from re-reading it.

- "Growing Object-Oriented Software, Guided by Tests", by Steve Freeman and Nat Pryce

[193]http://youtu.be/pi_I7oD_uGI

[194]http://www.threeriversinstitute.org

Heavily focused on using `@Test` method code to write and understand your code. It also covers mock objects very well.

This book helped change my coding style, and how I approach the building of abstraction layers.

The official homepage for the book is growing-object-oriented-software.com[195]

Covert Java

"Covert Java : Techniques for Decompiling, Patching and Reverse Engineering", by Alex Kalinovsky starts to show its age now as it was written in 2004. But highlights some of the ways of working with Java libraries that you really wouldn't use if you were a programmer.

But sometimes as a tester we have to work with pre-compiled libraries, without source code, and use parts of the code base out of context.

I found this a very useful book for learning about reflection and other practices related to taking apart Java applications.

You can usually pick this up quite cheaply second hand. There are other books that cover decompiling, reverse engineering and reflection. But this one got me started, and I still find it clear and simple.

Java Concurrency in Practice

Concurrency is not something I recommend trying to work with when you are starting out with Java.

But at some point you will probably want to run your code in parallel, or create some threads to make your code perform faster. And you will probably fail, and not really understand why.

I used "Effective Java" to help me get started. But "Java Concurrency in Practice" by Brian Goetz, was the book I read when I really had to make my automation abstraction layer work with concurrent code.

Core Java: Volume 1

The Core Java books are massive, over 1000 pages. And if you really want to understand Java in depth then these are the books to read.

---

[195]http://www.growing-object-oriented-software.com

I find them to be hard work and don't read them often. I tend to use the JavaDoc for the Java libraries and methods themselves.

But, periodically, I want to have an overview of the language and understand the scope of the built in libraries, because there are lots of in-built features that I don't use, that I would otherwise turn to an external library for.

Every time I've flicked through "Core Java", I have discovered a nuance and a new set of features, but I don't do it often.

Mastering Regular Expressions

We didn't cover the full power of Regular Expressions in this book.

I tend to try and keep my code simple and readable so I'll use simple string manipulation to start with.

But over time, I often find that I can replace a series of `if` blocks and string transformations with a regular expression.

Since I don't use regular expressions often I find that each time, I have to re-learn them and I still turn to "Mastering Regular Expressions" by Jeffrey E.F. Friedl.

As an alternative to consider: "Regular Expressions Cookbook" by Jan Goyvaerts, which is also very good.

I sometimes use the tool RegexMagic regexmagic.com[196], written by Jan Goyvaerts when writing regular expressions, it lets me test out the regular expression across a range of example data, and generate sample code for a lot of different languages.

Jan also maintains the web site regular-expressions.info[197] with a lot of tutorial information on it.

Recommended Videos

The videos produced by John Purcell at caveofprogramming.com[198] have been recommended to me by many testers.

I've looked through some of them, and John provides example coding for many of the items covered in this book, and in the "Advancing Concepts" section.

---

[196] http://www.regexmagic.com

[197] http://www.regular-expressions.info

[198] http://www.caveofprogramming.com

John's approach is geared around writing programs, and I think that if you have now finished this book, you will benefit from the traditional programmer based coverage that John provides.

Recommended Web Sites

For general Java news, and up to date conference videos, I recommend the following web sites.

- theserverside.com[199]
- infoq.com/java[200]

Make sure you subscribe to the RSS feeds for the above sites.

I will remind you that I have a web site javaForTesters.com[201] and I plan to add more information there, and links to other resources over time. I will also add additional exercises and examples to that site rather than continue to expand this book.

Remember, all the code used in this book, and the answers to the exercises is available to download from github.com/eviltester[202].

Next Steps

This has been a beginner's book.

You can see from the "Advancing Concepts" chapter that there are a lot of features in Java that I didn't cover. Many of them I don't use a lot and I didn't want to pad out the book with extensive coverage that you can find in other books or videos.

I wanted this book to walk you through the Java language in an order that I think makes sense to people who are writing code, but not necessarily writing systems.

Your next step? Keep learning.

I recommend you start with the books and videos recommended here, but also ask your team mates.

---

[199]http://www.theserverside.com
[200]http://www.infoq.com/java
[201]http://javafortesters.com
[202]https://github.com/eviltester/javaForTestersCode

You will be working on projects, and the type of libraries you are using, and the technical domain that you are working on, may require different approaches than those mentioned in this book.

I hope you have learned that you can get a lot done quite easily, and you should now understand the fundamental classes and language constructs that you need to get started.

Now:

- start writing `@Test` methods which exercise your production code
- investigate how much of your repeated manual effort can be automated

Thank you for your time spent with this book.

I wish you well for the future. This is just the start of your work with Java. I hope you'll continue to learn more and put it to use on your projects.

My ability to use automation to support my testing and add value on projects continues to increase, the more I learn how to improve my coding skills. I hope yours does too.

References

- Java For Testers
  - github.com/eviltester/javaForTestersCode[203]
  - JavaForTesters.com[204]
- Joshua Bloch
  - en.wikipedia.org/wiki/Joshua_Bloch[205]
  - youtu.be/pi_I7oD_uGI[206]
- Kent Beck
  - twitter.com/kentbeck[207]
  - "Three Rivers Institute" threeriversinstitute.org[208]
- Growing Object Oriented Software, Guided by Tests
  - growing-object-oriented-software.com[209]

---

[203]https://github.com/eviltester/javaForTestersCode
[204]http://www.javafortesters.com
[205]http://en.wikipedia.org/wiki/Joshua_Bloch
[206]http://youtu.be/pi_I7oD_uGI
[207]https://twitter.com/kentbeck
[208]http://www.threeriversinstitute.org
[209]http://www.growing-object-oriented-software.com

  - Steve Freeman's Blog higherorderlogic.com[210]
  - natpryce.com[211]
- Core Java Book
  - horstmann.com/corejava.html[212]
- Java Concurrency In Practice
  - jcip.net.s3-website-us-east-1.amazonaws.com/[213]
- Regular Expressions
  - Mastering Regular Expressions home page regex.info[214]
  - regular-expressions.info/[215]
  - regexmagic.com[216]
  - regexpal.com[217]
  - www.regexr.com[218]

---

[210]http://www.higherorderlogic.com
[211]http://www.natpryce.com
[212]http://www.horstmann.com/corejava.html
[213]http://jcip.net.s3-website-us-east-1.amazonaws.com
[214]http://regex.info
[215]http://www.regular-expressions.info
[216]http://www.regexmagic.com
[217]http://regexpal.com
[218]http://www.regexr.com

Appendix - IntelliJ Hints and Tips

Throughout the book I mentioned hints and tips, and shortcuts for using IntelliJ.

I collate all of those in this appendix for easy reference, and add some additional information on using IntelliJ with this book.

Shortcut Keys

This table contains the shortcut keys that I use most often.

Function	Windows	Mac
Create New	`alt + insert`	`ctrl + n`
Intention Actions	`alt + enter`	`alt + enter`
Intention Actions	`alt + return`	`alt + return`
Run JUnit Test	`ctrl + shift + F10`	`ctrl + shift + F10`
Show Parameters	`ctrl + p`	`cmd + p`
Show JavaDoc	`ctrl + q`	`ctrl + j`
Code Completion	`ctrl + space`	`ctrl + space`
Find by class	`ctrl + n`	`ctrl + n`
Find by filename	`ctrl + shift + n`	`ctrl + shift + n`
Find by symbol	`ctrl + shift + alt + n`	`ctrl + shift + alt + n`

JetBrains IntelliJ have supporting documentation on their website:

- Reference pdf for Windows and Linux
  - jetbrains.com/idea/docs/IntelliJIDEA_ReferenceCard.pdf[219]
- Reference pdf for Mac OS X
  - jetbrains.com/idea/docs/IntelliJIDEA_ReferenceCard_Mac.pdf[220]

And the help files have "Keyboard shortcuts you cannot miss"

- jetbrains.com/idea/help/keyboard-shortcuts-you-cannot-miss.html[221]

[219] https://www.jetbrains.com/idea/docs/IntelliJIDEA_ReferenceCard.pdf

[220] https://www.jetbrains.com/idea/docs/IntelliJIDEA_ReferenceCard_Mac.pdf

[221] https://www.jetbrains.com/idea/help/keyboard-shortcuts-you-cannot-miss.html

Code Completion

Code completion is your friend. You can use it to explore APIs and Libraries.

All you do is start typing and after the `.` you will see context specific items you can use.

You can force a start of code completion if you close the pop-up menu by pressing:

- `ctrl + space`

Navigating Source Code

`ctrl + click`

For any method in your code, either a built in method, or a library method, or even one that you have written. You can hold down `ctrl` and *left mouse click* on the method name to jump to the source of that method.

You might be prompted to allow IntelliJ to download the source for external libraries.

This can help when working with the example source code for this book as you can navigate to the domain objects from within the `@Test` method code.

Finding Classes and Symbols

If in this book you see a method name or a class name, but don't know where to find it in the source code then you can use the find functionality in IntelliJ to help.

To find a class by name, use the keyboard shortcut:

- `ctrl + n`

This can perform partial matching, so you don't have to type in the full name of the class.

If you want to find a 'file' in the project then use keyboard shortcut:

- `ctrl + shift + n`

If you want to find a method name, or variable name (symbol) then use the keyboard shortcut:

- `ctrl + shift + alt + n`

Running a JUnit Test

Annotating methods with `@Test` makes it easy for us to 'run' the methods we write. You can right click on the method name or class and choose to `Run` as JUnit test. Or use shortcut key:

- `ctrl + shift + F10`

Loading Project Source

The easiest way to load a project into IntelliJ, and this applies to the book example source code, is to use:

- `File \ Open` and select the `pom.xml` file.

Help Menu

The help menu does more than offer a link to a help file.

Find Action

The menu option `Help \ Find Action` allows you to type an action and IntelliJ will provide menu options and short cut keys to help.

e.g.

- Select `Help \ Find Action`
- type "junit" and you will see a list of 'settings' you can use to help configure JUnit in IntelliJ
- type "run" and you will see a list of options for running code, or tests

The list isn't just for information, you can click on the items in the list and you will be taken to the functionality in IntelliJ or run the command.

Enable Auto Importing

Auto Importing can help faster coding as it will add `Import` statements automatically, and download maven dependencies when you amend the `pom.xml` file.

You will probably see an onscreen prompt to switch this on, but if you miss it then you can use the settings to enable it.

- `Settings` and `Maven. Importing`[222] to switch on the Maven pom.xml importing automatically.
- `Settings` and `Editor. Auto Import`[223] to amend the Java import settings.

You can use the `Find Action` to help you locate these options if a future version of IntelliJ has moved them.

Use the Terminal in IntelliJ

IntelliJ has a built in terminal. The button for this is shown at the bottom of the GUI.

This is very useful for quickly issuing `mvn` commands or any of the other terminal commands mentioned in this book.

Productivity Guide

The `Help \ Productivity Guide` menu option shows a dialog with common productivity improvements.

You can click on the items in the list to see what it does, and you can also see which ones you have used, and which you haven't.

This can help you learn the basics of IntelliJ very quickly.

Summary

IntelliJ offers a lot of flexibility in how we work with code. Over time you will learn to make your work with Java faster as you learn more about the IDE.

Over time I will add videos and information to JavaForTesters.com[224] to demonstrate more functionality with IntelliJ that I do not have space to add to this book.

[222]https://www.jetbrains.com/idea/help/maven-importing.html

[223]https://www.jetbrains.com/idea/help/auto-import.html

[224]http://javafortesters.com

Appendix - Exercise Answers

This appendix contains answers to, and commentary on, the exercises in the book.

All the code found here, can also be found in the supporting source code github repository:

- https://github.com/eviltester/javaForTestersCode

Chapter Three - My First JUnit Test

Check for 5 instead of 4

When I ran the JUnit test I saw console output informing me of an Assertion Error.

```
java.lang.AssertionError: 2+2=4 expected:<5> but was:<4>
        at org.junit.Assert.fail(Assert.java:88)
        at org.junit.Assert.failNotEquals(Assert.java:743)
        at org.junit.Assert.assertEquals(Assert.java:118)
        at org.junit.Assert.assertEquals(Assert.java:555)
        at com.javafortesters.chap003myfirsttest.examples.MyFirstTest.
                   canAddTwoPlusTwo(MyFirstTest.java:19)
```

The actual message was longer than this.

It is important to note that in IntelliJ I could click on the hypertext in the error message `MyFirstTest.java:19` and I will be taken to the line of code in the editor that threw the exception. Did you try clicking on the link? It makes debugging a lot easier.

Create additional `@Test` methods to check

```
    @Test
    public void canSubtractTwoFromTwo(){
        int answer = 2-2;
        assertEquals("2-2=0", 0, answer );
    }

    @Test
    public void canDivideFourByTwo(){
        int answer = 4/2;
        assertEquals("4/2=2", 2, answer );
    }

    @Test
    public void canMultiplyTwoByTwo(){
        int answer = 2*2;
        assertEquals("2*2=4", 4, answer );
    }
```

Check the naming of the *Test* classes

In the example code you will see that I have written the JUnit tests that do not run from Maven, as failing methods i.e. the assertions fail. Just to make the point that naming is very important.

```
public class NameClass {
    @Test
    public void whenClassNameHasNoTestInItThenItIsNotRun(){
        // this test will not run from maven so i can make
        // a failing test... it fails in the IDE
        assertTrue("whenClassNameHasNoTestInItThenItIsNotRun",
                    false);
    }
}
```

```
public class NameClassTest {
    @Test
    public void whenClassHasTestAtEndThenTestIsRun(){
        // this test will run from maven so it needs to pass
        assertTrue("whenClassHasTestAtEndThenTestIsRun",
                    true);
    }
}
```

```
public class NameTestClass {
    @Test
    public void whenClassHasTestInMiddleThenTestIsNotRun(){
        // this test will not run from maven so i can make
        // a failing test... it fails in the IDE
        assertTrue("whenClassHasTestInMiddleThenTestIsNotRun",
                    false);
    }
}
```

```
public class TestNameClass {
    @Test
    public void whenClassHasTestAtFrontThenTestIsRun(){
        // this test will run from maven so it needs to pass
        assertTrue("whenClassHasTestAtFrontThenTestIsRun",
                   true);
    }
}
```

Chapter Four - Work With Other Classes

Convert an int to Hex

```
@Test
public void canConvertIntToHex(){
    assertEquals("hex 11 is b", "b",
            Integer.toHexString(11));
    assertEquals("hex 10 is b", "a",
            Integer.toHexString(10));
    assertEquals("hex 3 is b", "3",
            Integer.toHexString(3));
    assertEquals("hex 21 is b", "15",
            Integer.toHexString(21));
}
```

Confirm MAX and MIN Integer sizes

```
@Test
public void canConfirmIntMinAndMaxLimits(){

    int minimumInt = -2147483648;
    int maximumInt = 2147483647;

    assertEquals("integer min", minimumInt, Integer.MIN_VALUE);
    assertEquals("integer max", maximumInt, Integer.MAX_VALUE);
}
```

Chapter Five - Work With Our Own Classes

Experiment with the code

When you replace the `String` with an `int`, you should see a syntax error because an `int` does not satisfy the method declaration which needs a `String`

When you replace the `String` literal `"http://192.123.0.3:67"` with `null`, you won't get a syntax error because `null` is a valid object reference, but if you run the `@Test` method it should fail.

Convert from Static Usage to Static Import

The example source shows the individual imports of `DOMAIN` and `PORT`, if I comment those two imports out and add in the import for `TestAppEnv.*` then I have imported everything statically and then have the option to remove the `TestAppEnv` prefix from `getUrl`, but I don't have to.

I normally would not import `TestAppEnv` statically as I don't think it is as readable as a simple `import` of the class.

```
import com.javafortesters.domainobject.TestAppEnv;
import org.junit.Assert;
import org.junit.Test;

// I could import everything on TestAppEnv statically, and then
// I don't need to prefix getUrl with TestAppEnv
/*
import static com.javafortesters.domainobject.TestAppEnv.*;
*/
// If I just import the DOMAIN and PORT then I still need to
// prefix getUrl with TestAppEnv
import static com.javafortesters.domainobject.TestAppEnv.DOMAIN;
import static com.javafortesters.domainobject.TestAppEnv.PORT;


public class TestAppEnvironmentNoStaticImportTest {

    @Test
    public void canGetUrlStatically(){
        Assert.assertEquals("Returns Hard Coded URL",
                "http://192.123.0.3:67",
                TestAppEnv.getUrl());
    }

    @Test
    public void canGetDomainAndPortStatically(){

        Assert.assertEquals("Just the Domain",
                "192.123.0.3",
                DOMAIN);

        Assert.assertEquals("Just the port",
                "67",
                PORT);
    }
}
```

Chapter Six - Java Classes Revisited: Constructors, Fields, Getter & Setter Methods

Experiment with the package structure

When I have the Junit *Test* class in the same package as the `User` class then I do not need to import it. Even though we are in different source hierarchies i.e. one in `src\test` and one in `src\main`.

```
package com.javafortesters.domainentities;

import org.junit.Test;

import static org.junit.Assert.assertEquals;

public class UserTest {
```

If I change the package then I have to add the import for the `User` class.

```
package com.javafortesters.chap006domainentities.exercises.differentpackage;

import com.javafortesters.domainentities.User;
import org.junit.Test;
import static org.junit.Assert.assertEquals;

public class UserTest {
```

I would also have to add the import if there were multiple `User` classes in my code base, in order to tell Java which one I want to use.

Experiment with private and public fields

When a class has *fields* which are public:

```
public class User {
    public String username;
    public String password;

    public User(){
        username = "admin";
        password = "pA55w0rD";
    }
}
```

Then it doesn't really need getter or setter methods.

But the `User` class has no control over its data. Later we add checks on the setter and getter methods so that we can't add invalid data to the object. If you make the fields `public` then you don't have those safeguards.

```
    @Test
    public void canConstructWithUsernameAndPassword(){
        User auser = new User();
        auser.username = "bob";
        assertEquals("not default username",
                "bob",
                auser.username);
    }

    @Test
    public void canSetNameToInvalidValue(){
        User auser = new User();
        auser.username = "12345£$%$";
        assertEquals("invalid username",
                "12345£$%$",
                auser.username);
    }
```

Experiment with the field and parameter names

When you remove `this.` from the *constructor*:

```
    public User(String username, String password) {
        username = username;
        password = password;
    }
```

When Java sees the line:

```
        username = username;
```

It executes it, but assigns the value passed in as the *parameter* to the *parameter*, and not to the *field*, so our *field* called `username` is never assigned a value and so is `null`, as reported by the assertion message:

`java.lang.AssertionError: given username expected expected:<admin> but was:<null>`

When we rename the parameters:

```
    public User(String aUsername, String aPassword) {
        username = aUsername;
        password = aPassword;
    }
```

Then we do not need the `this` keyword. The *parameters* and *fields* have different names, so they will not clash.

It is up to you which style you choose to adopt for your coding.

I use both and switch between them at different times. By naming the *parameter* the same as the *field*, and using the `this` keyword to distinguish them, when I use code completion in the constructor, the code completion shows me `username` and `password` making it easy for me to see what the *parameters* refer to. This code completion use case is the main decision maker for me, when I choose whether or not to use `this` or rename the *parameters*.

Chapter Eight - Selections and Decisions

Cat or Cats? Ternary Operator

Write an `@Test` method that uses a ternary operator to return "cats" if a `numberOfCats` equals `1`. And return `"cat"` if the `numberOfCats` is not `1`

```
@Test
public void catOrCats(){

    int numberOfCats = 1;

    assertEquals("1 == cat",
            "cat",
            (numberOfCats == 1) ? "cat" : "cats");

    numberOfCats = 0;
    assertEquals("0 == cats",
            "cats",
            (numberOfCats == 1) ? "cat" : "cats");

    numberOfCats = 2;
    assertEquals("2 == cats",
            "cats",
            (numberOfCats == 1) ? "cat" : "cats");
}
```

When I rewrite the code so that it uses a method, then the code is cleaner and avoids the repetition.

```
@Test
public void catOrCatsAsMethod(){

    assertEquals("1 == cat", "cat", catOrCats(1));

    assertEquals("0 == cats", "cats", catOrCats(0));

    assertEquals("2 == cats", "cats", catOrCats(2));
}

private String catOrCats(int numberOfCats){
    return (numberOfCats == 1) ? "cat" : "cats";
}
```

AssertTrue if true

```
@Test
public void truthyIf(){
    boolean truthy=true;

    if(truthy)
        assertTrue(truthy);

    if(truthy){
        assertTrue(truthy);
        assertFalse(!truthy);
    }
}
```

AssertTrue else AssertFalse

For a single statement I do not need to add the braces:

```
@Test
public void truthyIfElse(){
    boolean truthy=true;

    if(truthy)
        assertTrue(truthy);
    else
        assertFalse(truthy);
}
```

When there is more than one statement in the `if` or the `else` then I need to add the `{}` braces:

```
@Test
public void truthyIfElseBraces(){
    boolean truthy=true;

    if(truthy){
        assertTrue(truthy);
        assertFalse(!truthy);
    }else{
        assertFalse(truthy);
    }
}
```

I can choose to leave off the braces for the `else` because there is only one condition, but in practice I would not do this because I might want to expand the number of statements on the else condition in the future, and I make the code harder to review:

```
@Test
public void truthyIfElseOnlyOneSetOfBraces(){
    boolean truthy=true;

    if(truthy){
        assertTrue(truthy);
        assertFalse(!truthy);
    }else
        assertFalse(truthy);
}
```

Nested If Else Horror

If you ever find yourself writing code like the following then I guarantee that you have done something wrong, and have not thought through the problem properly.

I decided to pull the main logic out into a separate method so that I could call it more easily with the different combinations of `true` and `false` for `truthy` and `falsey`.

I also added a set of `System.out.println` so that I could see the truth table combinations. It was fortunate I did this because I actually made a mistake in the nested `if/else` statements when I first wrote my answer - how did you check your answer?

```
@Test
public void nestedIfElseHorror(){
    horrorOfNestedIfElse(true, true);
    horrorOfNestedIfElse(true, false);
    horrorOfNestedIfElse(false, true);
    horrorOfNestedIfElse(false, false);
}

public void horrorOfNestedIfElse(boolean truthy, boolean falsey){

    if(truthy){
        if(!falsey){
            if(truthy && !falsey){
                if(falsey || truthy){
```

```
                        System.out.println("T | F");
                        assertTrue(truthy);
                        assertFalse(falsey);
                    }
                }
            }else{
                System.out.println("T | T");
                assertTrue(truthy);
                assertTrue(falsey);
            }
        }else{
            if(!truthy){
                if(falsey){
                    System.out.println("F | T");
                    assertTrue(falsey);
                    assertFalse(truthy);
                }else{
                    System.out.println("F | F");
                    assertFalse(falsey);
                    assertFalse(truthy);
                }
            }
        }
    }
```

Switch on Short Code

I added a `break`, after the `default`. Remove the `break` to verify for yourself if it is required or not, and decide if there is any difference in the readability of the code.

Also, remove some of the `break` statements and verify that the results are not as expected.

```
    @Test
    public void countrySwitch(){

        assertEquals("United Kingdom", countryOf("UK"));
        assertEquals("United States", countryOf("US"));
        assertEquals("United States", countryOf("USA"));
        assertEquals("United States", countryOf("UsA"));
        assertEquals("France", countryOf("FR"));
        assertEquals("Sweden", countryOf("sE"));
        assertEquals("Rest Of World", countryOf("ES"));
```

```
        assertEquals("Rest Of World", countryOf("CH"));
    }

    private String countryOf(String shortCode) {

        String country;

        switch(shortCode.toUpperCase()){
            case "UK":
                country= "United Kingdom";
                break;
            case "US":
            case "USA":
                country = "United States";
                break;
            case "FR":
                country = "France";
                break;
            case "SE":
                country = "Sweden";
                break;
            default:
                country = "Rest Of World";
                break;
        }

        return country;
    }
```

Switch on `int`

This exercise was designed to allow you to `switch` on variables other than `String`, and also to see what creative approach you adopted for the `> 4` and `< 1` conditions.

In my answer below, you can see that I added a set of `if` statements in the `default` block.

```
@Test
public void integerSwitch(){

    assertEquals("One", integerString(1));
    assertEquals("Two", integerString(2));
    assertEquals("Three", integerString(3));
    assertEquals("Four", integerString(4));
    assertEquals("Too big", integerString(5));
    assertEquals("Too big", integerString(Integer.MAX_VALUE));
    assertEquals("Too small", integerString(0));
    assertEquals("Too small", integerString(Integer.MIN_VALUE));
}

private String integerString(int anInt) {

    String valReturn="";

    switch(anInt){
        case 1:
            valReturn = "One";
            break;
        case 2:
            valReturn = "Two";
            break;
        case 3:
            valReturn = "Three";
            break;
        case 4:
            valReturn = "Four";
            break;
        default:
            if(anInt < 1){
                valReturn = "Too small";
            }
            if(anInt > 4){
                valReturn = "Too big";
            }
            break;
    }

    return valReturn;
}
```

And for the extra points, you explored writing a `switch` statement without using `break;`.

In this example, because the method is so simple, the code actually reads quite well, and succinctly. I did have to add an extra `return "";` line, which will never be executed, in order to satisfy the method's declaration of returning a `String`.

```
    private String integerStringUsingReturnOnly(int anInt) {
        switch(anInt){
            case 1:
                return "One";
            case 2:
                return "Two";
            case 3:
                return "Three";
            case 4:
                return "Four";
            default:
                if(anInt < 1){
                    return "Too small";
                }
                if(anInt > 4){
                    return "Too big";
                }
        }

        return "";
    }
```

I could also have removed the `if(anInt > 4)` block in the default switch and instead of returning `""` I could have returned `"Too big"`.

Chapter Nine - Arrays and For Loop Iteration

Create an Array of Users

In order to work with the `User` objects, I first had to import the `User` class.

```
import com.javafortesters.domainentities.User;
```

Then I created the array and added the users.

```
@Test
public void createAnArrayOfUsers(){
    User[] users = new User[3];

    users[0] = new User("bob","bA55Word");
    users[1] = new User("eris","eA55Word");
    users[2] = new User("ken","kA55Word");

    assertEquals("bob", users[0].getUsername());
    assertEquals("eris", users[1].getUsername());
    assertEquals("ken", users[2].getUsername());
}
```

Note that I added asserts on the username to check that I had added the users correctly. Did you add asserts to your `@Test` method? If not, how did you know it worked?

Iterate over the Array of Users

I added the following code to my `@Test` method above, to iterate over the array and print out the values in the array:

```
    for(User aUser:users){
        System.out.println(aUser.getUsername());
    }
```

Create an array of 100 users

In my sample answer, I chose to `System.out.println` the array to check.

I could have put a breakpoint after the loop and used the debugger to check by running the code in debug mode.

I added assertion code, which uses the *for each* so I iterate over every item, and count each item, using the count `userId` to check the username and password. Since I know that there are supposed to be `100`, when I exit the *for each* loop, I expect my `userId` to equal `101`.

You may have chosen another method. That's fine. There are many ways to do this.

```
@Test
public void exerciseCreateAnArrayOf100Users(){
    User[] users = new User[100];

    for(int userIndex =0; userIndex<100; userIndex++){
        int userId = userIndex + 1;
        users[userIndex] = new User("user" + userId,
                                    "password" + userId);
    }

    // check creation
    for(User aUser:users){
        System.out.println(aUser.getUsername() +
                           ", " +
                           aUser.getPassword());
    }

    // bonus points assert creation
    int userId = 1;
    for(User aUser : users){
        assertEquals("user" + userId, aUser.getUsername());
        assertEquals("password" + userId, aUser.getPassword());
        userId++;
    }
    // check the last one output was 100, i.e. next would be 101
    assertEquals(userId, 101);
}
```

Sort Workdays Array and Assert Result

The text is sorted in alphabetical order[225], and since all the strings start with uppercase, the words are in the order we would expect.

[225]http://en.wikipedia.org/wiki/Alphabetical_order

```
@Test
public void sortWorkdaysArrayAndAssertResult(){
    String[] workdays = {"Monday", "Tuesday", "Wednesday",
            "Thursday", "Friday"};

    Arrays.sort(workdays);

    assertEquals(workdays[0], "Friday");
    assertEquals(workdays[1], "Monday");
    assertEquals(workdays[2], "Thursday");
    assertEquals(workdays[3], "Tuesday");
    assertEquals(workdays[4], "Wednesday");
}
```

After amending the day names, I expect the words starting with lower case letters to come after the words with uppercase letters.

```
@Test
public void sortWorkdaysMixedCaseArrayAndAssertResult(){
    String[] workdays = {"monday", "Tuesday", "Wednesday",
            "thursday", "Friday"};

    Arrays.sort(workdays);

    assertEquals(workdays[0], "Friday");
    assertEquals(workdays[1], "Tuesday");
    assertEquals(workdays[2], "Wednesday");
    assertEquals(workdays[3], "monday");
    assertEquals(workdays[4], "thursday");
}
```

Understand how `print2DIntArray` method works

```
1   public void print2DIntArray(int [][]multi){
2       for(int[] outer : multi){
3           if(outer==null){
4               System.out.print("null");
5           }else{
6               for(int inner : outer){
7                   System.out.print(inner + ",");
8               }
9           }
10          System.out.println("");
11      }
12  }
```

- line 01 : declare the method as accepting a 2 dimensional `int` array as parameter
- line 02 : iterate over the outer array
- line 03 : if the outer array is null, then ...
  - line 04 : output `"null"`, we do not try and process the contents of this array
- line 05 : the outer array is not null, therefore...
  - line 06 : iterate over the contents of this array
    * line 07 : output the contents of the array cell
- line 10 : output a blank line

Create a Triangle

To create a triangle, I create the array to allow a ragged array.

Then loop over the array, and assign an array to each cell in the array.

For each of the new arrays, I loop over the cell contents and insert the index value.

```
@Test
public void createTriangle2dArray(){

    int[][]triangle = new int [16][];

    for(int row=0; row<triangle.length; row++){
        triangle[row] = new int[row+1];
        for(int i=0; i< (row+1); i++){
            triangle[row][i] = i;
        }
    }
```

```
        print2DIntArray(triangle);
    }

    public void print2DIntArray(int [][]multi){
        for(int[] outer : multi){
            if(outer==null){
                System.out.print("null");
            }else{
                for(int inner : outer){
                    System.out.print(inner + ",");
                }
            }
            System.out.println("");
        }
    }
```

Chapter Ten - Introducing Collections

Use a `for` loop instead of a `while` loop

```
@Test
public void useAForLoopInsteadOfAWhile(){

    String[] someDays = {"Tuesday","Thursday",
            "Wednesday","Monday",
            "Saturday","Sunday",
            "Friday"};

    List<String> days = Arrays.asList(someDays);

    int forwhile;
    for(forwhile=0; !days.get(forwhile).equals("Monday"); forwhile++){
    }
    assertEquals("Monday is at position 3", 3, forwhile);
}
```

Create and manipulate a `Collection` of `Users`

```java
@Test
public void createAndManipulateACollectionOfUsers(){
    Collection<User> someUsers = new ArrayList<User>();

    User bob = new User("bob", "Passw0rd");
    User eris = new User("eris", "Cha0sTime");

    assertEquals(0, someUsers.size());
    assertTrue(someUsers.isEmpty());

    someUsers.add(bob);
    someUsers.add(eris);

    assertEquals(2, someUsers.size());
    assertFalse(someUsers.isEmpty());

    Collection<User> secondUsers = new ArrayList<User>();
    User robert = new User("robert", "9assword");
    User aleister = new User("aleister", "Pass5word");
    secondUsers.add(robert);
    secondUsers.add(aleister);
    assertEquals(2, secondUsers.size());

    someUsers.addAll(secondUsers);
    assertEquals(4, someUsers.size());
    assertTrue(someUsers.containsAll(someUsers));
    assertTrue(someUsers.contains(aleister));

    secondUsers.removeAll(someUsers);
    assertEquals(0, secondUsers.size());

    someUsers.clear();
    assertEquals(0, someUsers.size());
}
```

Create and manipulate a `List` of `User`s

```
@Test
public void createAndManipulateAListOfUsers(){
    List<User> someUsers = new ArrayList<User>();

    assertEquals(0, someUsers.size());

    User bob = new User("bob", "Passw0rd");
    User eris = new User("eris", "Cha0sTime");

    someUsers.add(bob);
    assertEquals(1, someUsers.size());

    someUsers.add(0, eris);
    assertEquals(2, someUsers.size());

    assertEquals(1, someUsers.indexOf(bob));
    assertEquals(0, someUsers.indexOf(eris));

    someUsers.remove(0);
    assertEquals(0, someUsers.indexOf(bob));
    assertEquals(1, someUsers.size());
}
```

Create and manipulate a `Set` of `User`s

```
@Test
public void createAndManipulateASetOfUsers(){
    Set<User> someUsers = new HashSet<User>();

    assertEquals(0, someUsers.size());

    User bob = new User("bob", "Passw0rd");

    someUsers.add(bob);
    assertEquals(1, someUsers.size());

    someUsers.add(bob);
    assertEquals(1, someUsers.size());
}
```

Create and manipulate a `Map` of `User`s

```
@Test
public void createAndManipulateAMapOfUsers(){
    Map<String, User> someUsers = new HashMap<String, User>();

    assertEquals(0, someUsers.size());

    User bob = new User("bob", "Passw0rd");
    User eris = new User("eris", "Cha0sTime");

    someUsers.put(bob.getUsername(), bob);
    assertEquals(1, someUsers.size());

    someUsers.put(bob.getUsername(), eris);
    assertEquals(1, someUsers.size());
}
```

Chapter Eleven - Introducing Exceptions

Fix the `NullPointerException` in the code

All I had to do was take the code listed earlier in the chapter, and assign `18` to the `age` variable before trying to access it.

```
@Test
public void noLongerThrowANullPointerException(){
    Integer age=18;

    String ageAsString = age.toString();

    String yourAge =
            "You are " + ageAsString + " years old";

    assertEquals("You are 18 years old", yourAge);
}
```

Uninitialised variables, and parameters are a common source of exceptions.

Use a different exception instead of `NullPointerException`

When I replaced `NullPointerException` with `ArithmeticException`.

The `NullPointerException` is thrown because there was no code to catch it.

```
@Test(expected = NullPointerException.class)
public void catchADifferentException(){

    Integer age=null;
    String ageAsString;

    try{
        ageAsString = age.toString();

    }catch(ArithmeticException e){
        age = 18;
        ageAsString = age.toString();
    }

    String yourAge =
            "You are " + age.toString() + " years old";

    assertEquals("You are 18 years old", yourAge);
}
```

You can see I used the `expected` parameter to allow me to check for this Exception thrown by the `@Test` method.

Don't fix the cause of the exception

When I remove the `age = 18;` statement from within the catch block and run the code. The code threw a `NullPointerException` because we added no `try catch` block inside the `catch` block.

```
@Test(expected = NullPointerException.class)
public void testNotFixedStillThrowsNullPointer(){

    Integer age=null;
    String ageAsString;

    try{
        ageAsString = age.toString();

    }catch(ArithmeticException e){
        //age = 18;
        ageAsString = age.toString();
```

```
    }

    String yourAge =
            "You are " + age.toString() + " years old";

    assertEquals("You are 18 years old", yourAge);
}
```

Catch a Checked Exception

When I used `NoSuchMethodException` instead of `NullPointerException`. I received a syntax error.

```
@Test
public void thisTriggersASyntaxErrorBecauseExceptionIsNotDeclared(){

    Integer age=null;
    String ageAsString;

    try{
        ageAsString = age.toString();

    }catch(NoSuchMethodException e){
        age = 18;
        ageAsString = age.toString();
    }

    String yourAge =
            "You are " + age.toString() + " years old";

    assertEquals("You are 18 years old", yourAge);
}
```

I received a syntax error on the `NoSuchMethodException` line:

```
    }catch(NoSuchMethodException e){
```

`NoSuchMethodException` is a checked exception and needs to be declared as thrown by methods. The `toString` method does not declare that it will throw a `NoSuchMethodException` so I receive a syntax error.

`NullPointerException` and `ArithmeticException` are unchecked exceptions and don't need to be declared as thrown by methods.

Use Exception as an object

When I add the code to use the methods on the exception:

```
@Test
public void useExceptionAsAnObject(){
    Integer age=null;
    String ageAsString;

    try{
        ageAsString = age.toString();

    }catch(NullPointerException e){
        System.out.println("getMessage - " +
                e.getMessage());
        System.out.println("getStacktrace - " +
                e.getStackTrace());
        System.out.println("printStackTrace");
        e.printStackTrace();
    }
}
```

I receive the following output, I have cut down the output to save space so `...` represents some missing output:

```
getMessage - null
getStacktrace - [Ljava.lang.StackTraceElement;@4ea3c69a
printStackTrace
java.lang.NullPointerException
        at com.javafortesters.exceptions.exercises.IntroducingExceptionsExercisesTest.
        useExceptionAsAnObject(IntroducingExceptionsExercisesTest.java:99)
    ...
        at java.lang.reflect.Method.invoke(Method.java:601)
        at com.intellij.rt.execution.application.AppMain.main(AppMain.java:120)
```

From this I can see that `getMessage` on a `NullPointerException` does not return a message, so we need to use the stack trace to figure out what went wrong. Other exceptions do return messages, and when you start creating your own exceptions, I recommend that you add a message to make it easier for other people to understand the problem in the code.

The `getStacktrace` is an array of `StackTraceElement` objects, so I could access element [0], which is the most recent item on the Array, and use it to find information about that part of the stack trace e.g.

- `getClassName`
- `getFileName`
- `getLineNumber`
- `getMethodName`

```
System.out.println("Stack Trace Length - " +
                    e.getStackTrace().length);
System.out.println("Stack Trace [0] classname - " +
                    e.getStackTrace()[0].getClassName());
System.out.println("Stack Trace [0] filename - " +
                    e.getStackTrace()[0].getFileName());
System.out.println("Stack Trace [0] linenumber - " +
                    e.getStackTrace()[0].getLineNumber());
System.out.println("Stack Trace [0] methodname - " +
                    e.getStackTrace()[0].getMethodName());
```

which would display:

```
Stack Trace Length - 27
Stack Trace [0] classname - com.javafortesters.exceptions.exercises
IntroducingExceptionsExercisesTest
Stack Trace [0] filename - IntroducingExceptionsExercisesTest.java
Stack Trace [0] linenumber - 100
Stack Trace [0] methodname - useExceptionAsAnObject
```

For more information on the StackTraceElement you can read the official documentation:

- docs.oracle.com/javase/7/docs/api/java/lang/StackTraceElement.html[226]

[226]http://docs.oracle.com/javase/7/docs/api/java/lang/StackTraceElement.html

Chapter Twelve - Introducing Inheritance

Create a `User` that is composed of `TestAppEnv`

I have multiple approaches for implementing this.

I can:

- create a `TestAppEnv` object within my `User` object, or
- re-use `TestAppEnv` statically from within my `User` object
- create a new `EnvironmentUser` object which extends object and uses `TestAppEnv`

Create a `TestAppEnv` object within my `User` object

To create a `TestAppEnv` object within my `User` object I could:

- add a new `TestAppEnv` field,
- instantiate the object in the constructor, and
- implement a `getUrl` method on the object.

```
public class User {
    private String username;
    private String password;
    private TestAppEnv testAppEnv;

    public User(){
        this("username", "password");
    }

    public User(String username, String password) {
        this.username = username;
        this.password = password;
        this.testAppEnv = new TestAppEnv();
    }

    public String getUsername() {
        return username;
    }
```

```
    public String getPassword() {
        return password;
    }

    public void setPassword(String password) {
        this.password = password;
    }

    public String getUrl(){
        return this.testAppEnv.getUrl();
    }
}
```

Re-use `TestAppEnv` statically from within my `User` object

Since `TestAppEnv` was originally designed to be accessed statically, I don't need to declare a field or instantiate an object, I could just:

- add a `getUrl` method to `User`
- delegate to the `static` method on `TestAppEnv`

```
    public String getUrl(){
        return TestAppEnv.getUrl();
    }
```

Create a new `EnvironmentUser`

Since the `EnvironmentUser` is a special case of user, I don't need to amend the `User` object at all. I could create a new object called `EnvironmentUser` which extends `User`, and then add a new method to the `EnvironmentUser` which statically uses the `TestAppEnv` object.

```
package com.javafortesters.chap012inheritance.exercises;

import com.javafortesters.domainentities.User;
import com.javafortesters.domainobject.TestAppEnv;

public class EnvironmentUser extends User {

    public String getUrl(){
        return TestAppEnv.getUrl();
    }
}
```

And I would use the object in an `@Test` method as follows:

```
    @Test
    public void createAnEnvironmentUser(){
        EnvironmentUser enuser = new EnvironmentUser();

        assertEquals("username", enuser.getUsername());
        assertEquals("http://192.123.0.3:67", enuser.getUrl());
    }
```

Create a `ReadOnlyUser`

To create a `ReadOnlyUser` which has the permission `ReadOnly`, with the same default "username" and "password" from `User`. I first wrote an `@Test` method which checked for the correct implementation.

```
    @Test
    public void readOnlyUserPrivsAndDefaults(){

        ReadOnlyUser rod = new ReadOnlyUser();
        assertEquals("ReadOnly", rod.getPermission());
        assertEquals("username", rod.getUsername());
        assertEquals("password", rod.getPassword());
    }
```

Then I implemented the `ReadOnlyUser`. This was a very simple class which `extends` the `User`, and implements an `@Override` of `getPermission`

```
package com.javafortesters.chap012inheritance.exercises;
import com.javafortesters.domainentities.User;

public class ReadOnlyUser extends User {

    @Override
    public String getPermission() {
        return "ReadOnly";
    }
}
```

Chapter Thirteen - More Exceptions

Create an `InvalidPassword` exception

Part of 'helping' people use the `User` domain object is to alert them to validation and exceptions that they might encounter using the class. We can do this through documentation, and we can do this through custom exceptions.

By creating an `InvalidPassword` exception we alert people to the validation rules around setting the password on a user.

As you saw in the chapter, I create a class with the code for an `InvalidPassword`:

```
public class InvalidPassword extends Exception {
    public InvalidPassword(String message) {
        super(message);
    }
}
```

In my `User` class, I make the `setPassword` method throw the `InvalidPassword` when it fails the password length check:

```
public void setPassword(String password) throws InvalidPassword {
  if(password.length()<7){
     throw new InvalidPassword("Password must be > 6 chars");
  }

  this.password = password;
}
```

You can see in the code that I pass in a message to the `InvalidPassword` exception to describe the circumstances under which the exception was thrown.

In order to check all of this, I create a class with `@Test` methods which will check:

- the `InvalidPassword` exception is thrown in the constructor
- the `InvalidPassword` exception is not thrown in the default constructor
- the error message thrown by the exception contains the text "Password must be > 6 chars"
- the `InvalidPassword` exception is thrown on `setPassword`

To check that the `InvalidPassword` exception is thrown in the constructor, I use the `expected` parameter to check for the thrown exception. Since the exception is a checked exception I have to add the `throws` keyword in the method declaration:

```
@Test(expected = InvalidPassword.class)
public void constructUserWithException() throws InvalidPassword {
    User aUser = new User("username", "p");
}
```

To check that the default constructor does not throw an exception, all I do is create the `User` and assert that the default password was created.

```
@Test
public void createDefaultUserWithNoThrowsInvalidPasswordException() {
    User aUser = new User();
    assertEquals("password",aUser.getPassword());
}
```

My thinking around this was:

- Since the exception is Checked, I can't write the code if the exception is thrown since I would have to either add a `try catch` block or add the `throws` statement to the method.
- I assert that the `User` was created correctly because if the creation failed then the assertion would fail.
- If an exception is thrown then the `@Test` method will fail

To check for the error message, I `try` and `catch` the exception, then check the error message:

```
@Test
public void createUserWithInvalidPasswordExceptionMessages(){
    User aUser;

    try {
        aUser = new User("username", "p");
        fail("An Invalid Password Exception should have been thrown");

    } catch (InvalidPassword e) {
        assertTrue(e.getMessage().startsWith("Password must be > 6 chars"));
    }
}
```

Note in the above that I add a `fail` statement in the `try` block:

- I do this because the exception is supposed to have been thrown and this fail statement should never be reached.
- If the `fail` statement is reached then the exception was not thrown and I need to force an `@Test` failure.
- If I did not add the `fail` statement and an exception was not thrown then the `@Test` method would pass, but for the wrong reasons.

I also make sure that the `setPassword` method throws the exception.

```
@Test
public void setPasswordWithInvalidPasswordExceptionMessages(){
    User aUser = new User();

    try {
        aUser.setPassword("tiny");
        fail("An Invalid Password Exception should have been thrown");

    } catch (InvalidPassword e) {
        assertTrue(e.getMessage().startsWith("Password must be > 6 chars"));
    }
}
```

To do this, I create the `User` with the default constructor since I know that will not throw the exception. Then wrap the `setPassword` with a `try catch`. And I repeat the text assertion in the catch block. Note that I also add the `fail` statement.

This exercise is a good example of why the `fail` statement is important. Without the fail statement my `@Test` methods could pass because they did not throw the exception.

Chapter Fourteen - JUnit Explored

Create an `@Test` method which uses all of the asserts

```
@Test
public void junitHasAssertions(){
    assertEquals(6, 3 + 3);
    assertEquals("3 + 3 = 6", 6, 3 + 3);

    assertFalse("false is false", false);
    assertFalse(false);

    assertTrue("true is true", true);
    assertTrue(true);

    int [] oneTo10 = {1,2,3,4,5,6,7,8,9,10};
    int [] tenToOne = {10,9,8,7,6,5,4,3,2,1};
    Arrays.sort(tenToOne);
    assertArrayEquals(oneTo10, tenToOne);

    assertNotNull("An empty string is not null", "");
```

```
        assertNotNull("");

        assertNotSame("An empty string is not null", null, "");
        assertNotSame(null, "");

        assertNull("Only null is null", null);
        assertNull(null);

        assertSame("Only null is null", null, null);
        assertSame(null, null);
    }
```

Replicate all the JUnit Asserts using `assertThat`

```
    @Test
    public void assertThatWithHamcrestMatchers(){

        assertThat(3 + 3, is(6));

        /* failing assert used to generate message in book
        assertThat(3 + 3, is(7));
        */

        assertThat("3 + 3 = 6", 3 + 3, is(6));

                /* failing assert used to generate message in book
        assertThat("3 + 3 = 6", 3 + 3, is(7));
        */

        assertThat("false is false", false, equalTo(false));
        assertThat(false, is(false));

        assertThat("true is true", true, equalTo(true));
        assertThat(true, is(true));

        int [] oneTo10 = {1,2,3,4,5,6,7,8,9,10};
        int [] tenToOne = {10,9,8,7,6,5,4,3,2,1};
        Arrays.sort(tenToOne);
        assertThat(oneTo10, equalTo(tenToOne));

        assertThat("An empty string is not null", "",
                is(not(nullValue())));
```

```
        assertThat("", is(not(nullValue())));
        assertThat("",is(notNullValue()));

        assertThat("Only null is null", null, is(nullValue()));
        assertThat(null, nullValue());
    }
```

Use all of the Hamcrest matchers listed

```
    @Test
    public void useTheListedHamcrestMatchers(){

        assertThat(3, is(equalTo(3)));
        assertThat(3, is(not(4)));
        assertThat("This is a string", containsString("is"));
        assertThat("This is a string", endsWith("string"));
        assertThat("This is a string", startsWith("This is"));
    }
```

Chapter Fifteen - Strings Revisited

Try using the other escape characters

```
    @Test
    public void tryUsingTheOtherEscapeCharactersOutputToConsole(){
        System.out.println("New lines, and Tabs");
            String firstLine = "|first line\n";
            String secondLine = "|\tsecond line\n";
            String thirdLine = "|\t\tthird line\n";
            String fullLine = firstLine + secondLine + thirdLine;
        System.out.println(fullLine);

        System.out.println("Carriage return after each word");
        System.out.println("one\rtwo\rthree\rfour\rfive\r");

        System.out.println("Backspace after each word");
        System.out.println("one\btwo\bthree\bfour\bfive\b");

        System.out.println("Quotes and slashes");
        System.out.println("Bob\'s toy said \"DOS uses \'\\\'\"");
    }
```

You probably won't notice much effect of some the characters when output to the console. i.e. \r and \b

And sometimes when you output text to the console you don't see exactly what you expect due to buffering and flushing the output to the console, so don't naturally assume that your `System.out.println` is showing you a bug, investigate any potential bug in the debugger or write an assert to check.

Construct a String

```
@Test
public void canConstructStrings(){

    String empty = new String();
    assertThat(empty.length(), is(0));

    char[] cArray = {'2','3'};
    assertThat(new String(cArray), is("23"));
    assertThat(new String(cArray, 1, 1), is("3"));

    byte[] bArray = "hello there".getBytes();
    assertThat(new String(bArray, 3, 3), is("lo "));

    byte[] b8Array = new byte[0];
    try {
        b8Array = "hello there".getBytes("UTF8");
        assertThat(new String(b8Array, 3, 3, "UTF8"), is("lo "));
    } catch (UnsupportedEncodingException e) {
        e.printStackTrace();
    }

    String hello = new String("hello" + " " + "there");
    assertThat(hello, is("hello there"));
}
```

You can see that I used the Hamcrest matches and `assertThat` to make the code more readable.

Use `regionMatches`

```
@Test
public void exerciseUseRegionMatches(){
    String hello = "Hello fella";
    assertTrue(hello.regionMatches(true, 9,"young lady",6,2));
}
```

I find `regionMatches` painful to use. I made several mistakes trying to get the matching syntax lined up when writing the book and exercises.

Remember, the first integer is the start index in the String we are matching, this must match the first character of the String we want to find.

The second two integers are the index in the matching string we want the matching substring region to start at, and the final integer the length of the substring region.

Make sure you wrap your `regionMatches` in an assert to check you created it correctly.

Find positions of all occurrences in a `String`

using `indexOf`

```
private List<Integer> findAllOccurrences(String string,
                                         String substring) {

    List<Integer> results = new ArrayList<Integer>();

    if(string==null || substring==null){
        throw new IllegalArgumentException("Cannot search using null");
    }

    if(substring.isEmpty()){
        throw new IllegalArgumentException(
                                  "Cannot search for Empty substring");
    }

    // set search to the start of the string
    int lastfoundPosition = 0;

    do{
        // try and find the substring
        lastfoundPosition = string.indexOf( substring,
                                            lastfoundPosition);
```

```
            // if we found it
            if(lastfoundPosition!=-1){

                // add it to the results
                results.add(lastfoundPosition);

                // next start after this index
                lastfoundPosition++;
            }

         // keep looking until we can't find it
        }while(lastfoundPosition!=-1);

        return results;
    }
```

I may have added more parameter checks than you did, but since I'm releasing the code in a book, I'm the one on the receiving end of emails that say "You can't code. When I pass an empty substring in then there is an infinite loop" etc. etc.

It is worth getting in the habit of trying to make your code as robust as you can.

It might also help to see the code that I wrote first, to help me construct this method.

```
@Test
public void canFindAllOccurrencesInStringUsingIndexOf(){
    List<Integer> results;
    results = findAllOccurrences("Hello fella", "l");

    assertThat(results.size(), is(4));

    assertThat(results.contains(2), is(true));
    assertThat(results.contains(3), is(true));
    assertThat(results.contains(8), is(true));
    assertThat(results.contains(9), is(true));

    assertThat(results.get(0), is(2));
    assertThat(results.get(1), is(3));
    assertThat(results.get(2), is(8));
    assertThat(results.get(3), is(9));
}
```

In the above code you can see that I have two checks for the values, using the `.contains`

```
assertThat(results.contains(2), is(true));
```

And using the `.get`

```
assertThat(results.get(0), is(2));
```

My feeling was that I first wanted to make sure that the correct values were in the list, and then I wanted to check if they were in the right order.

This way, if I somehow did them in the wrong order, only the `.get` would fail. But if I failed to find the occurrence then the `contains` would fail.

It might seem redundant to have both `contains` and `get`, but I think that by doing this the `@Test` method will most likely help me in the future if I refactor and somehow get the order of the return values wrong.

Having written the above code, I started to think about what other parameters the method might be expected to handle, and wrote the `@Test` methods which 'stress' the method.

These helped me add the parameter checking code.

```
@Test
public void worksWhenNothingToFind(){
    List<Integer> results;
    results = findAllOccurrences("Hello fella", "z");
    assertThat(results.size(), is(0));

    results = findAllOccurrences("", "z");
    assertThat(results.size(), is(0));
}

@Test(expected = IllegalArgumentException.class)
public void cannotSearchForEmpty(){
    List<Integer> results = findAllOccurrences("", "");
}

@Test(expected = IllegalArgumentException.class)
public void cannotSearchForNullString(){
    List<Integer> results = findAllOccurrences(null, "hello");
```

```
}

@Test(expected = IllegalArgumentException.class)
public void cannotSearchForNullSubString(){
    List<Integer> results = findAllOccurrences("hello", null);
}

@Test(expected = IllegalArgumentException.class)
public void cannotSearchForNulls(){
    List<Integer> results = findAllOccurrences(null, null);
}
```

using `lastIndexOf`

To reverse the list I relied on the `lastIndexOf` method.

The main `@Test` method I used was:

```
@Test
public void canFindAllOccurrencesInStringUsingLastIndexOf(){
    List<Integer> results;
    results = findAllOccurrences("Hello fella", "l");

    assertThat(results.size(), is(4));

    assertThat(results.contains(2), is(true));
    assertThat(results.contains(3), is(true));
    assertThat(results.contains(8), is(true));
    assertThat(results.contains(9), is(true));

    assertThat(results.get(0), is(9));
    assertThat(results.get(1), is(8));
    assertThat(results.get(2), is(3));
    assertThat(results.get(3), is(2));
}
```

I have not included the additional methods that I used to check this method, but they are much the same as those used for the `indexOf` approach.

```
private List<Integer> findAllOccurrences(String string,
                                         String substring) {

    List<Integer> results = new ArrayList<Integer>();

    if(string==null || substring==null){
        throw new IllegalArgumentException("Cannot search using null");
    }

    if(substring.isEmpty()){
        throw new IllegalArgumentException(
                                "Cannot search for Empty substring");
    }

    // set search to the start of the string
    int lastfoundPosition = string.length();

    do{
        // try and find the substring
        lastfoundPosition = string.lastIndexOf(substring,
                                               lastfoundPosition);

        // if we found it
        if(lastfoundPosition!=-1){

            // add it to the results
            results.add(lastfoundPosition);

            // next start before this index
            lastfoundPosition--;
        }

     // keep looking until we can't find it
    }while(lastfoundPosition!=-1);

    return results;
}
```

Regular Expressions for `User setPassword`

```
public void setPassword(String password) throws InvalidPassword {

  if(password.length()<7){
     throw new InvalidPassword("Password must be > 6 chars");
  }

  if(!password.matches(".*[0123456789]+.*")){
     throw new InvalidPassword(
                        "Password must have a digit");
  }

  if(!password.matches(".*[A-Z]+.*")){
     throw new InvalidPassword(
                        "Password must have an Uppercase Letter");
  }

  this.password = password;
}
```

And of course I have to change the default constructor on User as well, otherwise it will fail the validation:

```
public User(){
        this("username", "Passw0rd", false);
}
```

Since the default password has to change, I had to amend the checking code surrounding this class as well.

Check `StringBuilder` resizes

```
@Test
public void capacitySizeIncreasesAutomaticallyWithAppend(){
    StringBuilder builder = new StringBuilder(5);
    assertThat(builder.capacity(), is(5));
    builder.append("Hello World");
    assertThat(builder.capacity() > 5, is(true));
}
```

Insert into a `StringBuilder`

```
@Test
public void writeATestToInsert(){

    StringBuilder builder = new StringBuilder();

    // insert at start
    builder.insert(0,"a");
    assertThat(builder.toString(), is("a"));

    // insert to end
    builder.insert(builder.toString().length(),"b");
    assertThat(builder.toString(), is("ab"));

    // insert to middle
    builder.insert(1,".");
    assertThat(builder.toString(), is("a.b"));
}
```

Chapter Sixteen - Random Data

Create `@Test` methods Which Confirm Random Limits

The basic `@Test` method I created looks like the following:

```
@Test
public void canGenerateRandomInt(){
    Random generate = new Random();

    for(int x=0; x<1000; x++){

        int randomInt = generate.nextInt();

        System.out.println(randomInt);
        assertThat(randomInt<Integer.MAX_VALUE, is(true));
        assertThat(randomInt >=Integer.MIN_VALUE, is(true));
    }
}
```

I use `System.out.println` to display the values to the console, just so I can see the random range. And I assert on the conditions mentioned in the documentation.

All other methods take the same form, with a different random generation approach.

For the boolean checks, I count the true and false values to make sure that both values are generated, and assert on the total:

```
@Test
public void canGenerateRandomBoolean(){
    Random generate = new Random();
    int countTrue = 0;
    int countFalse = 0;

    for(int x=0; x<1000; x++){

        boolean randomBoolean = generate.nextBoolean();

        if(randomBoolean)
            countTrue++;

        if(randomBoolean==false)
            countFalse++;

        System.out.println(randomBoolean);
    }

    System.out.println(
            String.format("Generated %d as true", countTrue));
```

```
// randomly generate a byte array between 0 and 99 length
int arrayLength = generate.nextInt(100);
byte[] bytes = new byte[arrayLength];
generate.nextBytes(bytes);  // fill bytes with random data
Assert.assertEquals(arrayLength, bytes.length);
String viewbytes = new String(bytes);
System.out.println(bytes.length + " - " + viewbytes);
```

Note that I randomly generate the size of the byte array.

Checking for Int Range

```
int randomIntRange = generate.nextInt(12);
System.out.println(randomIntRange);
assertThat(randomIntRange<=11, is(true));
assertThat(randomIntRange >=0, is(true));
```

Note that I generate below `12` so my assertion is from `0` to `11` inclusive

Create an `@Test` method which generates 1000 numbers inclusively between 15 and 20

```
@Test
public void generateRandomIntGivenRangeNot0(){
    Random generate = new Random();

        int minValue = 1;
        int maxValue = 5;
        int randomIntRange = generate.nextInt(
                maxValue - minValue + 1) + minValue;

        assertThat(randomIntRange<=maxValue, is(true));
        assertThat(randomIntRange >=minValue, is(true));
}
```

In the above code, I loop around 1000 times in order to make sure that I don't just hit one lucky number that passes my assertions.

I store the generated numbers in a set:

- this prevents duplicates so each number generated will only appear once
- this means that the size of the set is the number of different integers generated

I assert on the size of the set, because I know that 6 numbers are supposed to be generated.

I assert that each of the numbers {15, 16, 17, 18, 19, 20} has been generated.

Write an `@Test` method that shows the distributions

```
@Test
public void canGenerateRandomGaussianDistributionDouble(){
    Random generate = new Random();

    int standardDeviationCount1 = 0;
    int standardDeviationCount2 = 0;
    int standardDeviationCount3 = 0;
    int standardDeviationCount4 = 0;

    for(int x=0; x<1000; x++){

        double randomGaussian = generate.nextGaussian();

        //System.out.println(randomValue);
        if(randomGaussian > -1.0d && randomGaussian < 1.0d)
            standardDeviationCount1++;

        if(randomGaussian > -2.0d && randomGaussian < 2.0d)
            standardDeviationCount2++;

        if(randomGaussian > -3.0d && randomGaussian < 3.0d)
            standardDeviationCount3++;

        if(randomGaussian > -4.0d && randomGaussian < 4.0d)
            standardDeviationCount4++;
    }

    float sd1percentage = (standardDeviationCount1/1000f) * 100f;
    System.out.println("about 70% one standard deviation = " +
            sd1percentage);

    float sd2percentage = (standardDeviationCount2/1000f) * 100f;
    System.out.println("about 95% two standard deviation = " +
```

```
        sd2percentage);

    float sd3percentage = (standardDeviationCount3/1000f) * 100f;
    System.out.println("about 99% three standard deviation = " +
            sd3percentage);

    float sd4percentage = (standardDeviationCount4/1000f) * 100f;
    System.out.println("about 99.9% four standard deviation = " +
            sd4percentage);

    Assert.assertTrue(sd1percentage < sd2percentage);
    Assert.assertTrue(sd2percentage < sd3percentage);
    // I do not assert that sd3 and sd4 are different
    // because of the small % difference, they do overlap
}
```

Write an `@Test` method which generates 1000 ages using `nextGaussian`

```
@Test
public void canGenerate1000AgesUsingDeviation(){

    Random generate = new Random();
    Map<Integer, Integer> ages =
            new HashMap<Integer, Integer>();

    for(int x=0; x<1000; x++){
        int age = (int)(generate.nextGaussian() * 5) + 35;

        int ageCount = 0;
        if(ages.containsKey(age)){
            ageCount = ages.get(age);
        }
        ageCount++;
        ages.put(age,ageCount);
    }

    SortedSet<Integer> agesSorted = new TreeSet(ages.keySet());

    for(int age : agesSorted){
        System.out.println(age + " : " + ages.get(age));
    }
}
```

Create an `@Test` method for Random with Seed

```
@Test
public void canGenerateRandomNumbersWithSeed(){

    for(int x=0; x<10; x++){

        Random generate = new Random(1234567L);

        assertThat(generate.nextInt() , is(1042961893));
        assertThat(generate.nextLong() , is(-6749250865724111202L));
        assertThat(generate.nextDouble() , is(0.44762832574617084D));
        assertThat(generate.nextGaussian() , is(-0.11571220872310763D));
        assertThat(generate.nextFloat() , is(0.33144182F));
        assertThat(generate.nextBoolean() , is(false));
    }
}
```

In order to identify the values I needed to assert on, I first created a `System.out.println` for each of the lines, then used the value output to the console as the value to assert on.

Generate a Random String 100 chars long

```
@Test
public void generateARandomString(){

    String validValues = "ABCDEFGHIJKLMNOPQRSTUVWXYZ ";

    StringBuilder rString;

    Random random = new Random();

    rString = new StringBuilder();
    for(int x=0; x<100; x++){
        int rndIndex = random.nextInt(validValues.length());
        char rChar = validValues.charAt(rndIndex);
        rString.append(rChar);
    }

    System.out.println(rString.toString());
    Assert.assertTrue(rString.length()==100);
```

```
        Assert.assertTrue(rString.toString().matches("[A-Z ]+"));
    }
```

You can see that I assert on the length of the `String`, and use a regular expression to check that the characters in the string are from A-Z or space i.e. "[A-Z]+"

I also use a `StringBuilder` to help me construct the string by appending each of the randomly generated characters.

Chapter Seventeen - Dates & Times

Re-write the timing `@Test` method using nanoTime

```
    @Test
    public void nanoTime(){
        long startTime = System.nanoTime();

        for(int x=0; x < 10; x++){
            System.out.println("Current Time " + System.nanoTime());
        }

        long endTime = System.nanoTime();
        System.out.println("Total Time " + (endTime - startTime));
    }
```

Use currentTimeMillis to create a unique name with no numbers

There are lots of ways of implementing this exercise.

```
    @Test
    public void createAUniqueUserIDAllChars(){

        String initialUserID = "user" + System.currentTimeMillis();
        System.out.println(initialUserID);

        String userID = initialUserID;

        for(int x = 0; x< 10; x++){
            String charReplacement = "" + ((char)('A'+x));
            String intToReplace = String.valueOf(x);
```

```
12             userID = userID.replace( intToReplace, charReplacement);
13         }
14 
15         assertThat(userID.contains("0"), is(false));
16         assertThat(userID.contains("1"), is(false));
17         assertThat(userID.contains("2"), is(false));
18         assertThat(userID.contains("3"), is(false));
19         assertThat(userID.contains("4"), is(false));
20         assertThat(userID.contains("5"), is(false));
21         assertThat(userID.contains("6"), is(false));
22         assertThat(userID.contains("7"), is(false));
23         assertThat(userID.contains("8"), is(false));
24         assertThat(userID.contains("9"), is(false));
25 
26         assertThat(initialUserID.length(), is(userID.length()));
27 
28         System.out.println(userID);
29     }
```

- line 10 - I made it simple and easy by using the fact that 'A' (a `char`) can be added to an integer to get a new ascii character, then cast the `int` to a `char` and then concatenate it with an empty `String` to create a character string that represents a number.
- line 11 - I convert the `int` to a `String`
- line 12 - I then replace all the integer representations in the `String` with this calculated character e.g.
  - `'A' + 0` would equal `'A'`, and I would replace all `0` in the `String` with `'A'`
  - `'A' + 1` would equal `'B'`, and I would replace all `1` in the `String` with `'B'`
  - etc.

The rest of the code contains assertions to check that no digits are in the name.

Write the `toString` to console

```
@Test
public void writeCalendarToStringToConsole(){
    Calendar cal = Calendar.getInstance();
    System.out.println(cal.toString());
}
```

Use the other Calendar constants

```
@Test
public void useOtherCalendarConstants(){
    Calendar cal = Calendar.getInstance();

    cal.set(2013, Calendar.DECEMBER, 15, 23,39, 54);
    assertThat(cal.get(Calendar.MONTH), is(Calendar.DECEMBER));
    assertThat(cal.get(Calendar.YEAR), is(2013));
    assertThat(cal.get(Calendar.DAY_OF_MONTH), is(15));
    assertThat(cal.get(Calendar.HOUR_OF_DAY), is(23));
    assertThat(cal.get(Calendar.MINUTE), is(39));
    assertThat(cal.get(Calendar.HOUR), is(11));
    assertThat(cal.get(Calendar.AM_PM), is(Calendar.PM));
}
```

Experiment with other constants

```
@Test
public void experimentWithCalendarConstants(){
    Calendar cal = Calendar.getInstance();
    cal.set(2013, Calendar.DECEMBER, 15, 23, 39, 54);


    assertThat(cal.get(Calendar.DAY_OF_WEEK), is(1));
    assertThat(cal.get(Calendar.DAY_OF_WEEK), is(Calendar.SUNDAY));
    assertThat(cal.get(Calendar.DAY_OF_YEAR), is(349));

    // week of month depends on first day of week
    // some places use SUNDAY as first day
    // set to MONDAY for our calculation
    // and control Minimal Days in First Week
    cal.setFirstDayOfWeek(Calendar.MONDAY);
    cal.setMinimalDaysInFirstWeek(6);
    assertThat(cal.get(Calendar.WEEK_OF_MONTH), is(2));
```

```
        System.out.println(
                String.format("Generated %d as false", countFalse));

        assertThat(countTrue>0, is(true));
        assertThat(countFalse>0, is(true));
        assertThat(countTrue + countFalse, is(1000));
    }
```

Since all other `@Test` methods take the same form, I have not included the full code below, just the subset that has the random generation and the assertions.

Checking for Long

```
        long randomLong = generate.nextLong();
        System.out.println(randomLong);
        assertThat(randomLong<Long.MAX_VALUE, is(true));
        assertThat(randomLong >=Long.MIN_VALUE, is(true));
```

Note that the documentation for `nextLong` reports that the algorithm will not return all `long` values.

Checking for Float

```
        float randomFloat = generate.nextFloat();
        System.out.println(randomFloat);
        assertThat(randomFloat<1.0f, is(true));
        assertThat(randomFloat >=0.0f, is(true));
```

Note that the upper limit check is exclusive (<) and the lower limit check is inclusive (>=).

Checking for Double

```
        double randomDouble = generate.nextDouble();
        System.out.println(randomDouble);
        assertThat(randomDouble<1.0d, is(true));
        assertThat(randomDouble >=0.0d, is(true));
```

Note that the upper limit check is exclusive (<) and the lower limit check is inclusive (>=).

Checking for Byte

```
        // Week of the year, similarly requires the
        // config to control first day
        assertThat(cal.get(Calendar.WEEK_OF_YEAR), is(50));
    }
```

Increment and Decrement other Fields

```
    @Test
    public void incrementAndDecrementOtherFields(){
        Calendar cal = Calendar.getInstance();
        cal.set(2013, Calendar.DECEMBER, 15, 23,39, 54);

        cal.add(Calendar.YEAR,-2);
        cal.add(Calendar.MONTH, -6);
        cal.add(Calendar.DAY_OF_MONTH, -12);

        assertThat(cal.get(Calendar.YEAR), is(2011));
        assertThat(cal.get(Calendar.MONTH), is(Calendar.JUNE));
        assertThat(cal.get(Calendar.DAY_OF_MONTH), is(3));

        cal.set(2013, Calendar.DECEMBER, 15, 23,39, 54);

        // bump it forward to 3rd June 2014,
        // then pull it back
        cal.add(Calendar.DAY_OF_MONTH, 19);
        cal.add(Calendar.MONTH, 5);
        cal.add(Calendar.YEAR,-3);

        assertThat(cal.get(Calendar.YEAR), is(2011));
        assertThat(cal.get(Calendar.MONTH), is(Calendar.JUNE));
        assertThat(cal.get(Calendar.DAY_OF_MONTH), is(3));
    }
```

Confirm `add` Moves the Year

```
@Test
public void rollCalendar(){
    Calendar cal = Calendar.getInstance();
    cal.set(2013, Calendar.DECEMBER, 15, 23,39, 54);

    cal.roll(Calendar.DAY_OF_MONTH,17);

    assertThat(cal.get(Calendar.YEAR), is(2013));
    assertThat(cal.get(Calendar.MONTH), is(Calendar.DECEMBER));
    assertThat(cal.get(Calendar.DAY_OF_MONTH), is(1));

    cal.set(2013, Calendar.DECEMBER, 15, 23,39, 54);

    cal.add(Calendar.DAY_OF_MONTH,17);
    assertThat(cal.get(Calendar.YEAR), is(2014));
    assertThat(cal.get(Calendar.MONTH), is(Calendar.JANUARY));
    assertThat(cal.get(Calendar.DAY_OF_MONTH), is(1));
}
```

Chapter Eighteen - Properties and Property Files

Create and List a `Properties` object

```
@Test
public void canCreateAndListTheProperties(){

    Properties properties = new Properties();
    properties.setProperty("name", "bob");
    properties.setProperty("gender", "male");
    properties.setProperty("password", "paSSw0rd");

    assertThat(properties.stringPropertyNames().size(), is (3));

    for( String key : properties.stringPropertyNames()){
        System.out.println("Key: " + key + " " +
                "Value: " + properties.getProperty(key));
    }

    properties.list(System.out);

    Assert.assertTrue(properties.containsKey("gender"));
```

```
        Assert.assertEquals("bob", properties.getProperty("name"));
        Assert.assertEquals("Admin",
                    properties.getProperty("permission", "Admin"));
    }
```

Store and Load a Saved Properties File

```
    @Test
    public void canSaveAndLoadAPropertiesFile() throws IOException {

        String tempDirectory = System.getProperty("java.io.tmpdir");
        String tempResourceFilePath = new File(tempDirectory,
                                    System.currentTimeMillis() +
                                    System.nanoTime() +
                                    ".properties").getAbsolutePath();

        Properties saved = new Properties();

        long nanoTime = System.nanoTime();
        long millis = System.currentTimeMillis();

        saved.setProperty("nanoTime", String.valueOf(nanoTime));
        saved.setProperty("millis", String.valueOf(millis));

        FileOutputStream outputFile =
                new FileOutputStream(tempResourceFilePath);

        saved.store(outputFile, "Time Data When File Written");
        outputFile.close();

        FileReader propertyFileReader =
                new FileReader(tempResourceFilePath);
        Properties loaded = new Properties();

        try{
            loaded.load(propertyFileReader);
        }finally{
            propertyFileReader.close();
        }

        assertThat(loaded.getProperty("nanoTime"),
                is(String.valueOf(nanoTime)));
```

```
    assertThat(loaded.getProperty("millis"),
            is(String.valueOf(millis)));

    new File(tempResourceFilePath).delete();

}
```

Chapter Nineteen - Files

Create a Temp File and Vary the Parameters

```
@Test
public void createTempFileVaryTheParameters() throws IOException {
    // on Windows these files are in %TEMP%
    // on Mac these files are in $TMPDIR
    File temp1 = File.createTempFile("temp1", null);
    File temp2 = File.createTempFile("temp2OutFile", ".out");

    assertThat(temp1.exists(), is(true));
    assertThat(temp2.exists(), is(true));

    temp1.deleteOnExit();
    temp2.deleteOnExit();
}
```

You can see that I cheated and used the `exists` method to check for existence, and I used the `deleteOnExit` to remove the created temp files when the code execution completes.

But note that, had something gone wrong during the execution and an exception thrown, the files probably would not have been deleted. I should really use a `try/finally` block when working with files.

Write out the roots

```
@Test
public void writeOutTheFileListRoots(){
    File[] roots = File.listRoots();
    Assert.assertTrue(roots.length > 0);

    for(File aFile : roots){
        System.out.println(aFile.getAbsolutePath());
    }
}
```

Create a Temporary File With Custom Code

```
@Test
public void createATempFileWithCustomCode() throws IOException {

    String directory = System.getProperty("java.io.tmpdir");
    String fileName = "prefix" + System.currentTimeMillis() + ".tmp";

    File aTempFile = new File(directory, fileName);
    assertThat(aTempFile.exists(), is(false));

    aTempFile.createNewFile();
    assertThat(aTempFile.exists(), is(true));

    aTempFile.delete();
    assertThat(aTempFile.exists(), is(false));
}
```

Write an `@Test` method To Check Canonical Conversion

```
@Test
public void writeATestToCheckCanonicalConversion() throws IOException {

    File absolute1 = new File("C:/1/2/3/4/../../..");
    File absolute2 = new File("C:/1/2/../../1");
    File canonical = new File("C:/1");

    assertThat(trimOsStuff(
                    canonical.getAbsolutePath()),
            is(trimOsStuff(
                    canonical.getCanonicalPath())));
    assertThat(trimOsStuff(
```

```
                canonical.getAbsolutePath()),
            is(trimOsStuff(
                absolute1.getCanonicalPath())));
    assertThat(trimOsStuff(
                canonical.getAbsolutePath()),
            is(trimOsStuff(
                absolute2.getCanonicalPath())));

    assertThat(absolute1.getAbsolutePath().contains(".."), is(true));
    assertThat(absolute2.getAbsolutePath().contains(".."), is(true));
}

// The above code runs fine on a Mac and Windows without needing
// trimOsStuff
// but on Linux, it seems to add a ./ in the middle of the absolute path
// e.g. /home/travis/build/eviltester/javaForTestersCode/./source/C:/1
// So I add the following method to trim out the operating system addition to
// the path e.g. anything before the C:
private String trimOsStuff(String absolutePath) {
    int posOfDrive = absolutePath.indexOf("C:");
    String pathWithoutOsPrefixes = absolutePath.substring(posOfDrive);
    System.out.println(String.format(
            "trimOsStuff: %s became %s",absolutePath, pathWithoutOsPrefixes));
    return pathWithoutOsPrefixes;
}
```

Check that the Temp Directory is a Directory

```
@Test
public void checkThatTheTempDirectoryIsADirectory(){
    File tempDir = new File(System.getProperty("java.io.tmpdir"));

    assertThat(tempDir.isDirectory(), is(true));
    assertThat(tempDir.isFile(), is(false));
}
```

Write to a PrintWriter then Append

```
@Test
public void exerciseWriteToAPrintWriterThenAppend() throws IOException {
    File outputFile = File.createTempFile("printWriterPrint", null);

    System.out.println("Check file " + outputFile.getAbsolutePath());

    FileWriter writer = new FileWriter(outputFile);
    BufferedWriter buffer = new BufferedWriter(writer);
    PrintWriter print = new PrintWriter(buffer);

    print.println("Append Print to Buffered Writer");

    print.close();

    // append to the file
    writer = new FileWriter(outputFile, true);
    buffer = new BufferedWriter(writer);
    print = new PrintWriter(buffer);
    print.println("===============================");
    print.close();

    String lineEnd = System.lineSeparator();
    long fileLen = 62L + lineEnd.length() + lineEnd.length();
    assertThat(outputFile.length(), is(fileLen));
}
```

Create a File and Calculate the length

```
@Test
public void spaceMethods() throws IOException {

    File temp = new File(System.getProperty("java.io.tmpdir"));

    long freeSpace = temp.getFreeSpace();
    long totalSpace = temp.getTotalSpace();
    long usableSpace = temp.getUsableSpace();

    File outputFile = writeTheTestDataFile(5);
    assertThat(outputFile.length(), is(expectedFileSize(5)));

    System.out.println("Length " + outputFile.length() );
    System.out.println("Free " + freeSpace );
```

```
        System.out.println("Total " + totalSpace );
        System.out.println("Usable " + usableSpace);
    }

    private long expectedFileSize(int lines){
        String lineEnd = System.lineSeparator();
        return (("line x".length() + lineEnd.length())*lines);
    }

    private File writeTheTestDataFile(int lines) throws IOException {
        File outputFile = File.createTempFile(
                                    "forReading" + lines + "_", null);
        PrintWriter print = new PrintWriter(
                                new BufferedWriter(
                                        new FileWriter(outputFile)));
        for(int line=0; line<lines; line++){
            print.println("line " + lines);
        }
        print.close();
        return outputFile;
    }
```

Use `listFiles` to show the Temp Directory contents

```
    @Test
    public void listTempDirectory(){
        File tempDir = new File(System.getProperty("java.io.tmpdir"));
        File[] fileList = tempDir.listFiles();

        for(File fileInList : fileList){
            String outputString = "";
            if(fileInList.isDirectory()){
                outputString = outputString + "DIR: ";
            }else{
                outputString = outputString + "FIL: ";
            }

            outputString = outputString + fileInList.getName();
            System.out.println(outputString);
        }
    }
```

Output Attributes of Files In Temp Directory

```
@Test
public void listTempDirectoryAttribs(){
    File tempDir = new File(System.getProperty("java.io.tmpdir"));
    File[] fileList = tempDir.listFiles();

    for(File fileInList : fileList){
        String outputString = "";
        if(fileInList.isDirectory()){
            outputString = outputString + "DIR: ";
        }else{
            outputString = outputString + "FIL: ";
        }

        if(fileInList.canRead()){
            outputString = outputString + "r";
        }else{
            outputString = outputString + "-";
        }

        if(fileInList.canWrite()){
            outputString = outputString + "w";
        }else{
            outputString = outputString + "-";
        }

        if(fileInList.canExecute()){
            outputString = outputString + "x";
        }else{
            outputString = outputString + "-";
        }

        outputString = outputString + " - " + fileInList.getName();

        SimpleDateFormat sdf = new SimpleDateFormat("y M d HH:mm:ss.SSS");
        String lastModified =
                        sdf.format(new Date(fileInList.lastModified()));

        outputString = outputString + " => " + lastModified;
        System.out.println(outputString);
    }
}
```

copy And move a File

```
@Test
public void copyFile() throws IOException {
    File copyThis = writeTheTestDataFile();
    File toThis = new File(copyThis.getCanonicalPath() + ".copy");

    assertThat(toThis.exists(), is(false));

    Files.copy(copyThis.toPath(), toThis.toPath());

    assertThat(toThis.exists(), is(true));
    assertThat(copyThis.length(), is(toThis.length()));
}

@Test
public void moveFile() throws IOException {
    File moveThis = writeTheTestDataFile();
    File toThis = new File(moveThis.getCanonicalPath() + ".moved");

    assertThat(moveThis.exists(), is(true));
    assertThat(toThis.exists(), is(false));

    Files.move(moveThis.toPath(), toThis.toPath(),
                REPLACE_EXISTING, ATOMIC_MOVE);

    assertThat(toThis.exists(), is(true));
    assertThat(moveThis.exists(), is(false));
}

private File writeTheTestDataFile() throws IOException {
    File outputFile = File.createTempFile("forReading", null);
    PrintWriter print = new PrintWriter(
                            new BufferedWriter(
                                    new FileWriter(outputFile)));
    for(int lineNumber = 1; lineNumber < 6; lineNumber++){
        print.println("line " + lineNumber);
    }
    print.close();
    return outputFile;
}
```

Chapter Twenty - Math and BigDecimal

Convince Yourself of `BigDecimal` or `int`

```
@Test
public void convinceYourselfOfBigDecimalUsage(){

    try{
        double total = 5 - 0.3 - 0.47 - 1.73;
        System.out.println("2.5 != " + total);
        assertThat(total, is(2.5));
        fail("Expected the assert to fail");

    }catch(java.lang.AssertionError e){}

    int inPennies = 500 - 30 - 47 - 173;
    assertThat(inPennies, is(250));

    BigDecimal bdTotal = new BigDecimal("5").
                                subtract(new BigDecimal("0.30")).
                                subtract(new BigDecimal(("0.47"))).
                                subtract(new BigDecimal("1.73"));
    assertThat(bdTotal, is(new BigDecimal("2.50")));
}
```

Basic Arithmetic with BigDecimal

```
@Test
public void basicArithmeticWithBigDecimal(){

    BigDecimal bd = BigDecimal.ZERO;
    bd = bd.add(BigDecimal.TEN);
    bd = bd.multiply(BigDecimal.valueOf(2L));
    bd = bd.subtract((BigDecimal.TEN));
    bd = bd.divide(BigDecimal.valueOf(2L));

    assertThat(bd, is(BigDecimal.valueOf(5L)));
}
```

On my system, the result of the double calculation came to `"2.5000000000000004"` which would not equal 2.5. So always remember to use `BigDecimal` when comparing with the results of external systems or for financial and currency transactions.

Compare TEN and ONE

```
@Test
public void bigDecimalCompareTenAndOne(){
    assertTrue( BigDecimal.TEN.compareTo(BigDecimal.ONE) > 0);
    assertTrue( BigDecimal.ONE.compareTo(BigDecimal.TEN) < 0);
    assertTrue( BigDecimal.TEN.compareTo(BigDecimal.TEN) == 0);
    assertTrue( BigDecimal.TEN.compareTo(BigDecimal.ONE) != 0);
    assertTrue( BigDecimal.TEN.compareTo(BigDecimal.ONE) >= 0);
    assertTrue( BigDecimal.TEN.compareTo(BigDecimal.TEN) >= 0 );
    assertTrue( BigDecimal.TEN.compareTo(BigDecimal.TEN) <= 0);
    assertTrue( BigDecimal.ONE.compareTo(BigDecimal.TEN) <= 0);
}
```

Chapter Twenty One - Collections Revisited

Remove `if(val==0)`

```
userSortedList.add(bob);
userSortedList.add(dupebob);
userSortedList.add(rich);
userSortedList.add(dupebob2);
assertEquals(2, userSortedList.size());
userSortedList.add(mrBeer);
assertEquals("Mr Beer could not be added", 2, userSortedList.size());
```

Without the `val==0` lines in the `Comparator` I cannot add the `mrBeer` object to the `SortedSet`

```
// if(val==0){
//     val = user1.getUsername().compareTo(user2.getUsername());
// }
```

Disallow Duplicate UserNames

The code I created:

```
    @Test
    public void sortedSetWithComparatorForUser(){
        User bob = new User("Bob", "pA55Word");    // 11
        User dupebob = new User("Bob", "hello");
        User rich = new User("Richie", "RichieRichieRich"); // 22
        User dupebob2 = new User("Bob", "BobsMightyBigBobPassword");
        User mrBeer = new User("Stafford", "sys"); // 11

        SortedSet<User> userSortedList =
                 new TreeSet<User>(new UserComparatorDisallowDupes());

        userSortedList.add(bob);
        userSortedList.add(dupebob);
        userSortedList.add(rich);
        userSortedList.add(dupebob2);
        userSortedList.add(mrBeer);

        assertEquals(3, userSortedList.size());

        User[] users = new User[userSortedList.size()];
        userSortedList.toArray(users);

        assertEquals(bob.getUsername(), users[0].getUsername());
        assertEquals(mrBeer.getUsername(), users[1].getUsername());
        assertEquals(rich.getUsername(), users[2].getUsername());
    }
```

And the associated `UserComparatorDisallowDupes` class:

```
public class UserComparatorDisallowDupes implements Comparator {

    public int compare(Object oUser1, Object oUser2) {
        User user1 = (User)oUser1;
        User user2 = (User)oUser2;

        if(user1.getUsername().compareTo(user2.getUsername())==0){
            return 0;
        }

        int user1Comparator = user1.getPassword().length() +
                              user1.getUsername().length();
```

```
        int user2Comparator = user2.getPassword().length() +
                              user2.getUsername().length();

        int val =  user1Comparator - user2Comparator;

        if(val==0){
            val = user1.getUsername().compareTo(user2.getUsername());
        }

        return val;
    }
}
```

User `class` implements Comparable

The basic changes I made to the `User` class were to the class definition:

```
public class User implements Comparable {
```

Then I also added the compareTo method:

```
    @Override
    public int compareTo(Object oUser2) {
        User user2 = (User)oUser2;

        if(this.getUsername().compareTo(user2.getUsername())==0){
            return 0;
        }

        int user1Comparator = this.getPassword().length() +
                              this.getUsername().length();

        int user2Comparator = user2.getPassword().length() +
                              user2.getUsername().length();

        int val =  user1Comparator - user2Comparator;

        if(val==0){
            val = this.getUsername().compareTo(user2.getUsername());
        }
```

```
        return val;
    }
```

Then I created a `@Test` to use demonstrate it:

```
    @Test
    public void sortedSetWithComparableUser(){
        User bob = new User("Bob", "pA55Word");   // 11
        User dupebob = new User("Bob", "hello");
        User rich = new User("Richie", "RichieRichieRich"); // 22
        User dupebob2 = new User("Bob", "BobsMightyBigBobPassword");
        User mrBeer = new User("Stafford", "sys"); // 11

        SortedSet<User> userSortedList = new TreeSet<User>();

        userSortedList.add(bob);
        userSortedList.add(dupebob);
        userSortedList.add(rich);
        userSortedList.add(dupebob2);
        userSortedList.add(mrBeer);

        assertEquals(3, userSortedList.size());

        User[] users = new User[userSortedList.size()];
        userSortedList.toArray(users);

        assertEquals(bob.getUsername(), users[0].getUsername());
        assertEquals(mrBeer.getUsername(), users[1].getUsername());
        assertEquals(rich.getUsername(), users[2].getUsername());
    }
```

See the sort in action

When I added the line:

```
            System.out.println("Compare " + user1.getUsername() +
                    " with " + user2.getUsername() + " = " + val);
```

The output from the execution showed:

```
Compare Richie with Bob = 11
Compare Stafford with Bob = 17
Compare Stafford with Richie = -11
```

This means that I only reached the 'dupe' check for three `add` calls. All the other calls the result of the comparison was based on the duplicate username check.

Access Values in Map in Key order

```
@Test
public void exerciseCanGetAllKeysAsSortedSet(){
    Map<String,String> map = new HashMap<>();

    map.put("key4", "value4");
    map.put("key2", "value2");
    map.put("key1", "value1");
    map.put("key3", "value3");

    SortedSet<String> keys = new TreeSet<String>(map.keySet());

    int valSuffix = 1;
    for(String key : keys){
        assertEquals("value" + valSuffix,
                    map.get(key));

        valSuffix += 1;
    }
}
```

In the above code I add the values out of order into a `Map`. Not a `SortedMap`, so I know I can't rely on the order.

I construct a `TreeSet` from the `Set` returned by `map.keySet()`, so I now have a `SortedSet` of keys.

To demonstrate that the sort has worked, I predict the value I expect by incrementing `valSuffix` from `1` to `4`, then iterate over the keys to check that the value from the map is the value I predicted.

Printed in Great Britain
by Amazon